BALL DON'T LIE!

In the series *Sporting*, edited by Amy Bass

BALL DON'T LIE!

Myth, Genealogy, and Invention
in the Cultures of Basketball

YAGO COLÁS

TEMPLE UNIVERSITY PRESS
Philadelphia · Rome · Tokyo

TEMPLE UNIVERSITY PRESS
Philadelphia, Pennsylvania 19122
www.temple.edu/tempress

Library of Congress Cataloging-in-Publication Data

Colás, Santiago, 1965–
  Ball don't lie! : myth, genealogy, and invention in the cultures of
basketball / Santiago Colás.
    pages cm—(Sporting)
  Includes bibliographical references and index.
  ISBN 978-1-4399-1242-3 (cloth : alk. paper) — ISBN 978-1-4399-1243-0
(pbk. : alk. paper) — ISBN 978-1-4399-1244-7 (e-book)
  1. Basketball—United States—History. 2. Basketball—Social aspects—
United States. I. Title.
  GV883.C65 2016
  796.3230973—dc23

                                                      2015022911

Printed in the United States of America

02122019

For Papá (1928–2014), who first introduced me to
the basketball universe

For Mamá (1929–2015), who always saw the joy in my play

And for Claire, who so joyfully helped me find my way back
to it and to so much more

Detroit Sheed, cut paper, by Nathan McKee. (Fakeyrowndeath.com and Makemtakem.com; Dr_Dawg_MD [Twitter]; Nathan_Mckee [Instagram].)

A NOTE ON THE
FRONTISPIECE IMAGE

originally intended to use the image that appears on the facing page as the cover art for this book. The illustration depicts Rasheed Wallace wearing the uniform of the National Basketball Association's (NBA's) Detroit Pistons, for whom he played for several years. Wallace's mouth is open. We do not know, of course, why that is. But I imagined him shouting, "Ball don't lie!" the slogan for which he is so well known. As I explain in the Introduction to this book, this phrase expresses the autonomous, creative spirit of basketball players—particularly African American basketball players (since the adage originated on urban playgrounds)—who challenge attempts by institutions and corporations to corral and capitalize on their abilities. *Ball Don't Lie!* is written squarely in solidarity with this spirit.

Nathan McKee, the artist who created the image, graciously agreed to its inclusion on the cover and in promotional materials for the book. Unfortunately, a legal representative for the NBA informed the team at Temple University Press that because the image includes the NBA logo and a recognizable player, it would be necessary to secure a number of releases, including one from Rasheed Wallace. We determined instead to proceed with the superb alternative design produced by the cover designer, Bruce Gore, and to reproduce McKee's artwork in the book's interior—where it now appears and where the NBA, apparently, does not object to its use.

The ironies of this episode, however, seemed too rich to go unnoted. As I document throughout this volume, the NBA behaved very much as it has throughout its history, carefully controlling the image (and, indeed, the speech) of its players, especially its most independent players. I relocate the image here not to capitulate to the NBA's authority but, rather, to echo the elusive autonomy of players, who have always found a way to get free.

CONTENTS

PREFACE

In Praise of Heresy

My wife, Claire, often makes heretical statements when we watch sports.

Like me, she loves in sports the exhibition of what a human body can do, as well as the revelation sports so often offer that we are in fact one, a body-mind, working in graceful, confident harmony. Unlike me, Claire has not spent her life swimming in the culture of sports. She did not play sports competitively, did not watch them obsessively, did not read sports pages and sports magazines and sports books. Her observation of sports rattles along innocently, unconfined by the well-worn grooves of thought and discourse that experience and repetition have carved into those of us who have spent our lives in sports culture. The combination of her passion for what is going on and her inexperience in the habits of sports culture gives rise, then, as I say, to these heretical outbursts.

For example, a few years ago we were watching a Detroit Pistons NBA game on TV. It may have been a playoff game. A foul was called against the Pistons' forward Rasheed Wallace. Wallace vehemently disagreed with the call, and the referee promptly whistled him for a technical foul for unsportsmanlike conduct. Claire decried the unfairness of both calls. That is not the heretical part. On the contrary, that is a time-honored tradition within sports culture. But then she went to the dangerous place: "Why do they even *need* refs?" I laughed. She flashed, indignant: "*What?*" I laughed more. "I'm serious!" she insisted. I could not stop laughing. I laughed in part because I found her earnest outrage completely charming but also because her heresies make me nervous.

They unsettle me because they illuminate the areas of sports culture that I have come to accept as natural and necessary and so have stopped questioning. "Why do we *need* refs?" I might have sputtered, "*Why?* Well, of course, it is quite obvious, you see; if we did not have refs, well, then, why, you know . . ." It is not that there was no answer to the question. There was an answer to the question: I could see it in my mind, but as I stumbled toward it, it began to repel me, so it never quite made it out of my mouth. It is a bit like introducing a spectacular new friend to your family: when you see your family through the eyes of your friend, it may look better in some ways or it may look worse, but it will never look the same. Some of the things to which Claire draws attention, when I think about them under the hot spotlight of her heresy, do stand the test of critical reflection. Others do not. When they do not, I feel a little embarrassed for sports for being that way, and for myself for not having noticed.

More specifically, I feel embarrassed because basketball, in particular, has been my home for all of my life, and the people of basketball are my people. My family put up a hoop in the driveway when I was four, and I was chasing my older siblings around on that court soon after. I was seven when I saw Wilt Chamberlain and Kareem Abdul-Jabbar, Oscar Robertson and Jerry West go head to head at the Dane County Coliseum in Madison, Wisconsin; I was probably around seven, too, when I painted sideburns and a mustache on my face and scrawled "Knicks" on the front of a T-shirt and "Frazier" and the number "10" on the back. I think I was twelve when a classmate procured for me a personally autographed copy of John Wooden's Pyramid of Success. When I was fourteen, I plastered my walls with Magic Johnson posters, made a Magic Johnson scrapbook, and wrote to the Lakers asking for Magic's home address. (They did not give it to me.) At sixteen, I made room on the wall for Isiah Thomas. I was seventeen when, as the point guard and captain of my high school varsity, I lost a state tournament game in overtime on the same floor where Kareem and Oscar had won a world championship thirteen years before, and afterward I cried in the same locker room. At twenty, I got not one but two pairs of the original Air Jordans.

Years—decades—have passed, slicing not inches but feet off my vertical leap. But time has not dulled my enthusiasm for the game in all its forms. The heroes have changed, but still I watch their games and buy the shoes they hawk. And still I lace up those shoes at least twice a week in my noon pickup run. Moreover, the very myths of the culture of basketball that I critique in this book and the values they harbor formed my experience of the game and shaped my personality, even off the court. I believed in them then, and even if I no longer do now, I still feel their emotional pull. So Claire's questions sometimes unsettle my heart and disorient me, as though the rightness of my very being were suddenly thrown into question.

Fortunately, she is a gentle, capacious, and loving heretic, so none of this gets in the way of our continuing to love what we love in sports, just as they are. In fact, I find that her heresies have shown me a way to expand and enrich my encounter with sports, much as any relationship grows stronger and more durable when it expands to flexibly accommodate a variety of types and intensities of feelings such as wonder, doubt, frustration, and disappointment. I am writing this book guided by my wife's spirit of loving heresy and in the hope that my reflections on some of the cherished myths of basketball culture will similarly unsettle my readers, whether they are natives of basketball, long-standing residents, or just passing through. But also, as with Claire's sporting heresies, I hope that, supported by history and enhanced by fanciful inventions, mine will not cause readers to love basketball less, but only to love it better.

ACKNOWLEDGMENTS

Before this was a book, it was a course. And before it was a course, it was a tweet. And before it was a tweet, it was a fit I threw after a visit to the Half Moon used bookstore in Kingston, New York, on my birthday in 2010. And before it was a fit, it was a desire I could not recognize, and so I certainly could not act on it. And as William Blake once wrote, "He who desires but acts not breeds pestilence." But wait. Acknowledgments really are not the place for confessional tales. Suffice it to say that the path to the completion of this book has been long, and many times I wandered ignorant and confused and doubtful. It is like one of those paths they say that you make by walking. I like this book a lot. I have put my whole heart and mind into it, and I am proud of it. But I know I would never have gotten to this moment without the contributions of many people.

Before this was a book, it was a course, so my first debt is to the many students who have taken my course on the cultures of basketball at the University of Michigan. By now, in my sixth semester teaching the course, they number about two hundred, so I cannot name them all individually. But all of them have made a contribution to what you are about to read through their dedication and intelligence and, especially, through their belief in the course and their willingness to accompany me with affirmations, arguments, questions, and good humor as I led them clumsily through what was for me too often uncharted terrain. Not only these students but also those who have taken other sports studies courses I have offered since then, and still others, graduate and undergraduate, who have so generously—indeed, enthusiastically—indulged my hoops digressions in graduate seminars on French philosophers or undergraduate literature courses on innocence and experience have helped me keep open the windows of the gym, as it were, allowing refreshing crosscurrents of literature, art, music, philosophy, history, and social theory to invigorate my thinking about the sport and its culture.

But among this inspiring crowd of students I want to thank a few by name—with hope that the others will not feel slighted in the process—either for serving as guinea pigs by using the manuscript as their course textbook or for giving special time and attention to conversations about these topics with me inside and outside the classroom: Muhammad-Ali Abdur-Rahkman, Danny Ackerman, Spike Albrecht, Christiana Allen-Pipkin, Maximillian Alvarez, Ryan Armbruster, Josh Bartelstein, Ronald Beach, Robert Bell, Tim Bergsma, Shaun Bernstein, Max Bielfeldt, Kelsey Blake, Allison Boevers, Steven Braid, Jonah Brandhandler, Lauren Brandt, Erik Braun, Allie Breitfeller, Lucas Brockner, Peter Brown, Trey Burke, Basak Candar, Kam Chatman, Suphak Chawla, Abby Cole, John D'Andrea, Elliott Darvish, Ally Davis, Matt Davis, Aubrey Dawkins, Seba Díaz, Stuart Douglass, Ricky Doyle, Nicole Dressler, Kyle Duckitt, Jordan Dumars, Luke Dwyer, Ryan Feeley, Tom Fleming, Nate Gallant, Pavel Godfrey, Matt Gordon, Erica Gray, Adam Grinwis, Miles Gueno, Megan Hibler, Lily Hochman, Randeep Hothi, Roxanne Ilagan, Connor Jaeger, Chantel Jennings, Zaryn Jennings, Albert Karschnia, Ari Kefgen, Peter Kraus, Mack Ladd, Caris Levert, Hillary Levinson, Chris Love, Dan Madwed, Maegan Mathew, Teresa Mathew, Blake McCliman, Matt McCool, Mitch McGary, Chris Meade, Will Meter, Rico Miller, Stephen Molldrem, Will Morgan, Kelly Murphy, Gil Naamani, Joshua Nance, Tony Natoci, Michael Parker, Alex Petrone, Andrew Portnoy, Katie Prchlik, Glenn Robinson III, Karly Rolls, John Rowland, Rachel Salle, Geoff Simpson, Ramon Stern, Ronnie Trower, Sai Tummala, Matt Vogrich, Ella Webb, Robert Wells, Emily Willer, D. J. Wilson, Jordan Wynne, Matt Yoder, and Michael Zhu.

Of course, none of these conversations would have occurred had it not been for the enthusiastic encouragement and material support of my colleagues and administrators and of staff members at the University of Michigan. Among those I should single out are, in the Residential College, Naomi Andre, Charlie Bright, Angela Dillard, Jennifer Myers, and Cindy Sowers for never batting an eyelash at the idea of basketball forming part of the Arts and Ideas in the Humanities curriculum and, in

Comparative Literature, Yopie Prins and Silke Weineck for encouraging me to develop and expand that course into other courses and avenues of research. Many staff members at Michigan have supported this process in small and large ways. But Paula Frank, Judy Gray, Charles Murphy, and especially Nancy Harris have been steadfast throughout the process, hacking through bureaucratic thickets so I could wander undisturbed. In addition, colleagues and friends at Michigan, such as Vincenzo Binetti, James Neal, and Stefan Szymanski, informally shared my interest in sports and helped keep the embers stoked. My former colleague and dear friend Jason Young, over more than twenty years, nourished even my failed intellectual experiments and inspired me with his successes. The generous support of an Associate Professor Support Fellowship from the College of Literature, Science, and the Arts helped not only materially but also by showing me that my project was legible to and valued by my academic community.

Outside Ann Arbor, a number of scholars from various disciplines, most sharing my love for sports and my commitment to studying it but vastly exceeding my knowledge and experience in that endeavor, astonished me time and again with their generous willingness to nurture half-baked ideas and to share resources that I ought to have known enough to already have. Pablo Alabarces, David Andrews, Kristina Aurelyiate, Patricio Boyer, Ana Cara, Ben Carrington, Noah Cohan, Sebastiaan Faber, Eric Falk, Grant Farred, Héctor Fernández-L'Hoeste, Aram Goudsouzian, Jack Hamilton, Robert McKee Irwin, David Leonard, Alejandro Meter, William Morgan, Joshua Nadel, Patrick O'Connor, Juan Poblete, Theresa Runstedler, Anya Spyra, Orin Starn, Abe Stein, and Lucia Trimbur have all heard or read and responded to early versions of various parts of this work, pointed me to useful resources in the field, put me in touch with like-minded scholars, and helped me think through the connections among sport, culture, and society.

Among these, I particularly acknowledge Grant Farred. Anyone who knows this academic field knows that he is now a luminary: a provocative thinker and eloquent stylist whose work on various figures and issues at the intersection of sports, politics, and culture has influenced a generation of young scholars. His work has inspired me, as well, and he has generously supported my efforts. But twenty years ago, Grant and I were just two assistant professors in comparative literature at the University of Michigan. Although we were colleagues for only a short time, a love for basketball, as well as shared literary, philosophical, and political affinities, cemented a friendship that, despite long periods without seeing or even talking with each other, has endured and deepened. Around 1996, when he invited me to write an essay about Dennis Rodman, Grant seemed to know where I wanted to head before I did. He was waiting for me with a smile when I got there, nearly two decades later, and first reached out to share with him my ideas about this book.

These people helped me shape the raw materials of my thinking about basketball into a proposal that I could share with Micah Kleit and Amy Bass at Temple University Press. I am grateful to both of them—and to two anonymous readers for improving the work with their constructive criticism—for seeing the value in that embryonic proposal, for pushing me to make it into the book that I really wanted to write rather than the one I believed was expected of me, and for being so unsparing in their admiration for what emerged. I could not have asked for a more professional, expert, or congenial editorial team. I am grateful to the rest of the production staff at Temple for guiding me kindly and skillfully through the myriad choices that have gone into making the object that you hold in your hands.

Before this was a book, it was a course. And before it was a course, it was a tweet sent out to a loose community of writers devoted, often in their spare time, to producing stimulating, intelligent, thoughtful, informed, and entertaining writing about basketball for blogs and other Internet publishing venues. It was their writing that helped me see that I was not alone in wanting to think about sports when I started out, and their writing to this day makes me consider very carefully the value of esoteric academic jargon I might be inclined to use. They are smart and accessible and inspire me to try to be both, as well. I value them all as public intellectuals. Kevin Arnowitz, Danny Chau, Paul Flannery, Eric Freeman, Nathaniel Friedman, Dennis G., Lisa Hickey, David Hill, Kelly Innes, Toby Jochheim, Rich Kraetsch, Zach Lowe, Jessica Luther, Rob Mahoney, Jason Mann, Beckley Mason, Nathan McKee (whose artwork is included as the frontispiece for this book), Andrew McNeil, Matt Moore, Ryan O'Hanlon, Neil Paine, Seth Partnow, Brian Phillips, Sebastian Pruiti, Tomás Ríos, David Roth, Tim Varner, Matt Watson, Jacob Weinstein, Alexander Wolff, Miles Wray, and Tom Ziller not only produce exemplary work for public consumption but have also corresponded with me, guided me, edited me, provided me with venues to share my work with much broader audiences than would otherwise be possible, and offered feedback on the project from its earliest stages through the final manuscript.

Among these inspiring writers, I must single out Nathaniel Friedman (a.k.a. Bethlehem Shoals) as deserving special thanks. Although he would be quick to share the credit, Nathaniel more or less singlehandedly created a genre of cultivated basketball writing, grounded in the emotional, stylistic, and cultural aspects of the game and aimed at the thoughtful basketball fan, without which I really doubt I would have been able to imagine my own contributions. Moreover, my students use and love the book he co-wrote with his FreeDarko Collective, *The Undisputed Guide to Pro Basketball History*, and as my numerous citations in the pages that follow attest, I do, as well.

Before this was a book, it was a course. And before it was a course, it was a tweet. And before it was a tweet, it was a desire. The desire was, for lack of a better word, for integration: integration of body and mind, past and present, passion and intellect—of all that I am, working gracefully together in the service of making something new. The first place I experienced this integration, as a young boy, was in the driveway of my family's home in Madison, Wisconsin, when the hoop went up the summer I turned four. However sophisticated the intellectual tools I have brought to bear in this book, its driving heart lies in my experiences as a basketball player and the deep gratitude and respect those experiences have inspired in me for the dedication, talent, creativity, and integration that basketball players display every time they step onto the court. So I thank my teammates and competitors on playgrounds from Madison to Durham, Ann Arbor, St. Louis, and Oberlin. I have had many, but a few stand out in my memory for having appreciated me as a player, even though, as now, I tend to overthink on the court: Nate Anderson, Julio Ariza, Johnny (J-Train) Austin, Marvin Barges, Dwayne Blue, Andy Brabson, Tyrone Braxton, Bull, Isaiah Cavaco, Eli Cohen, Nate Cole, Casi Donelan, Laurence Edem, Flint Fleming, Allison Gannon, Big Dave Hopkins, Danny Johnson, Derrian Jones, Derrick Jones, Robb Lee, Chris Love, Mike Mancini, Tim McCrory, Chris Meade, Mike, Miles, Jon Morgan, Jerry Pettinger, Davy Rothbart, John Rowland, Sam, Matt Schemmel, Fred Schernecker, Michael Speaks, Ramon Stern, Vic, Travis Wilson, and Turf Wilson.

Inspiring me on the court all along were dozens of teams and players who are far more dedicated and skilled than I could ever have hoped to become. Some are the subject of my writing in this book, but even when they are not, their infectious creativity and excellence have made me want my writing to do for readers what their play on the court has done for me: the 1971 Bucks, especially Kareem Abdul-Jabbar and Oscar Robertson, as well as the Bucks' voice on the radio, Eddie Doucette; Clyde Frazier; Wilt Chamberlain; the dominant University of California, Los Angeles (UCLA), teams of John Wooden; the 1977 Blazers *and* the 1977 Sixers; Bill Walton *and* Dr. J (not to mention Darryl Dawkins); Nancy Lieberman-Kline; Magic Johnson; Phil Ford; Wes Matthews; Isiah Thomas and Joe Dumars; Cheryl Miller; Michael Jordan; the Fab Five; AI; Steve Nash; Manu Ginobili; the early 2000s Pistons; Rasheed Wallace; LeBron; Chris Paul; Russ; KD; Maya Moore; and Britney Griner.

To say that I found my first experiences of integrated desire on the basketball court is to say that basketball was always more to me than simply a recreational activity or a competitive sport. At its best, it became the place where I could exercise capacities and dispositions within myself that I found frightening to exhibit in my life off the court. At its worst, it became the place where I reinforced my own inhibitions. But in either case, and to this day, basketball play furnishes me with the most legible and productive vocabulary and images for understanding myself, and making myself understood, off the court. It is a form of thought and expression. Undoubtedly—and, perhaps, to some degree unwittingly—this book conveys the deeply personal nature of my relationship to the game. I hope that this manifests not as a flaw but as an element that contributes to its power.

If so, it will be because of the encouragement, love, and support of family and friends who enthusiastically embraced and applauded my efforts to integrate my love for this sport with my professional life. My in-laws, first of all—the late Morris Solomon, Millie Solomon, Mark Solomon and Deanna Stickler Laurentz; Louisa Solomon and Miller Oberman, Nicole Solomon and Shawn Setaro, Jeanie and Bruce Coopersmith, and Michael Coopersmith—have each in different ways recognized the value of what I was doing and demonstrated this by throwing a news item my way, engaging me in conversation, sharing memories, reading drafts, promoting my work, or watching or playing ball with me. My mother-in-law, Diane Welch, planted a seed of inspiration by giving me Eduardo Galeano's *Soccer in Sun and Shadow*. It is not the book I have written, but I have aspired to match the poetry of its style. Her late father, Leonard Welch, generously shared memories and mementos of his championship playing career in the 1930s at what is now the University of Wisconsin, Superior. Among the dear friends who have responded to this work with enthusiasm and joy, I thank in particular Grant Farred, Jimmy King, Tim McCrory, Eli Oberman, and Jason Young.

My siblings were my first teachers, opponents, and teammates, on and off the court. Toño Colás, my oldest brother, was always the best athlete of us all. His successes on the court when I was a small child, and especially his incredible leaping ability, thrilled me and probably first instilled in me the desire to be on the court with a ball in my hands. Juan, next in line, with and against whom I have probably played more basketball games than anyone else in my life, taught me to be dogged and challenged me with his trash talk to develop psychological toughness. He and his wife, Amy, were, after my parents, my biggest fans during my playing career. From Chinca, my big sister, I learned to respect every opponent: it is not what you may be thinking; it is because, even when I was little, she treated me like I was competition and our competition like it was life or death. And from her late husband, Randy, I learned that the game was for fun and laughter.

My younger son, Adam, and I have not really communicated much during the period of incubation and composition of this book. But my relationship with him before this time helped to shape me into the person who could write this book, paradoxically by, among other things, his interest in almost everything except basketball (with the exception of a brief foray into Pistons fandom around 2005). Adam's independent interests further developed in me a curiosity and breadth of interest that have been vital to my approach to the sport in this book.

My older son, Owen, shared with me a love of sports and of competition in his childhood and later, even after he had given up playing sports, continued in his teen years to share and stoke my enjoyment in watching basketball—particularly such iconoclastic players as Rasheed Wallace, whose jersey was the first one I bought him. More recently, as he has continued to bravely blaze unconventional trails as an independent, young adult, he has imparted to me his delight and pride in my becoming a "basketball scholar" or "*basketballphilosoph*," a pride and delight that I have come to be able to take as my own and that has further inspired me.

My father passed away just as I was beginning this manuscript, and my mother passed away almost exactly one year later, as I was finishing it. My mother, who had no athletic experience or knowledge, played with me when nobody else would (even when, in recent years, the terrible course of Alzheimer's meant that she was not sure who she was playing with), drove me to practices and to games, cheered when I won and hugged me when I lost, and, perhaps most important and unforgettable, always made me feel as though my simply playing the game was a gift of joy to her. My father was a scholar and a basketball fan, although he also was not a player. We watched countless pro and college games together on TV and in person and, toward the end of his life, over FaceTime, when he agreed to wear a Michigan beanie I bought him, despite his long-standing devotion to Wisconsin. To my embarrassment and secret relish, from my first competitive game to my last, he yelled at the refs on my behalf and used his exceptional intelligence to track and help me understand my stats. Even long after that, in the last months and weeks of his life, when my only games were informal and recreational, he inquired with interest, gave advice, and showed pride. Throughout my life, each nourished my love for basketball and for thought and writing, and I hope they would be proud of this book—my attempt to bring it all together.

The debt I owe to my wife, Claire Solomon, is both intellectual and personal and in both cases far greater than I can possibly reflect in words. I have tried to acknowledge her work in the places where it had a direct impact on my thinking. But Claire's intellectual influence on this book is far more pervasive than endnotes can register. She is the smartest person, the finest writer, and the most effective teacher I know. Claire possesses a remarkable capacity to invite and accommodate many and, perhaps, contradictory points of view on an issue and in this way to cultivate ambiguity, nuance, and complexity. Because that is not always easy for me in areas, such as basketball, that I care about deeply, Claire's lessons in this regard have been indispensable. Through her own scholarly work and by personal example, Claire also has shown me what it means to see history against the grain, how we imprison others and ourselves with language and stories and how to use language, stories, and other tools to fight for freedom for ourselves and for others. She helped me to see how these struggles were already present in the things—basketball and philosophy—that I knew and cared about. Without her example and guidance, I doubt I would ever have come to see the stories I analyze as myths and these myths as bearing harmful political implications or known how to expose the sources of their emergence and their pull on us, or how to counter them with inventive stories that affirm the creativity and autonomous potency of players. Indeed, more than once she has spotted the emancipatory potential of a play or player before I did, not just because she has fresh eyes for basketball, as I indicate in the Preface, but especially because she has sharp eyes for freedom.

She also taught me how all that I was thinking about that I thought of as out there—all those stories, with their tensions and conflicts and joys—was also inside me, in my own heart. When I threw a fit on my birthday in 2010, it was Claire who encouraged me to reflect on my vocation, to think deeply about what I desired and about how I might be keeping myself from manifesting it out of fear. I was able to allow myself to return to sports directly because of that encouragement. From that first encouraging response and through all of the many subsequent twists and turns and successes and setbacks along the way, Claire has believed in my desire and in my talent. She has become a basketball fan (and sometime player), and she has heard more about basketball and sporting culture than I suspect she ever thought she would. And she has unfailingly and lovingly carried and coaxed, challenged and cajoled me in the direction of what I want—but inexplicably resist. Driving this book is the affirmation that basketball play at its core is an embodied, dynamic, and experimental expression of human creativity, desire, and freedom. I owe to Claire the great gift of putting me back in touch with that in myself and for helping me to see and articulate it in the play of others. That is the heart of this book, and of me, and that heart belongs to Claire.

INTRODUCTION

"BALL DON'T LIE!"

December 2, 2012

It's kind of like a slave and master or father
and son. You've got your little son and [you say],
"Don't say nothing back to me"—and to me,
that's totally wrong.—**Rasheed Wallace**

L ate in the first quarter of a 2012 NBA game between the New York
Knicks and the Phoenix Suns, the Suns guard Goran Dragic stepped
to the free-throw line and bricked his foul shot off the back of the
rim. As the errant free throw caromed off the iron, the veteran Knicks
forward Rasheed ("Sheed") Wallace called out, "*Ball* don't lie!" and was
immediately assessed a technical foul and ejected from the contest. This
was neither the first time that Wallace had received a T nor the first time
that he was ejected from a game. In fact, he had received one just moments
before, and these two together were numbers 316 and 317 of his career
and the ejection, his thirtieth. (Both figures top the NBA's list of all-time
career leaders in these categories.)

However, this was the quickest ejection of his career and the first time
he had been ejected for saying, "Ball don't lie!"—the phrase he had made
famous as a slogan of protest against bad calls. For years, when an opposing player missed a free throw, Wallace would call out, "Ball don't lie!"
He would not shout this every time, only when he felt the free throw had
resulted from a bad call, although it is true that Sheed seemed often to
have felt that way. In any event, the opposing free-throw shooter might
clang a brick off the iron, and there was Sheed, shaking his head and
laughing or raising his innocently aggrieved face to heaven: "*Ball* don't lie!"
picked up by courtside microphones and broadcast to viewers everywhere.

But this time, for some reason, though early in a meaningless game played early in the season, hearing "Ball don't lie!" prompted the game's referee to assess the second T and eject Wallace from the game.

Most observers view "Ball don't lie!" as Sheed's way to assert that higher powers govern the outcome of basketball plays and express their will through the ball, to validate his complaint, and, in effect, to overturn the decision of a referee. "Ball don't lie!" renders the hapless free-throw shooter a mere pawn in a cosmic tribunal that pits the referee, discredited mundane authority figure, against Sheed, maligned mouthpiece speaking truth to that earthly power in the name of a justice that has not been done. Sheed is a warrior for truth and justice, a soldier for the basketball gods, and "Ball don't lie!" is his battle cry. In that case, maybe the ref who T'd Sheed for saying, "Ball don't lie!" hoped to regain the authority whose emptiness Sheed exposed. And perhaps, to those inclined to believe the ref ever had it, he succeeded. But for the rest of us, his petty, vain attempt amounted to a humiliating clutch at empty air and served only to lay all the more bare the despicable true dynamics of power at work in the situation. "Ball don't lie!" indeed![1]

I feel this. I can even get excited about it. But this excitement runs aground on the reefs of my agnosticism when it comes to the existence of basketball gods and my pragmatism when it comes to issues of truth and justice. "Ball don't lie!"—at least when interpreted in this usual way— appeals to those transcendent basketball gods and fixed ideals of truth and justice in which I just do not want to believe. No matter how exciting it may be when Rasheed invokes them, transcendent gods and fixed ideals carry too much force in the imagination. I worry about them falling into less judicious hands than Sheed's. Curiously, when I set aside this conventional interpretation, "Ball don't lie!" stirs me all the more.

What Is a Foul Call?

Let us look more closely at the kind of situation that might lead Sheed to cry, "Ball don't lie!" It is common enough, occurring nearly one hundred thousand times over the course of an NBA season: the referee's shrill whistle pierces the ambient sound cloud of the bouncing ball, murmuring spectators, chattering players, and squeaking sneakers, and, as the movement of players grinds grudgingly to a halt, the referee takes center stage. "Foul!" he calls, before signaling to the scorer's table the nature of the foul and the identity of the perpetrator.

Terry Eagleton has explained, "Common sense holds that things generally have only one meaning and that this meaning is usually obvious, inscribed on the faces of the objects we encounter."[2] Moreover, "common sense" holds that its "obvious" interpretation is "common"—that is, universally shared, independent of perspective and of the particularities of diverse social experiences. What I call "*basketball* common sense" holds that referees have the right to ensure that the rules of the game are followed. Basketball common sense further maintains that, in the event of a foul call, a referee has determined that a player has violated one of the rules and should therefore justly be penalized. This sounds reasonable, perhaps even obviously and undeniably true. But there is another, equally reasonable perspective on the foul call that illuminates issues obscured by basketball common sense, issues that clear the path for understanding the philosophical and, ultimately, political meanings of "Ball don't lie!"

The word "foul" first appears in the *Official NBA Rulebook for 2013– 2014* in a description of the powers of the referee: "When a personal foul or violation occurs, an official will blow his whistle to terminate play. The whistle is the signal for the timer to stop the game clock. If a personal foul has occurred, the official will indicate the number of the offender to the official scorer, the type of foul committed and the number of free throws, if any, to be attempted."[3] This provides a clearer sense of how the NBA defines a referee—namely, *functionally*, as the person endowed with the power to render decisions concerning an infraction of the rules prohibiting "personal fouls." This is important, as will emerge, but to make it more meaningful, it still requires a definition of "personal foul."

A definition does appear under "Rule No. 4—Definitions," where, in "Section III—Fouls," the very first clause tells us, "A common personal foul is illegal physical contact which occurs with an opponent."[4] However, it does not explain how one is to distinguish "illegal physical contact" from legal physical contact. That explanation appears in Rule No. 12, which provides a list of all of the prohibited forms of physical contact with an opponent (as well as the permitted exceptions): "A player shall not hold, push, charge into, impede the progress of an opponent by extending a hand, arm, leg or knee or by bending the body into a position that is not normal. Contact that results in the re-routing of an opponent is a foul which must be called immediately. . . . Contact initiated by the defensive player guarding a player with the ball is not legal. This contact includes, but is not limited to, forearm, hands, or body check."[5] Now it seems we have a clear-cut framework. During a game, players may intentionally or unintentionally make illegal contact with an opponent. The rules call this "a personal foul." They also tell us exactly what the referee is to do when this occurs: render a decision by blowing the whistle and verbally or manually communicating that decision to the scorer. So with all of this defined so clearly and in such detail, it might start to seem hard to see what Sheed used to get so worked up about. After all, it is all just common sense, right?

The problems arise—as with many of the myths in basketball culture—when you look at what is not said. In this case, the rules do not tell you that three other things have to have happened in the situation: the referee has to (1) see physical contact; (2) decide that what he or she has seen is in fact illegal physical contact; and (3) decide to blow his or her whistle and enforce the rule. I imagine that the NBA presumes that it goes without saying that these things happen. Yet any frustrated fan knows that they seem not to happen when they should and to happen when they should not. Even the league seems at least tacitly to acknowledge this by providing rules governing the expression of disagreement and the review of certain calls.

But despite justified concerns about such matters as racial or other biases among officials, fans' frustration and the league's attempt to eliminate its causes both miss—and, in fact, obscure—the point of what a foul call really is: *an exercise of the referees' profound power to bring fouls into being.*[6] Physical contact is merely physical contact and is neither legal nor illegal until the referee *makes it* illegal by blowing the whistle. In this way, the whistle augurs—like royal fanfare, but more shrill and less thrilling—the referee's power to bring the rules to bear on the players playing the game. Considering that those rules are backed by the hierarchical administrative structure and authority of the NBA (to fine or suspend players, for example), then whenever the referee blows a whistle to call a foul, he brings not only the rules but also their entire supporting structure to bear on the players and the game they are playing.

To emphasize the depth and reach of this power, it is useful to view a foul call as "a declarative illocutionary speech act" or, more briefly, "performative utterance" or "speech act."[7] These are acts of speech (or of nonverbal communication, like hand signals) that bring into being the state of affairs they describe. A commonly given example is a promise: when I say, "I promise to pay you back," my promise comes into being with the utterance. But a better sense of the power associated with speech acts may be gained by looking at some other common examples:

"I sentence you to fifteen years in a state penitentiary," whereby a judge brings the criminal sentence into being.

"This is my body," whereby a Catholic priest effects the transub-
stantiation of the wafer into the body of Christ.

"Let there be light," whereby God illuminates the cosmos.

"Foul!" works the same way in that by uttering the word, the referee
makes it so. Bearing this in mind, then, the causal chain of events the
rules prescribe actually reverses what occurs in reality: a foul does not
cause the whistle to blow (as the rules prescribe); *the whistle blowing causes
a foul to come into being.*

All of this—that the foul call is a speech act, the creative power that
this implies, the hierarchical administrative structure backing that
power, and the fun-house mirror inversion of reality entailed—is hidden
by the rules and by basketball common sense. And so it goes unseen by
the average observer who expects the referee will carefully observe the
play on the floor; remain unswayed by personal interests or the emotions
of players, coaches, and fans; and call "foul" only when physical contact
corresponds to what the rules describe as illegal. Even the category of the
"bad call"—the erroneous description of legal contact as illegal, or vice
versa—persists in making the error of assessing a speech act as if it were
an objective description.

By making this mistake and hiding the fact that it has been made, the
rules and basketball common sense confine debate to a narrow range of
possibility: was the statement true (a good call) or false (a bad call) or evil
(a biased call)? But neither the rules nor common sense acknowledge the
quasi-divine power to constitute illegality (and to classify players' behavior under that category) that basketball officials wield. Nor, since they
do not acknowledge that power, are they capable of challenging it, if they
were interested in doing so.

What Sheed Says When He Says,
"Ball Don't Lie!"

Sheed, however, understood, exposed, and challenged that power. In fact,
his 317 career technical fouls roughly gauge his success in conveying to
referees his intent to do so. It may seem at first glance that, like basketball
common sense, "Ball don't lie" also mistakes the referee's speech act as a
descriptive statement, one with which Sheed (or, actually, "Ball") merely
disagrees. But the outraging power of "Ball don't lie!" goes beyond disagreement. "Ball don't lie!" outrages by challenging and posing an alternative to the philosophical, cultural, and political underpinnings of the

foul call, basketball common sense, the NBA, and the broader societal dynamics of power these rely on and uphold.

Where foul calls are concerned, basketball common sense (and referees) adopt two fairly common, and commonly interrelated, philosophical positions: one, called "generic realism," about the nature of reality, and one, called "the correspondence theory," about the nature of truth. Generic realism holds that real things (such as tables) and the thing-ness that makes them what they uniquely are (such as table-ness) exist independently of anyone's belief, statements, or conceptual schemes.[8] As I argued above, basketball common sense believes that a foul is a real thing (made what it is by an intangible essence we might call "foul-ness") that exists prior to and independently of the referee's whistle. In this sense, the belief is a species of generic realism. The correspondence theory, meanwhile, defines truth as a relation between thoughts (or statements) and an independently existing reality to which these thoughts or statements faithfully correspond (or match, reflect, or mirror). When thoughts or statements correspond to reality, according to the correspondence theory, they are "true" (and, of course, when they do not, they are "false"). Our passionate arguments about whether a foul call was a good or bad call are, in effect, arguments over whether the ref's manifest belief that physical contact was illegal faithfully corresponds to reality. We are all—in this behavior, anyway—"generic realists" and "correspondence theorists."

Whatever the merits of generic realism more broadly, I have already argued that as applied to the foul call it entails a logical error. Far from existing independently, the foul by definition comes into being only when the referee blows his whistle and calls a foul. In doing so, he transforms physical contact into illegal physical contact and actually *causes* the foul to come into being. Given this, it makes little sense to speak of a correspondence between his belief and reality, since the latter is dependent on the former. Moreover, because of the circularity constituting the nature of fouls and the powers of the referee (and quite apart from league rules restricting protest), it is logically impossible for players to contest official rulings, at least from within the parameters of generic realism and the correspondence theory of truth that govern basketball common sense.

"Ball don't lie" eludes this trap by dissenting in a way that avoids both generic realism and the correspondence theory of truth and targets not only the particular call but also the entire structure undergirding the call's claim to legitimacy. The philosopher William James defined "truth" as "what it is better for us to believe." More precisely, he argued that those ideas or statements that help us to get a practical handle on the world are—so long as they do so—the ones we tend to call "true."[9] Sure, reality may be "out there," existing independently of our experiences and beliefs and statements about it (as generic realism maintains). But we cannot *know* anything about it without experience, belief, and language, so we cannot measure the truth of our experience, belief, and statements about reality *directly* against reality.

Because human beings do not have the standard of pure, unmediated reality by which to measure the validity of these experiences, beliefs, and statements, according to James, they measure them by the standard of what it is most practically useful to believe, and "truth" is the name given to that practical value. Truth, it follows, is not a thing or substance or essence that inheres in true ideas or statements. Instead, "truth," as James put it, "happens to ideas" through a process called "verification" (which means, etymologically, "truth making").[10] That complex process can occur in a variety of ways, but all involve definite situations governed by specific rules and criteria that are either explicitly or implicitly agreed on by the parties involved (or imposed forcefully by one party on another). In the NBA, as we have seen, the verification process for a foul call is circular: a referee calls "foul," which brings the real state of affairs "foul" into being, which in turn makes the call "foul" into a true description of the real state of affairs that the call initially brought into being.

"Ball don't lie!" offers an alternative verification process. It proposes that other powers, greater even than that of the referee, are weighing in, as well, which may implicitly remind us of the referee's powers. Indeed, the very absurdity of the ball making a call may draw our attention to the fact that the referee was not objectively describing a play but exercising what, within the universe of basketball, are quasi-divine powers to bring a foul into being. Sheed is not just disagreeing with the call; he is exposing the operation of these quasi-divine powers and, in doing so, calling into question the hierarchical structure of the sport whereby a referee is uniquely endowed with the powers to create and define reality. Perhaps the ejection with which I began this chapter occurred because Sheed, in applying "Ball don't lie!" to a technical foul call, challenged the referee's authority to enforce conformity with his decisions.

"Ball don't lie!" comes from the culture of recreational or "pickup" basketball. In such settings, without referees, players referee themselves, calling their own fouls and violations.[11] Of course, as in any formal game, disagreements may arise. Often, these are settled by one of the disputants taking an uncontested shot from the top of the free-throw circle. If the ball goes in, the claim is upheld; if it does not go in, the claim is rejected.

Either way the dispute is definitively settled because, well, as everyone on the playground knows and accepts: "Ball don't lie!"

In this sense already, even prior to an analysis of the racial dynamics of playground ball or the league, Sheed has made a stand in favor of autonomist (or horizontalist) politics.[12] By introducing a phrase from this setting into the NBA, Sheed reminds us that players can and do play basketball without refs and their transcendent powers. This, perhaps obviously, would be intolerable to refs and to the hierarchical regulatory structure they embody on the court, which may also contribute to the technical fouls against Wallace. Viewed from this angle, "Ball don't lie!" does not, as in the conventional interpretation of the phrase, invoke a transcendent power *higher* than that of the referees. It rejects the very idea of transcendent, ethereal power (including that of "basketball gods"). Instead, it invokes a *lower, material* power. More accurately, it invokes a power that circulates *horizontally* among equals rather than vertically from the top of a hierarchy to its bottom—that is, *the immanent, self-organizing autonomous power of basketball players.*

However, within the culture of basketball, pickup basketball is more than just "informal" play outside the sanction and control of hierarchically organized institutions such as the NBA. Identifying the historical, material, and symbolic specificity of pickup is crucial to grasping the racial dimensions of the politics of "Ball don't lie!" for while pickup occurs in a wide variety of settings hosting individuals of diverse racial, ethnic, and socioeconomic backgrounds—any of whom today might shout, "Ball don't lie!"—the phrase originated in games played on inner-city playgrounds, primarily by African American men who (or whose parents or grandparents) migrated to the core of America's northern cities beginning around the middle of the twentieth century.[13] This particular manifestation of pickup basketball has come to function, materially and symbolically, as the NBA's "supplement" or "Other," meaning that the NBA simultaneously depends on pickup basketball and the black men who play it and suppresses its dependence on pickup basketball through strategies that have emerged historically in response to specific changes in the sport and society.[14]

The NBA tends to treat "blackness" and its stereotypical signifiers as a kind of fluid cultural currency it wants flowing into the NBA in the form of talent and marketable cool, but it wants to control the tap.[15] "Ball don't lie!" unleashes this flow, as if uncapping a city fire hydrant on a hot summer's day so that everyone can enjoy the water. Sheed injects the racialized urban playground of white American fantasy directly back into the white middle-class mainstream of American culture—as a kind of overdose of the reality of urban black culture. In this way, "Ball don't lie!" resists the NBA's erstwhile defusing appropriations of blackness by directly challenging its regulatory authority and, in so doing, brings it to crisis. Simultaneously, "Ball don't lie!" affirms the autonomous self-governance of intersecting populations (basketball players, the poor, urban dwellers, African Americans in general, and young black men in particular) whose capacity for self-governance both public policy and popular culture attempt to hamper and then disingenuously pretend does not exist.

All of this has important consequences for language and for how we shape it into stories. The call "Foul!" is, after all, a piece of language and a miniature narrative about what just happened that claims to be true. In addition, the foul call's claim to be a true story depends on an interrelated group of beliefs, many of which themselves take the form of stories, though most are so commonly held that they go untold most of the time. In this particular case, the beliefs in play may be framed as a narrative proposition: "Referees are necessary, desirable, and qualified interpreters and enforcers of the rules of basketball, which rules, in turn, are necessary and desirable to ensure order and the highest possible quality of play. Without referees the game would disintegrate into an unwatchable, chaotic and possibly violent mess." I call this narrative proposition (and other examples like it throughout this volume) a "myth," by which I mean a kind of story that "accomplishes something significant for its adherents" and that, furthermore, may express a conviction that—though it may be true or false—is held tenaciously by its adherents.[16]

This particular myth primarily serves the purpose of justifying the present state of affairs, including the power dynamics therein. It does this by speculatively evoking a frightening state of affairs that must be avoided at all costs and presenting the refereed game as the only bulwark against the state of affairs. It holds that referees—competent or not—guard the line between basketball order and basketball chaos. And this myth implies another myth expressing the conviction that players cannot regulate their own play and arbitrate their own disputes. Both of these, finally, rest on other more complex myths prevalent in the culture of American sports and in American society more generally that express political convictions about the indispensability of hierarchical structures of power as well as about the nature of athletes and of African Americans and, in particular, about the nature of African American athletes.

When Sheed calls out, "Ball don't lie," he exposes these myths and thus challenges various forms of power embodied in the referee's foul call—

and in ways consistent with his outspokenness on league politics in other areas.[17] But the "truth" Sheed speaks to power is the truth of the pragmatist. "Ball don't' lie," as pragmatist truth, simply refuses to tangle with the ruse that refs' calls are inherently true *or* false descriptions of events that have occurred. "Ball don't lie!" does not really contend with the call, or try to plead that *truly*, reality is different from what the referee said. "Ball don't lie!" is not a petition at all. "Ball don't lie!" does imply a counter-truth, but it is of another category than the truth it would counter.

The key to the categorical difference lies in the *manner* or *form* of that counter-truth—the way it says what it says. Simply disputing a referee's call and asserting that it was blown would not carry the additional philosophical, political, and narrative force conveyed through the form of the phrase "Ball don't lie!" That form, in addition to subtly invoking playground scenarios and the politics of race in the basketball culture, also emphasizes the arbitrary, made-up, fabricated, or invented character of all calls and, in the process, with that final word "lie," hints that all of this involves traffic in fiction, fabrication, or invention of one sort or another. Moreover "Ball don't lie!" prioritizes the elementary, physical materiality of basketball by making the basketball itself the agent of discourse about the game. And it is not just the "ball" (as in the ball that clangs off the front of the rim) that points to the materiality of the game. It is also that "ball" metonymically means "basketball," as in the played game itself. So when Sheed says, "Ball don't lie!" the phrase echoes broadly, indeed. It affirms something like, "Regardless of whatever may be said about the game or its players (say, by referees or other purveyors of myth), the game itself—the play itself—does not lie."

Ball Don't Lie!—The Book

"Ball don't lie!" summarizes well my concerns, aims, and methods in this book. To begin with, it defines the topic of the book—the intersection of basketball and language—stakes a position within that intersection, and reminds us that this intersection involves dynamics of power. It exposes how cultural and philosophical convention conspire to stack the odds in favor of institutional authority and against players and that this process runs along racial and class lines, discriminating prejudicially against African Americans and the poor. It offers an alternative to this arrangement in affirming the capacity for autonomous self-governance among those same populations. It frames this alternative in an ironic and fanciful way that eludes the trap of a pseudo-objective debate between two equally plausible positions. And it invokes the disruptive force of the bodies at play in the game itself.

From its beginnings in 1891 and over the course of basketball's subsequent history, changes in society and in the sport have sparked sometimes contentious discussion of the nature of basketball, as well as of the techniques and tactics that ostensibly best embody and convey that nature. Investigating these discussions, I have identified clusters of recurrent stories, metaphors, and images arising around key events and personalities. These clusters make up the objects of study of my work, which I call "myths." I refer to them as myths not so much to lay bare their failure to correspond to reality as to emphasize that they have become tenaciously held, largely unexamined and influential "truths" within the culture of basketball. Speaking generally, the myths of basketball culture give narrative shape to a collective struggle with changes—particularly related to race—taking place in basketball and in society. Typically, they fabricate an idealized, timeless essence of the game and project it onto a succession of moments, individual players, coaches, and teams or, conversely, fantasize that a contrasting succession poses a destructive threat to that essence. Sometimes, the same myth simultaneously hails an embodiment of basketball's essence and decries an imagined threat to it.

In their proposal for critical sports studies, Mary McDonald and Susan Birrell formulated the basis for the approach I follow here. "The methodology of 'reading sport,'" they suggested, would involve "finding the cultural meanings that circulate within narratives of particular incidents and celebrities," as well as "uncovering, foregrounding, and producing counternarratives, that is alternative accounts of particular events and celebrities that have been decentered, obscured, and dismissed by hegemonic forces."[18] In my case, I excavate the "cultural meanings that circulate" within the myths of basketball by adapting Friedrich Nietzsche's historical method, which he called "genealogy."[19] The philosopher of sport William Morgan has described genealogy succinctly as "a way of trying to understand, explain, and evaluate a cultural practice by telling a story of how it came about or might have come about.[20] In telling this story, my genealogy looks not to understand the history of a myth *as it is given* but, rather, to expose *the conditions under which it came to be given*, or accepted as natural.

Although my genealogies partly inform the "alternative accounts" I subsequently offer, I do not counter the myths of basketball culture by replacing them with a story that I claim corresponds more faithfully to "what really happened." After all, historians and sociologists have already provided such accounts with little effect on the grip these myths hold on the culture of basketball. Though indispensable, historical and sociological research alone cannot dislodge the power of myth, because myth speaks to affect and imagination and such research speaks to reason. Destabilizing the power of myth requires storytelling that, while informed by the reason of scholarly research, also operates via affect and imagination. Therefore, I submit my "alternative accounts" in the form of what I call "inventions." Inventions tell a different story about the subjects of basketball myths by combining elements excavated by genealogy with close readings of the on-court phenomena that I find distinctive and compelling in those subjects.

I devote each chapter of *Ball Don't Lie!* to a key myth pertaining to a different era in basketball's history, with a specific date of symbolic importance to that myth identified in the chapter's title. Within each chapter, I first employ literary analysis to identify the key elements of the myth in question. I then draw on existing historical and sociological research to situate this myth in and against the overlapping contexts, in basketball and society, in which it emerged. Finally, I propose alternative narratives of the phenomena in question that attend to the specific tactical and stylistic innovations of particular players and the ways in which these might carry meaning beyond the boundaries of the basketball court and thereby disrupt the more confining myths that have crystallized around them.

I have organized the nine chapters that follow into three parts. Part I, "Myths of the Basketball Republic," examines myths that arose between 1891, when basketball was invented, and 1949, when, in the wake of its astonishingly rapid global spread, the NBA was formed. For much of this period, basketball underwent nearly constant change in terms of play, rules, and equipment; the demographic characteristics of players; and play venues. Moreover, although a few organizations emerged with aspirations to national scope toward the end of the period, most basketball was played in and between small, locally defined groups with the minimum organizational structure needed to foster competition. It is because of the primarily decentralized, locally based nature of the emergent and rapidly growing sport that I characterize this as the period of "the basketball republic."

The myths of this period, which appear in rulebooks, instructional manuals and promotional guides, institutional documents, and personal memoirs, as well as in popular and scholarly histories, maintain that basketball has a fixed and static athletic, moral, and aesthetic nature, born at the moment of the sport's invention, and that this essence is safeguarded by self-appointed institutional stewards who protect the game against chaotic forces of change wrought by entrepreneurs, spectators, and, most of all, players. These myths, which I examine in Chapter 1, "The Myth of Creation, December 21, 1891," and Chapter 2, "The Myth of Foundation, June 6, 1946," established a normative paradigm of basketball culture that equates tactical elements of game play (passing the ball and moving without it, defending aggressively and hustling cleanly after rebounds and other loose balls) with moral qualities (unselfishness, cooperation, hard work, humility). This complex was then naturalized as inherently pertaining to the white, Anglo-Saxon, Protestant, mostly middle-class men by and for whom the game was originally devised.

As the game rapidly grew in popularity and spread across the globe, played by women, foreigners, African Americans, Native Americans, ethnic immigrants, and the working class, anxieties about change intensified even as change was not only inevitable but also profitable and desirable to those whose sense of identity was threatened by it. The resulting tension gives rise to what I call the "white basketball unconscious" to indicate a hypothetical repository of psychological and cultural fears and fantasies arising from the fraught feelings that accompany these changes, the desires they stimulate, and the threat they appear to present to the stability of whiteness as a privileged identity. Because they remain unconscious, these fears and fantasies frequently express themselves subtly between the lines of basketball culture. In this sense, *Ball Don't Lie!* provides not so much a comprehensive history of basketball culture as site-specific critical analyses of—and alternatives to—the cultural productions emanating from the white basketball unconscious, with the proviso that "white" here refers to the race not necessarily of any individual but, rather, of the social group that stands to benefit from the widespread acceptance of the beliefs conveyed by the myth in question.

In Part II, "Myths of the Modern Basketball State," I take up a forty-year period from the middle of the twentieth century to 1991. By the beginning of this period, the major contemporary institutions of American basketball (state high school associations, the National Collegiate Athletic Association [NCAA], and the NBA) had emerged, consolidated regulatory power over basketball play, and achieved relative stability, forming what I call—to indicate the arrogation of resources, rights, and powers by these institutions—the "modern basketball state." During this period, whose beginning coincides roughly with the Civil Rights Movement and desegregation in American society at large, basketball at its highest levels of play experienced, first, desegregation (beginning at the professional level in 1950), then an influx of elite African American players who transformed the techniques, tactics, and style of basketball and its attendant cultures until, by the late 1970s, roughly 80 percent of the NBA's players were African American. For this reason, the history of the modern basketball state necessarily centers on race. The culture of basketball—invented as an instrument of white Anglo-Saxon Protestant social reform, institutionalized on the foundation of segregation, and buttressed by complex myths correlating techniques and tactics with moral qualities and these, in turn, with class, gender, and, especially, race and ethnicity—manifested its conflicting attitudes toward racial integration in a set of influential myths that unfolded from the late 1950s through the early 1980s.

The chapters in Part II address these myths as they crystallized first around Bill Russell and Wilt Chamberlain, the game's first black superstars in the late 1950s (Chapter 3, "The Myth of the Rivalry, November 7, 1959"); then around the racially diverse NBA champion New York Knickerbockers, who were lauded for their unselfishness, cooperation, and defense and celebrated as "the perfect team" in the early 1970s (Chapter 4, "The Myth of the Garden, May 8, 1970"); and finally around the rookie superstars Earvin "Magic" Johnson and Larry Bird, one black and one white, who purportedly saved the NBA from the perception that it was too black and, with their emotionally expressive love of the game, too cynically professional (Chapter 5, "The Myth of the Amateurs, March 26, 1979"). Throughout this period, the myths of basketball culture enabled the white basketball unconscious simultaneously to accommodate itself to a reality in which most basketball players and most of the best basketball players in the world were black while preserving the fantasy that the essential values constituting the sport were intrinsically associated with whiteness.

Part III, "Myths of the Basketball Empire," includes four chapters on myths that arose from the global cultural and economic expansion of basketball—the "basketball empire"—in the context of the end of the Cold War, the growth of multinational capitalism, new forms of mass media, and the widening and increasingly racialized gap between rich and poor in the United States during the Ronald Reagan years and beyond. In the basketball universe, this period is marked by four interrelated phenomena: (1) the globalization of basketball, sparked by the mega-celebrity of Michael Jordan and the NBA brand; (2) the infusion into basketball of cultural forms that originated in late twentieth-century African American urban communities; (3) the emergence and growing influence of international basketball players in the NBA; and (4) a growing entrepreneurial assertiveness on the part of players, amateur and professional. Chapters 6–9 identify and critically examine the key myths that have emerged around these phenomena.

As Jordan's career unfolded, a consensus formed around the claim that he was the greatest player of all time. I argue that this unverifiable claim presupposes that history, in a specific sense of the word, is over and that the global capitalist order, like Jordan, who is its metonym, is the greatest (social order) of all time, capable of bridging all differences and resolving all conflicts (Chapter 6, "The Myth of the Greatest of All Time, June 13, 1991").

Even as Jordan boosted the NBA to unprecedented levels of popularity and lucre, a new generation of African American players unapologetically displayed the cultural markers of their urban upbringing (tattoos, corn-rows, baggy shorts, hip-hop) while building on and raising to new levels technical and tactical innovations first developed in urban playgrounds in the 1950s and 1960s. The NBA sought to coopt this so-called hip-hop invasion in basketball by both capitalizing on the new markets it helped the league penetrate and carefully regulating the presentation of these players to the league's traditional white male consumers (Chapter 7, "The Myth of Blackness, March 12, 1997").

This rise to preeminence in the United States of this so-called hip-hop generation coincided with a dramatic improvement in the talent of basketball players abroad, who over the course of the 1990s gradually narrowed the gap between their teams and those representing the United States in international competition. Thus, in the wake of the U.S. men's national team's first loss in international competition in 2002, a new myth arose reasserting a tactical essence to basketball (called "playing the right way" and widely associated with the Hall of Fame coach Larry Brown) and equating it with moral virtues (Chapter 8, "The Myth of the Right Way, June 15, 2004"). This myth claimed that white foreign players better embodied the morally virtuous "right way" from which the deviant "hip-hop generation" had strayed, resulting in national disgrace in the context of a more general, post-9/11 insecurity concerning America's place in the world.

Finally, in 2010, LeBron James, the NBA's Most Valuable Player and a free agent, decided to leave his hometown Cleveland Cavaliers to join two other superstars (both also African American) with whom he had consulted before making his decision. This entailed, in effect, the players' exercising powers of team formation conventionally reserved for team owners (almost all white in the NBA) and general managers (still mostly white).

The subsequent racialized public backlash (Chapter 9, "The Myth of the Man, July 8, 2010") invoked a normative, hypermasculine fantasy figure ("The Man") to discipline James and so police the autonomy, mobility of, and interaction among black male bodies in the NBA, on and off the court.

Ball Don't Lie! thus critiques existing popular myths concerning the history of basketball, contextualizes them in relation to historical accounts that encompass developments internal to and beyond the world of basketball, and presents an alternative history of the sport grounded in innovations in play on the court. It emphasizes the creative prerogative of players and the ways in which their innovations are shaped by, and shape, broader cultural and social phenomena, ultimately disrupting the myths that would feed off and confine them. *Ball Don't Lie!* shows that basketball cannot be reduced to a single, fixed or timeless essence but, instead, is a continually evolving exhibition of physical culture that flexibly adapts to and sparks changes in American society.

I

MYTHS OF THE BASKETBALL REPUBLIC

(1891–1949)

THE MYTH OF CREATION

December 21, 1891

This is like Athena bursting out of Naismith's
head full-blown.—**Selby Kiffer**

On December 10, 2010, Sotheby's in New York held an auction for three items. The first was Robert Kennedy's copy of the Emancipation Proclamation signed by President Abraham Lincoln—one of forty-eight such copies originally made, of which about half remain. The second item was the last flag not captured during Custer's Last Stand at the Battle of Little Big Horn. And the last item sold that day were the two pages on which James Naismith, inventor of basketball, had a secretary type up the original thirteen rules of the game on the morning of December 21, 1891. The first two items sold for $3.8 million and $2.2 million, respectively. The original rules of basketball? They sold for $4.3 million—or about the same amount (adjusted for inflation) as the $4 million Sotheby's garnered in 2006 for a copy of Shakespeare's First Folio: the first copy, published in 1623, of his complete plays.

For anyone outside the culture of basketball (and for many, like me, steeped in it), the purchase may seem ludicrous. Understanding it as something more than the eccentric, self-indulgent caprice of an American multimillionaire requires an exploration of what I call basketball's "myth of creation." This myth of creation, which centers on this document, its creator, and the moment of its creation, elides the social and historical details of basketball's origin to put forth a static image of the game's core or essence, which it presents as essentially immune to historical change and social influence. The myth then supports misrepresentations of aspects of the sport's subsequent development. These misrepresentations, in turn, frequently entail racialized moral critiques of basketball innovations lamented as corrupt perversions of the core essence of the game supposedly codified by Naismith in the original thirteen rules on December 21, 1891. Examining the myth in light of the historical and social details it suppresses illuminates a different image of basketball and its history. Rather than the static and ethereal moral essence of the myth of creation, basketball appears as a necessarily dynamic, social, and embodied process of continual invention. And this image in turn invites ways to narrate the sport's beginning that better convey this dynamic and inventive nature.

Basketball's Myth of Creation

The purchaser of the original rules, David Booth, explained after the auction why he would, in his words, "pay more than anyone else in the world would pay or more than anyone in his right mind would pay" for those two typewritten pages. "The story of basketball," Booth said, "is Naismith inventing it and Phog Allen popularizing it."[1] Booth may have been unique in his willingness to value the document with piles of cold hard cash. But he is certainly not unique in his estimation of their importance. Others have conveyed their enthusiasm for the rules of basketball in the alternative currency of metaphor. The document Booth purchased for a higher price than any other piece of sports memorabilia in history has been called "the most important document in the history of sport" and "the crown jewel of basketball history." It has been compared to the U.S. Constitution, the Declaration of Independence, the Magna Carta, and the Ten Commandments.

As these comparisons suggest, at least part of the excitement this document generates comes from its foundational status as the origin point of a sport. Nearly every history of basketball begins with the fact that it, uniquely among the world's major sports, has a precise date (December 21, 1891) and location (Springfield, Massachusetts) of origin, a creator (James Naismith), and a founding document (the thirteen rules). The fact fascinates not only collectors such as Booth but also amateur and professional historians of basketball and, indeed, of sport more generally.[2]

These authors often ornament their fascination with some stylistic embellishment. Frequently, historians employ the term "birth" or birth imagery to portray the event. Instances appear from the first year after its origin through to the present day, from scholarly treatises on the game's history to coaching manuals and from amateur reflections on the game to the webpage of the Naismith Memorial Basketball Hall of Fame.[3] More specifically, the game regularly is said to have "sprung full-blown" from Naismith's head—an allusion to the most common version of the myth of the birth of Athena, which holds that the goddess was born full-grown and fully armed from the head of her father.[4]

Sotheby's Vice-President Selby Kiffer, referring to the original thirteen rules, provides the essential elements of the story. "This," he told a *New York Times* reporter, "is like *Athena bursting out of Naismith's head full-blown.*"[5] Elsewhere, Kiffer elaborated, "Nothing else like this exists that captures the origin of a sport. *One day there wasn't basketball. The next day there was.* You don't have that with football, baseball, lacrosse, golf. *This is the birth* of one of the most popular games in the world."[6] Kiffer's remarks nicely summarize the version of events that has appeared in many accounts of the game's invention over the past one hundred years, according to which basketball was born, full-grown, directly from the head of its father, James Naismith, in the form of thirteen written rules.

The meager details surrounding this spectacular—not to say, miraculous—birth tend to be given as follows. James Naismith, a mild-mannered, teetotaling Canadian divinity student turned physical education instructor, comes to the Springfield Young Men's Christian Association (YMCA). There, his boss assigns him an unruly class of students known as "the incorrigibles" and snappily challenges young Jim to come up with a safe, indoor form of recreation that will keep the young men entertained. After a couple of weeks, Proustian inspiration strikes Naismith in the form of the vivid childhood memory of playing a stone-tossing game called "Duck on a Rock." So inspired, Naismith rationally deduces the thirteen rules in a single evening. The next morning, he pins the two typewritten pages to the bulletin board, strides into the empty gym, nails peach baskets to each end of the gallery railing, ten feet above the floor, and informs "the incorrigibles" that he has a new game for them to try. Corrigible after all, as it turns out, the students take to the game with relish: "basket ball" is born, and the rest, as they say, is history. The rest may indeed be history, but for basketball civilization it is something more: it is our cosmogony. This is our myth of creation.

This is a little embarrassing to me personally as a lifelong citizen of basketball because, well, none of this is literally true—or, to put it differently, historically accurate. Basketball was not "born." It was invented. And it was not invented "full-grown" (i.e., in the form it is played today). The original version of the game bears little resemblance to the game as it is played today. Finally, while it is true that Naismith devised the original thirteen rules, he did so neither in isolation nor through an effort of pure intellect but, rather, in an extended process of experimental and sometimes haphazard collaboration with colleagues and students that included physical trial and error, conversation, study, *and* solitary reflection, not to mention despair.[7] We actually do not even know that any of this happened on December 21, 1891.[8] So what gives? If it is not accurate, and *we know it is not accurate*, why do we keep repeating it? What sort of broader, underlying cultural work might this myth be accomplishing for those who adhere to it?

The key to this puzzle lies in the image of Athena, born fully formed from the head of Zeus. On the one hand, the metaphor tells us that basketball, like Athena, was born and so is alive and must undergo growth and change. On the other hand, the metaphor tells us that basketball, like Athena, is immortal and emerged full-grown from the start, subject to no developmental changes, since "what she will become, she is from the start."[9] The metaphor first acknowledges change through the invocation of birth and then hastily suppresses that by emphasizing the timelessness of the thing born. Furthermore, since the version of the Athena birth myth invoked here involves her emerging directly from Zeus's head, the metaphor suggests that Naismith was (like Zeus) the game's sole progenitor. Creation myths involving solitary male creators suggest "a source outside of the generative cycle of birth, life and death; a source that is eternal and that by so being provides some sort of immortality to his creation."[10] Basketball's creation myth, in short, portrays the sport as beyond time, matter, and society. In this, the metaphor both reveals and suppresses a tension that runs through the entire history of the sport between a desire for growth and a desire for stability—or, to put it more concretely, between a desire to capture new participants, and markets, and a desire to police the technical, aesthetic, moral, and social impact these new participants would have on basketball.

Then, by portraying the sport as a *brainchild*, basketball's creation myth emphasizes the intellectual dimension of the sport's invention. Likewise, the myth exclusively equates inventing basketball with *writing* the original thirteen rules. But why not include the playing of the first game, on the morning after Naismith came up with the rules, as part of the invention? After all, then as now, there would be no basketball without players to play it. It could be that the myth's adherents find it easier to postulate basketball's immortality if they associate it with an act of mental deduction than with the confused, rough bustling of eighteen rowdy end-of-the-nineteenth-century male bodies. In this respect, the myth also internalizes and repeats a broader class-based preference for intellectual over manual labor in assigning creative agency to human activity.[11]

Now, historians and collectors fetishize the written rules as a record of that mental act, which is to say as mere transcriptions of the *intangible* stuff that is what really matters in the story: Naismith's mental conception of the game. In this respect, the idealist aversion to matter that leads to a preference for intellectual over manual labor extends further and expresses itself in relative disregard for the linguistic and textual materiality of the rules themselves. This allows adherents of the myth of creation to ignore, for example, that Naismith only hastily penned the rules and had his secretary type them up just before class as a mnemonic aid for his students. Or, more strikingly still, they ignore that Naismith had to amend Rule No. 8 by hand, inserting the phrase "into the basket" in the sentence describing the manner of goal scoring. These details suggest that Naismith saw the new game as a contingent work in progress. Ignoring them contributes to the myth of creation's central conceit: that the immaterial essence of basketball has persisted, immune to time and change, from the moment it appeared in Naismith's mind through to the present.

Moreover, by prioritizing the instructor's conception of rules rather than the players' game as the point of basketball's origin, the myth of creation promotes a hierarchized view of the sport's elements whereby players (and their play) are subordinated to institutions, their representatives, and their rules. Remember the *Official NBA Rulebook* I examined in the Introduction? It is sixty-six pages long. But guess how many rules it has. That's right: thirteen. What better way to emphasize the quasi-divine status of Naismith's original thirteen rules? After all, we still have just ten commandments. And it makes sense. If the condition triggering your myth is that players are "incorrigible"—and how many basketball players have been so characterized right up to the present day?—then what could be more important than rules? Rules and the firm, benevolent hand of older mentors and strong institutional structures to enforce them. Indeed, what does this aspect of our myth of creation teach if not that even the incorrigible can mend their ways under the guidance of a (divine) father figure?

So purveyors of basketball's myth of creation seem both to insist repeatedly on the precise date, place, and manner of basketball's origin and to push a view of the sport as beyond time, society, and matter. Given the apparent incommensurability of these two positions—not to mention the obvious evidence suggesting that basketball is not immutable, immaterial, or somehow beyond social influence—why do adherents to basketball's myth of creation cling to the image it promotes? The myth itself will not answer that question, not in any obvious way. However, its determined silence on matters of history, bodies, and society leads me to suspect that there may be something in a materialist, social history of the sport that threatens this idealized, immortalized image of basketball.

A Genealogy of Basketball Morals

When the Canadian-born Naismith left Montreal in the summer of 1890, carrying a freshly minted divinity degree from McGill University's Presbyterian College, to visit America for the first time, the country was a rapidly modernizing, emerging industrial power. Its cities were swelling with immigrants searching for better lives. But the unevenly distributed prosperity and rapid urban growth of the so-called Gilded Age worried many citizens and policy makers. Perhaps the most fundamental worry, for a country less than a quarter-century removed from the Civil War, was how to achieve social efficiency, organization, and, especially, cohesion in an increasingly dynamic and heterogeneous society. Or, conversely, perhaps it was how to continue to foster values of individual initiative and competition—seen as crucial to American industrial achievement—without imperiling values indispensable to social harmony such as unselfishness and cooperation.

Among the Progressive Era social reformers addressing these concerns, a cadre of new physical education professionals emerged, concerned especially with youth and, more specifically, with young men in growing cities.[12] They developed and implemented organized, supervised, rationalized, and competitive team sports as a tool for channeling what they saw as natural impulses (e.g., aggression, competition, or play) into positive social ends. As one historian puts it, physical education professionals believed that "intelligently designed and properly supervised sporting and athletic institutions could thereby instill and test a whole series of positive social values—manliness, character, efficiency, subsumation of the individual within the collective, and others."[13] Overlapping with this movement, a tendency known as "muscular Christianity" took root in the last quarter of the nineteenth century to promote sport within American Protestantism, where it had previously been viewed as a diabolical pursuit. Muscular Christianity fostered sport as a tool to attract and proselytize young urban men (many of them immigrants and others newly migrated to cities) and to cultivate in them a gentlemanly model of masculinity that navigated the perilous strait between upper-class effeminacy and working-class brutishness.[14]

Naismith cast his own vocational turn from the pulpit to physical education in similar terms: "My attention was directed to the fact that there were other ways of influencing young people than preaching. In games it was easily seen that the man who took his part in a manly way and yet kept his thoughts and conduct clean had the respect and the confidence of the most careless. It was a short step to the conclusion that hard clean athletics could be used to set a high standard of living for the young."[15] It is no surprise, then, that when he graduated Naismith took his training and experience to the YMCA Training Institute. There, in Springfield, Dr. Luther Gulick was pioneering his own version of muscular Christianity. Called the "greatest of YMCA philosophers," Gulick, upon assuming leadership of the school in 1887, sought to harmonize Protestant spirituality, late nineteenth-century science, and athletic endeavor. Gulick adopted— from the commandment in Deuteronomy (6:5) to "love the Lord thy God with all thine heart, with all thy soul, and with all thy might"—the slogan "Body, Mind, Spirit." He also designed the YMCA's logo, the inverted red triangle whose three sides, symbolizing the physical, mental, and spiritual dimensions of the human being, join to form a single whole.[16]

Basketball's invention occurred in the context of these social, cultural, and institutional developments and concerns, and Naismith, as the sport's inventor, embodied the concerns of Progressive Era social reformers and the beliefs of muscular Christianity and play professionals that scientifically devised, properly supervised, and organized athletic endeavors could contribute to solving late nineteenth-century social problems. Certainly, Naismith seemed to see it this way when he introduced the rules of the game in 1892 by emphasizing, "Basket Ball is not a game intended merely for amusement but is the attempted solution of a problem that has been pressing on physical educators."[17] The "problem" was not just the unruly class or even, as Naismith goes on to define it, the need for an easy-to-learn, indoor team sport. Or, if these were problems, they were seen as such because they indicated more significant moral problems rooted in social issues, moral problems for which sport could contribute solutions. Thus, Naismith wrote approvingly, "Games have been called the laboratory for the development of moral attributes."[18] Basketball specifically, Naismith claimed, cultivated a host of moral values, including initiative, agility, accuracy, alertness, cooperation, skill, reflex judgment, speed, self-confidence, self-sacrifice, self-control, and sportsmanship.[19]

The belief that basketball cultivates these and other virtues has been a staple of basketball culture from Naismith's time to the present.[20] As the former college All-American, NBA star, and U.S. Senator Bill Bradley put it in his book *The Values of the Game*, "Even though the game has changed, the old values still flow through it." Bradley's chapter titles—which include the words "discipline," "selflessness," and "courage"—form a list of those "old values" that Naismith would no doubt have been happy to add to his own.[21] John Wooden, the late esteemed coach of the University of California, Los Angeles, Bruins, crafted a legendary and often photocopied Pyramid of Success, with fifteen building blocks (such as "loyalty," "alertness," "team spirit," and "competitive greatness") "glued" together with values such as "adaptability," "reliability," and "faith."[22] More recently, Phil Jackson, a former NBA player, Hall of Fame coach, and now general manager of the New York Knicks, has given this discourse a New Age twist through popular books blending autobiography; basketball strategy and tactics; and a mix of fundamentalist Christianity, Lakota Sioux religion, and Zen Buddhism.[23] But given such unabashed promotion of the game's putative moral core, why should its myth of creation exclude the details of the sport's emergence out of the moral matrix of nineteenth-century Christianity, Progressive Era social reform, and professionalized physical education? Would these particular details not support the postulation of certain moral values as essential to the sport?

The answer is that these particular historical details reveal that the sport's moral values are neither timeless nor universal. My genealogy of basketball morals threatens the agenda of basketball's myth of creation by laying bare the *contingent* social and historical nature of the sport's putatively eternal moral essence. While basketball's creation myth eternalizes and universalizes this moral core, the game's moral and physical aspects were in fact conceived and designed to address specific social problems arising in a specific place and time. Thus, it would be reasonable to imagine modifications in the game's rules, strategies, tactics, or styles that would better address needs and circumstances other than those of late nineteenth-century America, not to mention agendas of those other than white, middle-class Anglo-Saxon Protestant men.

The contingency of basketball's original moral mission, however, is intolerable to adherents of the myth of creation. For them, when Naismith created basketball he also created, at one and the same time, a morally ordered universe. This means that introducing—or portraying the introduction of—a *technical* change to basketball as Naismith conceived it, whatever that change might be, would simultaneously tamper with the moral order of that universe. It may be unsurprising that a sport devised by Christians for purposes they explicitly articulated in Christian terms should give rise to a myth of creation that resembles Christianity's own.

But the resemblance is significant nonetheless. Changes to this athletic and moral order—no less than the changes introduced to the Garden of Eden in the Christian myth of creation—come to represent a dangerous corruption of an ideal, a fall from grace, metaphors used explicitly in myths I examine in subsequent chapters.[24] Indeed, while the fall from grace entails the loss of a particular quality such as innocence, at a deeper level it shatters illusions of permanence because the mere introduction of change, regardless of its content, obviously implies impermanence.

In addition to the intrinsic dangers posed to the religious-minded by the mutability of morality in general, the stability of this particular moral code was vital to American capitalist development at the end of the nineteenth century. The virtues baked into the rules of basketball were supposed to attenuate the extremes of capitalism, which, left unchecked, could lead to social disintegration or, worse, provoke revolution. The imperatives of this tightly bound technical, moral, and social order have driven some to lament elements of the game introduced after Naismith's time, such as the dunk, as aberrations tainted with the stain of moral degradation and linked inherently to particular socially marginalized racial or ethnic groups such as African Americans.[25]

If myths, as some have said, are "cultural dreams," and dreams fulfill unconscious wishes, then what sort of wish does basketball's creation myth fulfill? And what sort of unconscious has that wish? In response to the latter question, I posit what I call the "white basketball unconscious," a hypothetical container constituted by its contents: the wishes, terrors, and impulses related to race and basketball that the conventions of time and place require us to repress before we are even conscious of them.[26]

Let me take a moment here to be as precise as possible about what I mean and do not mean by this potentially provocative phrase. For Sigmund Freud, the unconscious was a hypothetical, explanatory concept whose value would be tested pragmatically in treatment. Although one could never empirically verify its existence, Freud believed that certain otherwise inexplicable behaviors could be understood, and modified, by positing the existence and operation of a mental realm that by definition was unknown to individuals because of their aversion to its contents. Fredric Jameson, building on the work of Freud, subsequent psychoanalytic thinkers, and Marxist philosophers, inflected this notion to coin the term "political unconscious." As with Freud's unconscious, Jameson argued that hypothetically positing the existence of a realm of thoughts, unknown to those individuals or broad sectors of society who hold them, that specifically pertain to class conflict could render intelligible certain cultural expressions (especially novels in Jameson's work) that otherwise remain baffling.

The premise of psychoanalytic treatment is that bringing unconscious thoughts to the surface of consciousness can mitigate symptoms caused precisely by the unconsciousness of those thoughts. Likewise, Jameson believed that bringing the contents of the political unconscious to the surface of narratives in which it operated could restore to the surface of texts the social reality they unwittingly disguise. In this spirit, in these pages I seek to read the myths of basketball to draw to the surface the hidden fears and fantasies that, I argue, lurk within the white basketball unconscious and that, as long as they remain unconscious and unarticulated, help to give these myths their cultural authority. Accordingly, I believe that shedding light on these fears and fantasies will help to defuse their harmful power.

Here I am introducing two modifications to the idea of an unconscious: "white" and "basketball." By the latter, I mean simply to suggest the existence of specific unconscious contents and operations that pertain to basketball. By itself this probably raises no serious objection. It is with the addition of the word "white" that problems may arise. So let me be clear: the white basketball unconscious is *not* a function of the skin tone of individuals. So I do *not* mean to suggest that all white people associated with the sport as players, fans, or coaches "possess" a white basketball unconscious. Nor do I mean to suggest that all black people associated with the sport are exempt from it. I use "white" in the phrase to identify the broader racial significance and implications of unconscious thoughts pertaining to the sport.

These specifically racial implications arise because unresolved racial tensions in the history of the sport and its culture are repressed. The tensions themselves, in turn, arise from the fact that a game originally designed by and for white men in relation to social and moral goals pertaining to a white majority society, and still primarily operated by white men for the entertainment of a white majority, evolved over time to be dominated, in terms of both on-court play and off-court cultural expression, by black men. *And*—this is crucial—this change was simultaneously feared and desired. So when here and elsewhere in the volume I refer to fantasies or fears of the white basketball unconscious, I am referring to the collective social source to which, hypothetically, I attribute particular assertions or broader myths, independent of the skin color of those uttering or espousing them.

The white basketball unconscious, then, fabricated this cultural dream of the game springing, full-blown like Athena, directly from the head of James Naismith as a means of expressing its unsavory wish that basketball *was in fact still played by white Christian men under the supervision of an appropriate authority figure to cultivate the moral values of the late twentieth-century American middle class.* It is as though if that dream could be real, then a century and a quarter of challenges to American white male privilege might just have been a nightmare from which the white basketball unconscious could now safely awaken. In fact, things are even more intolerable for the white basketball unconscious because at least some of the play elements and styles identified as a morally corrupt actually hew closely either to what Naismith wanted the game to be (fast-paced and full-court) or to what he was later glad it included (such as the dribble), as I show momentarily.[27]

What is more, these elements draw on precisely the *creative principles* that Naismith employed to conceive the game in the first place. In a seminar in psychology attended by Naismith, Gulick stated, "There is nothing new under the sun. All so-called new things are simply recombinations of things that are now existing." Naismith took the lesson to heart and applied it almost immediately, recombining Gulick's general observation that invention is combinatorial creativity with an earlier discussion of the need for a new sport. "Doctor," Naismith reported having replied, "if that is so, we can invent a new game that will meet our needs. All that we have to do is take the factors of our known games and recombine them, and we will have the game we are looking for."[28]

Gulick's and Naismith's particular usage of the term "invention" here derives from the classical art of rhetoric, where the word "invention" (Latin: *inventio*; Greek: *heuresis*) literally meant "to come upon," "find," or "discover"—among all the things that had already been said about an issue (called "the inventory")—the resources to construct the most persuasive new argument under the current circumstances. Rhetorical invention implies an awareness that creating an effective, novel argument involves not the creation of new words but the repurposing of old ones, the experimental recombination of existing facts and arguments for a decidedly pragmatic purpose: persuasion or, in other words, *verification*—truth *making* as a dialogic process. Invention, in other words, does not mean instantaneously creating something out of nothing (as in basketball's myth of creation). It means instead the process of rearranging the "things that are now existing" to come upon something new that suits the purpose at hand.[29]

Considering coming up with a new sport to entertain the class of "incorrigibles" as analogous to coming up with a new argument to persuade a skeptical interlocutor underscores just how closely Naismith's invention of basketball resembles the process of rhetorical invention. He consulted the inventory of existing sports (football, rugby, soccer, lacrosse) and tried them out. As each successive attempt failed to produce the desired effect in his audience, he adapted: dropping elements of one game, adding those of another—recombining, as Gulick had suggested, the elements of existing things in a back-and-forth, experimental process that took him from gymnasium (and his skeptical audience) to office and back. Moreover, Naismith recognized that the success of his invention would depend less on its intrinsic qualities than on the persuasiveness with which he could present it to leading (or most persuasive) students.[30] Thus, basketball was invented—and invented in the rhetorical sense of the term—as an *embodied form of rhetorical persuasion*.

Invention, therefore, in this same sense, is the very foundation of basketball, its lifeblood and its essence. But it is, I hasten to emphasize, a curious foundation and essence, for as an essence, basketball-as-invention dictates no particular form or result outside of what works in any given situation. Basketball, understood as invention, happens whenever a group of people gather and agree to call what they are doing basketball. There may be discussion and adaptation of the rules governing a given instance of this activity. Likewise, in any basketball setting, there may be lively debate about what constitutes sportsmanship, moral virtue, or aesthetic value. But what there is *not*—in basketball as invented by James Naismith—is a single form or style of play (much less a single skin tone) that embodies a fixed essence of the sport, because the essence of the sport is that it has no such fixed essence.[31]

Inventing Basketball

Considering the importance of invention to the sport, I propose that more suitable narratives of basketball's origin will adopt the pragmatic disposition of rhetorical invention and employ such fictive devices, literary figures, and rhetorical tropes as may be necessary to convey the inventive origin and character of the sport. John Grissmer's musical *The Perfect Game: Jim Naismith Invents Basketball* exemplifies this beautifully. Much of the musical follows the story as historians and Naismith himself recounted it, but it deviates from the historical record in one seemingly trivial but illuminating way: Grissmer portrays Naismith conceiving the dribble in its modern form as a critical step in inventing his new game and then calling it "the key" to the game.[32]

It may be tempting, and legitimate, to read this as yet another attempt to fabricate a continuity of identity between the contemporary game (which includes dribbling) and Naismith's original game (which did not). However, I want to read this particular historical fantasy differently. I submit that Grissmer's lie offers a critical truth: the dribble *may be the key* (or at least *a* key) to the game for reasons relating to the true history of basketball that Grissmer omits in his musical. Although today a practiced fundamental skill, a tactical maneuver, a form of artistic expression, and a means of social one-upmanship, the dribble was never imagined, expected, or planned. It just happened spontaneously and from there grew rapidly through myriad contingent factors into what it is today, what it is still becoming. According to Naismith's own later account, the dribble originated "when a player was facing the corner, for instance, and the other men were covered . . . and a player was right behind him, so there was not any chance for him to get rid of that ball. What he did was roll it across the floor and then run after it. Theoretically, we are not permitted to move with the ball in our possession. When I roll it, theoretically I let it out of my possession, but I follow it as closely as I can and get it. Then they began to bounce the ball, one bounce, and from one bounce they began to get a number of them." Naismith went on to add that he considered the dribble "one of the finest plays, one of the sweetest, prettiest plays in the whole bunch."[33]

In other words, a player's body responded to an intractable, seemingly insoluble problem encountered in the course of play—being trapped in a corner with the ball, surrounded by defenders, prohibited from running with it, and unable to pass it successfully—by breaking the rules and so inventing the game (again). In an instant, a player's body reflexively reinvented the game, and the game then accepted and assimilated that foreign body. Moreover, in doing so he was replicating on the floor the process by which Naismith invented the game in the first place. That Naismith himself delighted in the improvisational, inventive violation only emphasizes how distant was his understanding of *what* he had invented and *how* he had invented it from the static image portrayed in basketball's creation myth.

The sportswriter Leonard Koppett once argued that while the theoretical aim of basketball is throwing the ball through the hoop, in practical terms "you must 'deceive' your opponent in order to get a decent shot, and so basketball is a game in which various types of fakes and feints, with head, hands, body, legs, eyes, are proportionately more important than in other games." Working from a detailed, historically accurate version of the game's invention, Koppett concludes that the parameters

Naismith set for the game made the ability to deceive a defender to "get free" a basketball player's most important trait and greatest skill. This imperative to get free becomes the condition under which the dribble first emerged. Countering those who believe that so-called flashy embellishment contaminates Naismith's game, Koppett concludes that coupling the indispensable practical importance of deception with its connections to fabrication, style, and art explain why "any knowledgeable crowd will cheer louder for a fancy pass, behind the back, or through the legs, that does not lead to a score than it will for a routine basket."[34] Indeed, I can imagine Naismith himself—who celebrated the aesthetics of the dribble as "one of the sweetest, prettiest plays in the whole bunch"—there in such a crowd, loudly cheering a "fancy play."

It is hard indeed to find, among basketball's plays, a more appropriate emblem for the game than the dribble—the play that originated as a deceptive breaking of the rules to get free and that came to delight the inventor whose code it broke. From that vantage point, every single game of basketball, every single play, entails, at least on the micro level, myriad improvisational inventions of the game, myriad exhibitions of a body, in an instant of time, adapting itself and its circumstances into the shape of something we have not yet seen to solve a practical problem. The history of the dribble, in other words, shows as much as anything the lack of continuous, essential identity of basketball; it shows it to be a game evolving in multiple places at different times, through accidental and deliberate betrayals of its origins that, having been pragmatically tested, only later come to be accepted as valued parts of the game. The dribble, I am arguing, may be seen as a metonym for basketball itself: elusive, heterodox, deceptive, dynamic.

The dribble is a way to carry the ball without carrying it, to circumvent the rules without breaking them, to get free from existing constraints and, thereby, to create new patterns and possibilities on the basketball court. In these respects, the dribble is the basketball equivalent of metaphor. Metaphor, which etymologically refers to carrying meaning from one domain to another, likewise twists the rules of language without breaking them to the point of nonsense (so that "rose lips" can simultaneously be impossible and true). It liberates language from convention and, in so doing, leads us to new cognitive patterns and discoveries.[35] This secret resemblance of metaphor to dribbling—that basketball players' invention that emblematizes basketball's invention—may be why one of the most compelling narratives of basketball's origin offers a metaphorical tour de force.

Bethlehem Shoals's essay "Down by Law: James Naismith, the Peach-Basket Patriarch" offers a three-page gloss on basketball's myth of creation that is also a self-reflexive tour of metaphorical interpretations of the game's origin.[36] Shoals's rich parade of metaphors strews the supposedly singular event of the game's invention across thousands of years of history, around the world, and over several domains of human enterprise. Shoals thus converts the story of basketball's uniquely precise origin from a founding myth capable of grounding a particular essentializing, normative view of the game into a groundless, shifting matrix for kaleidoscopically generating endless variations, much like the game itself.

In the essay, Shoals ironically shuffles Naismith through a series of metaphorical comparisons, each of which he proffers, supports, and then pulls away. In dizzying succession, Naismith morphs from Moses ("lawgiving father") to Martin Luther ("basketball was a corrective measure") to a coldly rational Enlightenment engineer (who "cooked up basketball efficiently, even scientifically") to a fevered Romantic ("scribbling down basketball's rules by candlelight") to an American founding father, in which incarnation he rests briefly, before sloughing off the stars and stripes and becoming, finally, simply, "a Canadian." In the process of running Naismith through these metaphorical transformations, Shoals scatters basketball itself across multiple domains of human discourse (the religious, the scientific, the literary, and the political) and over a temporal landscape that stretches from the documented past back into the realms of religious myth. Although Shoals's essay offers the oft-repeated facts of basketball's invention, it eludes the traps of the myth of creation by self-consciously multiplying Naismith (and basketball's) possible identities.

Shoals's rhetorical style mimics the inventive improvisational elusiveness of basketball. Reading the essay, one may be tempted to latch onto any *one* of the particular metaphors he uses to convey the invention of the game as though that one figure captured the true identity of basketball. That impulse to latch on brings to mind a defender trying to lock down an offensive player in a basketball game. Like, say, LeBron James, whose diverse athletic abilities and offensive skills make him all but unguardable, Shoals eludes our interpretive grasp, going to the rhetorical basket again and again, but each time in a different way. Just when we think we have him, when we think we know what basketball is, Shoals reverses his tracks, changes directions, contradicts himself, equivocates, or ironizes and leaves us clutching air where we thought a fixed essential identity would be.

The exhibition of rhetorical elusiveness that has deprived us of any single, fixed identity for basketball has—by its very style and as a whole—

given us instead an experience of basketball as shape-shifting, improvisational, inventive performance. Shoals invites us to consider the origin of the game (and its inventor) from multiple, contradictory vantage points all at once. He thereby ironizes any attempt to identify the sport's fixed essence via an account of its origins and so relieves (or bereaves) us of our belief that we must know and name the essence of basketball to enjoy (or despise) any one of the myriad variations that is basketball.

Indeed, if we are left with anything at all, it is with a glimpse of what basketball culture might look like if we could understand and accept that basketball is, first and foremost, this endless, inventive, kaleidoscopic variation exhibited across different scales (over the course of its history; in any given era or level; in a single season, game, or even play) and then, second and as a response to this radical, foundational instability, that basketball is *also* the impulse—found in the white basketball unconscious— to arrest that variation, to fix it, label it, and so transform it into a thing to be loved or hated. Shoals's inventive rendering invites us to view what Naismith invented not as a total, ontological horizon distinguishing what is from what is not basketball, but as a set of combinatory elements that may be reconfigured inventively by subsequent generations. "Basketball," as such, is both a point of departure from which, in very definite historical, geographical, and social situations, the game would evolve in different ways and forms and an emergent property of a complex system.[37] Basketball, as a Nike campaign from 2011 reminded us, "never stops." Basketball is always on the move.

And this brings me back to Athena, but not so much Athena as we encountered her in basketball's creation myth: at the moment of her birth, bursting forth full-grown in stiff armor from the head of Zeus, a symbol of the timeless state power of Athens, which bears her name.[38] I am thinking instead—or, better yet, *also*—of the multiplicitous Athena who declares in the *Odyssey*, "I am preeminent among the gods for invention [Greek: *metis*] and resource."[39] This Athena's relevant parent is not Zeus but her mother, Metis, whose very name spans a range of meanings, including "many-coloured" and "shimmering," and is associated by some classicists with a "shifting world of multiplicity" and "deceit" and comes to mean an efficacious "way of conniving with reality," a way whose "suppleness and malleability give it the victory in domains where there are no ready-made rules for success, no established methods, but where each new trial demands the invention of new ploys, the discovery of a way out (Greek: *poros*) that is hidden."[40] Recall here the improvisational pragmatism of rhetorical invention that foregrounds the discovery of devices—such as new sports—that will effectively persuade, or the deceptive dribble that breaks the rules and gets the player free from a trap, or the frankly imaginative falsification of history that better conveys the truth of the past. All begin to appear as arts falling under the aegis of *metis* and so of Athena.

Of course, for basketball to exist at all, it must—like any other entity, cultural or otherwise—exist in a continual tension between stasis and movement, stability and flexibility, tradition and innovation. Basketball's myth of creation supports a vision of the game as static and stable, beyond the realms of matter, time, and society. Inventive modes of narrating the game's origin, however, emphasize the moving, flexible, and innovative facets of the sport. Basketball, in fact and inevitably, arises as a tension and an oscillation between the tendencies expressed through these two narrative modes.

However, I have here critiqued—as I do throughout the rest of this volume—the mythical and the static in favor of the inventive and the mobile because (as with many cultural forms in our world) the mythic and the static predominate in the imagination, supporting and supported by social structures, as if they were the natural, exclusive essence of basketball, obscuring the inventive and the mobile—and, more crucially, obscuring key historical forces and marginalized social actors associated with it. I emphasize the foundational importance of invention, then, as an affective, cultural, aesthetic, and political corrective to the tendency to hypostasize that aspect of the game.

Perhaps, if there must be a mythological emblem of basketball's origin, this multifaceted, ever moving Athena conveys more effectively and, yes, with more style the invention of a sport whose original parameters—designed to persuade a recalcitrant audience—put a premium on trickery, cunning, invention, and artfulness and so launched a proliferating evolution of all manner of form and style of play. A game whose players, of every color, gender, class, and country for more than a century have so insistently and joyfully improvised new means of deception to "get free," even when it meant breaking the rules, basketball deserves a symbol and stories of its inventive origin and subsequent development that can acknowledge continuity and tradition while matching this dazzling historical mutability, as well as the brilliant variety of its contemporary forms.

2

THE MYTH OF FOUNDATION

June 6, 1946

Do I make the game? Or do they make the game?
—**Donald Sterling**

If Naismith's invention of basketball was a physical form of persuasion, then his "argument" succeeded beyond his wildest dreams. By the middle of the twentieth century, basketball had become a major American sport at every level of competition. Over the course of the half-century following its invention, tens of millions the world over took to playing the new game: men, women, and children of all races and ethnicities, in rural and urban areas, recreationally and competitively, in a chaotic, rapidly shifting patchwork of formal and informal, variously stable amateur and professional teams and leagues.[1] Moreover, as the number of players swelled and the game spread geographically, so also swelled the ranks of spectators, initially curious about the new game but also eventually building spectatorship and fandom into the fabric of their daily lives. On this rising tide of popularity, a cluster of powerful institutions emerged—which I call "the modern basketball state"—to corral and control the basketball-playing producers of the game, regulate their product, and thus capitalize on their labor. In short, the modern basketball state emerged to capture the value—both economic and cultural—of basketball play.

I use the term "modern basketball state" to suggest, loosely, certain fundamental parallels in function between this network of basketball institutions and modern nation-states as they emerged, developed, and expanded in Europe and the Americas from the late eighteenth century through World War II. Briefly, I am referring to public entities and private capitalist interests cooperating to maximize the profits they can extract from labor, stabilize the system by which they do so, and foster the impression that this arrangement is not only desirable but also natural and, in any event, inevitable.[2] Among the cultural devices the modern basketball state employed to achieve these ends is what I call "the myth of foundation."

Nation-states employ foundational myths to selectively narrate their own origins so as to create an image of their past that leads seemingly inevitably, as if guided by destiny, to their present form.[3] In doing so, both modern nation-states and the modern basketball state tend to constrain our capacity both to remember and to imagine alternative forms of organization. "Getting its history wrong," as Ernest Renan put it, "is part of being a nation."[4] By making *themselves* the subject of historical narrative, states position themselves as agents of change while casting their citizens as passive objects. Like these, basketball's myth of foundation seeks both to make what is contingent (and thus changeable) appear necessary (and thus eternal) and to make the creative agents of history appear to be its passive consumers. But viewing basketball institutions as the modern basketball state can lead us to draw lessons from the alternatives that history has posed to modern state forms to learn about how to find and foster alternatives to the modern basketball state.[5]

If basketball is our world, then the NBA is its superpower. And if the myth of creation is the cosmogony of that world, the NBA's myth of foundation is the origin myth of that world's preeminent nation. The myth of creation narrated the origin of basketball to preserve—in the face of challenges to white male privilege—the fantasy of basketball as an unchanging configuration of athletic, tactical, aesthetic, and moral qualities. Similarly, the myth of foundation narrates the origin of professional basketball to preserve the fantasy that only control by capitalist owners prevents the sport from disintegrating into chaos at the hands of "incorrigible" basketball players. Of course, this myth, like its predecessor, also obscures the complex process by which basketball play became professionalized, as well as its own origins as a story. And we can invent an alternative narrative of professional basketball play by exploring the process the myth obscures from the perspective of those it seeks to disempower: the players.

The Myth of Foundation

June 6, 1946, emblematizes the myth of foundation because the NBA gives that as its date of origin. On that day, a group of wealthy hockey arena operators from various cities in the U.S. Northeast gathered to form an association with the explicit intention of capitalizing on the rising postwar popularity of college basketball to create a league of professional basketball teams that could fill their otherwise empty arenas when neither hockey games nor other events such as circuses were in town. As any number of versions of the myth of foundation tell the story, these owners sought to present fans with a big-city, major-league alternative to the existing National Basketball League (NBL), based in the Midwest.[6] After a couple of years of uneasy but mostly peaceful coexistence, four of the best NBL teams in large cities found the growth opportunities available in the new league enticing enough to jump to it for the 1948–1949 season. After that season, the story goes, the new league generously absorbed the last handful of insignificant NBL franchises. And that is the tale the NBA and basketball culture more generally tell about the origin of the NBA. That is its myth of foundation.

Just one thing: the NBA was *not* founded on June 6, 1946. What *was* founded on that day was a now defunct league called the Basketball Association of America (BAA). As newspapers reported on June 7, 1946, "The Basketball Association of America, a professional basketball league involving 13 cities in the United States and Canada, was organized here today with President Maurice Podoloff of the American Hockey league at its head."[7] The NBA was not formed until three years later, on August 3, 1949, as the result of a *merger* of the BAA and the NBL, and was reported that way in the papers.[8] What is more, of the seventeen franchises that made up the nascent NBA in 1949, only six were from the original BAA. In other words, almost two-thirds of the franchises in the new NBA had nothing to do with the BAA's original vision or its June 6, 1946, origin date. Yet the NBA, most fans, and many popular and scholarly historians of the sport—most of the basketball world, in short—persist in backdating the NBA's formation to June 6, 1946, when the BAA was formed.

As the former NBA Commissioner David Stern put it, referring implicitly to the formation of the BAA in 1946 in his introduction to *The NBA at Fifty*, "*Our creation* was based on the modest notion that a professional basketball league might provide additional dates for arena operators to complete their winter schedules."[9] Meanwhile, the "history" section of the NBA's official website includes season recaps going back to 1946, the BAA's first season but three years before the NBA would come into being.[10] Similarly, *The Official NBA Encyclopedia* offers, as its frontispiece, what it calls "The NBA Family Tree," listing all of the franchises constituting the league going back to 1946. A caption accompanying the photo essay that opens that volume acknowledges the existence of professional players and leagues prior to that time but relegates them to the role of "providing the roots" that would lead to the NBA, which the same caption unequivocally asserts "traces its beginning to 1946."[11]

Any number of popular and scholarly histories of the sport also repeat as fact the NBA's revisionist backdating or else implicitly trace the NBA's genesis solely back to the BAA's formation in 1946. In one of the more frequently cited popular histories of the NBA, for example, Connie Kirchberg refers to personnel and data from the BAA's three seasons as "NBA Champions."[12] The journalist Charley Rosen, in a work whose subtitle promises the story of the birth of the NBA and its first game, in fact tells the story of the BAA's first game on November 1, 1946.[13] Leonard Koppett reminds us that the National Basketball Association "began life under the name of Basketball Association of America," implying that they are one and the same entity distinguishable by only a change in name.[14] And perhaps the most popular book on basketball ever published, Bill Simmons's bestselling *The Book of Basketball*, while not explicitly addressing the formation of the NBA, dates the league's first era from 1946 to 1954.[15] Scholars narrating the emergence of the NBA within the framework of different disciplines also exhibit this particular tic of the myth of foundation.[16]

In other cases, even where the existence of both rival leagues and the facts and dates of the merger are cited accurately, the narrative structure itself attributes motive agency solely to the BAA and its owners. *The Official NBA Encyclopedia*'s article entitled "Roots" narrates the origin story from the point of view of the BAA, which is said to have absorbed the NBL franchises and then changed its name to NBA.[17] And Michael Schumacher, biographer of the early superstar center George Mikan, offers this account of the merger: "In August 1949, the BAA reached a merger agreement with the remaining NBL teams that would change the course of pro basketball history. The BAA would take in the NBL teams and a newly named league would be formed. . . . The new league would be called the National Basketball Association."[18] Schumacher acknowledges the fact of the merger and that the new league, named the NBA, was in fact a new league (and not simply a renamed version of an existing league). However, the subject of each sentence (and thus the agent driving the history these sentences depict) remains the BAA.

Unsurprisingly, given the pervasiveness of the myth of foundation in authoritative histories of the NBA, it has also taken hold in various locales in the popular consciousness, where it appears as simple truth. Thus, if one enters the search string "national basketball association founded" into Google, the first of the nearly two million results returned is a large box within which one finds, in the largest font on the page, the date "June 6, 1946," and the place name "New York City, NY." Below this is the caption "National Basketball Association founded" and, to the right, the logo of the NBA. Clicking on the logo takes you to the NBA's Google+ page. The second result is the Wikipedia entry for the National Basketball Association, which informs researchers, "The league was founded in New York City on June 6, 1946, as the Basketball Association of America. The league adopted the name National Basketball Association on August 3, 1949, after absorbing the rival National Basketball League."[19]

The negative impact of the myth of foundation manifested itself to me strikingly in the fall of 2011 while teaching my undergraduate Cultures of Basketball course at the University of Michigan. That semester, NBA owners locked the players out when negotiations over the terms of a new collective bargaining agreement reached an impasse. When we discussed the lockout and tried to imagine possible solutions, not a single student imagined the possibility of the players' simply forming a league of their own—not even a temporary league. Indeed, when I suggested it myself, they dismissed the possibility as laughably implausible—I think most of them literally laughed. That particular suggestion may or may not have been realistic at the time. But leaving that aside, why had not one of these bright and imaginative students been able to imagine anything other than minor reforms within the capitalist ownership model in professional basketball?

Among the possible reasons, one surely is the effectiveness with which the myth of foundation has purveyed and naturalized the belief that professional basketball reached its "maturity" only when properly organized, sponsored, and regulated by capitalist franchise owners operating in large media markets. All other elements of the history of professional basketball, whether earlier teams or forms of organization, rival leagues, or, of course, the players themselves—despite their initiative and excellence—become passive objects, mere role players in a story whose principal protagonist is the league as subject of basketball history. That history then gets boiled down to the actions of that league: sucking in capital from one part of the American economy, combining it with raw materials (infrastructure, communications technology, players' bodies) and bringing to consumers a product that was seemingly destined to capture markets at home and, eventually, around the globe. The naturalization of the myth of foundation—by which I mean our tendency to accept it as simply recording how things in fact *happened* rather than as a distorted re-presentation of events—has the effect of obscuring historical fact, disabling historical perspective, and inhibiting our ability to imagine alternative basketball futures.

The pervasive popularity of such a myth calls for a challenge, and its negative effects require remedy. The philosopher and cultural critic Walter Benjamin once wrote, "There is no document of civilization which is not at the same time a document of barbarism." The myth of foundation is a document of basketball civilization. While it may be too much (for some) to call it a document of basketball barbarism, there is no question that it obscures some unsavory and harmful dealings. That task of the historian in such cases, Benjamin concluded, was "to brush history against the grain" to destabilize the apparently solid foundations of an exalted origin by probing the silences and shadowed margins—the "most unpromising places"—in the story it tells of itself.[20] If so, then the genealogy of the NBA might as well begin with what its myth seems at pains to obscure: the National Basketball League.

A Genealogy of the NBA

The NBL originated in the fall of 1935 and played out two seasons under the name Midwest Basketball Conference (MBC), with franchises stretching from Chicago to Buffalo, including cities in Indiana, Michigan, Ohio, and Pennsylvania. In 1937, MBC officials renamed it the National Basketball League but operated on more or less the same basis as its predecessor. When it merged with the BAA in 1949, the league had played twelve full seasons (fourteen if you count the two it played as the MBC), surviving the tail end of the Great Depression and all of World War II, when both players and disposable income for sports spectatorship were in short supply. At its peak of popularity in the 1947–1948 season, its eleven franchises ranged from Syracuse in the east to Minneapolis in the west and played a sixty-game season and a three-round playoff.[21]

The NBL's longevity and stability, however, should not be taken as a sign of the breadth of its market appeal or of its viability as an economic growth enterprise. On the contrary, most of the NBL franchises broke even (or lost money), and even those that turned a profit were never principally moneymaking ventures. That is understandable, since most of the long-lasting NBL franchises were located in small- to medium-size midwestern cities. The median 1950 population for cities with NBL franchises during that 1947–1948 season was just 163,000, and no NBL city that year had a population larger than one million.[22] As you would expect for cities of this size, venues—usually college or high school gyms—were small. The largest might accommodate 7,500 fans, while the more standard size (and attendance figure) might be around 1,500–2,000. And, of course, there were no local, national, or cable television contracts to draw in fans from outside the franchise locale.

All of this, however, seems to have suited most NBL franchise owners, players, and fans, for most of the league's existence, quite well. According to Murry Nelson, "It cannot be emphasized enough that the NBL was founded to promote basketball and the communities that sponsored teams in the league. Though not unimportant, making money was not an initial concern of the owners in the league. They did not want to lose money, but profit was less of a concern for them than amity and sport."[23] Owners, players, and fans supported the league, in their various capacities, out of love of basketball, love of their communities, or both. Team operators and the business owners who sponsored them had developed a passion for the sport, in many cases having played in their youth, and saw supporting professional basketball as good publicity for their local businesses and as a boost to community pride. Fans rallied behind the local franchise, cheering on players who were their neighbors and co-workers. Players, meanwhile, were happy in the cash-strapped years of the Depression to augment their income and extend their careers playing a sport that many had played in college. As Nelson puts it, "The league and the community operated in a mutualistic relationship, with success for one leading to success for the other."[24]

Success certainly did come on the court. Most historians, including some who otherwise purvey the NBA's myth of foundation, regard the NBL as having had the best talent of any of the professional leagues (including the BAA).[25] The 1948 NBL champion Minneapolis Lakers also won that year's World Professional Tournament. In fact, the Lakers edged out perhaps the greatest professional basketball franchise in history, the legendary barnstorming all-black New York Rens, whose all-time win-loss record of 2,318–381, for a winning percentage (0.858), tops any in professional basketball history.[26] The Lakers would then join the BAA for the 1948–1949 season, winning that league's title before going on to win four of the NBA's first five championships. Nor was the NBL's talent confined to the Lakers. The other team to win an NBA title in the league's first five years—the Rochester Royals—was also of NBL origin. And sixteen of the twenty players selected to the all-league team in the NBA's first two seasons played for former NBL franchises.[27]

With its organizational impetus in a love for basketball, the NBL expressed perhaps the last gasp of a do-it-yourself entrepreneurial spirit that had inspired professional basketball from its inception.[28] As the membership rolls of local YMCAs in the 1890s swelled with young men interested in playing ball, interassociation play commenced pitting teams from neighboring towns in usually weekly contests.[29] Before long, YMCA executive boards saw basketball exhibitions as a cash cow whose revenues could subsidize other, less popular components of the Y's mission. In the case of the YMCA in Hartford, Connecticut, total attendance in one winter season was 10,000—the average around 550, and the largest more than 700. In all, the Hartford Y cleared $250 after expenses.[30] The rowdy crowds, however, spurred debate on the pages of YMCA publications about how best—from organizing leagues to banning basketball altogether from Y gymnasiums—to respond to the new phenomenon. Eventually, in 1896, the YMCA turned "official" administrative stewardship over to a committee under the auspices of the Amateur Athletic Union (AAU), an organization that had been founded in 1888 with the self-appointed mission of maintaining the purity of amateur ideals through the regulation of amateur sports in the United States.

But even as the power transfer occurred, YMCA players in cities where basketball had been restricted or banned took the game outside, renting venues and organizing competitions on their own. The Trenton Y's team, for example, was competing in games with both YMCA and college teams between Philadelphia and New York and traveled as far west as Nanticoke, Pennsylvania, and as far north as Hartford for matches, paying expenses out of modest gate receipts. Then on November 4, 1896, something different happened. Trenton's *Daily True American* carried an ad announcing the "Grand Opening of the Season of the National Champions." The Trentons, as the team called itself, would be hosting the Brooklyn YMCA at the Masonic Temple, where seats would cost twenty-five cents and standing room would cost fifteen cents. The difference this time was that the players—after subtracting the cost of hall rental, the fees for the referee and umpire, and the traveling expenses of their opponents—divided the gate receipts: the first professional basketball game. Those first pro basketball players received $5 for their efforts that night (roughly $140 in 2014 dollars), easily defeating the visitors 16–1 before a crowd of seven hundred.[31] The Trentons and other player/owner-operated squads in the Trenton-Philadelphia corridor soon formed the first professional basketball league: the National League of Professional Basketball, which lasted from 1898 to 1904.[32] And this, in turn, helped spur the proliferation of what one historian has dubbed "micro-leagues."[33]

The very ingredients—talented players finding a way to stage games, even despite scarce means of production, and drawing paying crowds (and interested sponsors) in the process—that connect the earliest profession-al players, teams, and leagues to the NBL also sharply *distinguish* the NBL from the BAA. This distinction helps illuminate why the NBA would dis-avow the NBL as a parent, preferring instead to identify itself fully with the BAA. NBL franchises, as we have seen, were low- or no-growth com-munity-based enterprises run for the mutual benefit of players, owners, and spectators (and in at least one case, cooperatively owned). By contrast, BAA franchise owners got into professional basketball, having observed the growing popularity of the sport, especially at the college level, primar-ily to augment the profits they could make from owning hockey arenas in large metropolitan areas. It is telling, in this regard, that the BAA formed only after the end of World War II, when Americans in a booming econo-my enjoyed greater disposable income for entertainment such as sporting events.

Whether or not BAA owners originally intended to coexist peacefully alongside the NBL, they quickly discovered that most of the best bas-ketball players—the ones fans wanted to pay to watch—were interested only in playing against the best, and the best were already playing in the NBL. Faced with losses, BAA owners stepped up the competition, using their deeper pockets, media connections, large metropolitan markets, and entertainment industry acumen to escalate bidding wars for the services of players and, eventually, luring larger-market NBL teams to jump to the BAA and its promise of big-money basketball on the nation's largest stages. After the merger, it took only one season for the smallest-market NBL franchises in the new NBA to fold. The BAA's larger capital forma-tion and greater potential for growth had succeeded in purchasing the player talent it needed to break those affective bonds connecting owners, players, and fans that had kept the NBL afloat for a dozen years. Whereas the NBL game was—and was understood by all to be—made through a cooperative effort of players, operators, and citizens, the BAA game was seen as a production conceived and created by capitalists monopolizing a labor pool to bring a product to a market of passive consumers.

In this respect, at least, today's NBA looks very much like the BAA, as a recent scandal reveals. On April 29, 2014, NBA Commissioner Adam Silver held a press conference to announce the results of the league's inves-tigation of Donald Sterling, owner of the Los Angeles Clippers franchise, who had been recorded making racist comments. Underexamined in the extensive media coverage was Sterling's rhetorical question asserting his creative importance as owner: "Do I make the game? Or do they make the game?" Sterling posed the question in the context of describing his compensation to players as an expression of paternalistic goodwill: "I support them and give them food, and clothes, and cars, and houses. Who gives it to them? Does someone else give it to them? . . . Who makes the game? Do I make the game, or do they make the game?"[34] Let me dwell for a moment on that rhetorical question at the center of these remarks: "Who makes the game?"

Although Sterling has appropriately been chastised, lampooned, and punished for his remarks and behavior, I believe he was also to some degree being scapegoated by other owners, league executives, the news media, and fans availing themselves of the easy opportunity to distance themselves from the kind of extreme and easily quotable form of racism that, too often, is the only form of racism acknowledged to exist in sports and in this country more broadly. As the journalist Tim Marchman has put it, "Sterling isn't some anomaly; he's the perfect representative of his class."[35] Indeed, we have seen that this claim that it is the owners, rather than the players, who "make the game"—and the racist logic from which it emerged, characterized as a "plantation" by the NBA star David West— expresses a key component of the myth of foundation that runs like a fault line back to the very foundation of the NBA.[36]

Inventing the Pro Basketball Player

This genealogy disturbs the NBA's myth of foundation by making visible the NBL and its role in the origin of the league. But it remains a story of an institution told from an institutional perspective and presumes that the history of the pro game is a history of owners and the associations they form. In other words, it tells the history of pro basketball from the perspective of the modern basketball state. Nonetheless, recalling the nature and role of the NBL still usefully reminds us that professional basketball players were more than merely passive tokens in a labor pool monopolized by one or two dozen of the wealthiest Americans. They were talented individuals, imaginatively reshaping the game through on-court innovation while seeking, equally imaginatively, to preserve their political and economic autonomy in a basketball universe increasingly crowded with wealthy and powerful institutions looking to capitalize on their talents and efforts. How would these same events look from the perspective of players? I am interested in *inventing* the history of the consolidation of the modern basketball state as if told *from below*, as it were, by the autonomous, creative agent that state came into being to subjugate: "the basketball player."

When James Naismith and his students invented basketball, they invented a world that shared certain important features with the world outside the gymnasium. Late nineteenth-century America was rapidly modernizing and, in the process, generating new experiences of time, space, and society. Whether alarmed, thrilled, or both, Americans during this period crafted or were drawn to visions and ideas that might help them get a handle on the modern world.[37] Basketball, as I showed in Chapter 1, was explicitly conceived as a tool to help guide young men in navigating the moral perils of modern America. Moreover, the sporting innovations built into the game's rules replicated some of modern America's distinctive spatiotemporal experiences—dramatically varied population density (in the varying spacing of players on the court), verticality, speed, fluidity, and a mix of individual and cooperative work. This made basketball into a kind of laboratory of modern life for its players.

The earliest reports of basketball play during the 1890s supported this view. YMCA physical directors, team managers, journalists, and players themselves praised the new sport for its fast pace, for the freedom of physical movement it privileged, and for cultivating qualities such as agility and quickness of thought and action that were—sometimes explicitly—identified as critical for adapting to the accelerating pace of modern life.[38] Even administrators' concerns about the roughness in the game and plans for ordering "the chaos" of basketball—usually by expanding their own power—indicate that it provided a distilled version of the temporal and spatial qualities of modern life.[39]

I call the distinctively modern spatiotemporal and social conditions built into the new sport and experienced by its new players "basketball modernity." Whether or not basketball, as one philosopher argues, "more than any other sport, opens space for humans to meaningfully live space and time," basketball's rules did constitute a universe with a distinctly modern experience of space and time and society, not least in that its players confront at one and the same time dramatic limitations and expanded possibilities.[40] Indeed, participants experienced new limits as an indirect result of experimenting with expanded powers and, conversely, augmented their powers in part through the confrontation with newly experienced limits.

In that case, I propose reframing the technical and stylistic innovations developed by participants to cope with the conditions of basketball modernity as varieties of "basketball modernism." Through such inventions as the dribble, the bounce pass, patterns of team play, the one-handed running shot, the hook shot, the jump shot, the dunk shot, trapping defenses, the fast break, defensive switches, and, especially, the assemblage of these into a single kaleidoscopic flow of play, men and women sought to make themselves *agents* of the spatiotemporal and social experiences offered by basketball modernity. To the degree that these basketball modernisms were successful, these *individuals who played basketball* transformed themselves into *basketball players*—that is, into active agents of basketball modernity.

While institutional histories depict battles between rival commercial enterprises (such as the BAA and NBL) or, in some cases, narrate a more sweeping, epic struggle between rapacious commercial interests and the guardians of the amateur ideal, from the point of view of the basketball player these same events look more like a story of increasing (even if implicit) cooperation among previously antagonistic parties working together—much as the state and private capital worked together to discipline labor in the United States in the wake of the Russian Revolution and in the course of the Great Depression—to wrest control over the game's players and the profits they generated through their labor power. But players were, as I have shown, *agents* who saw no reason that they should be forced to choose between playing for love and playing for money. On the contrary, most simply sought to find a way, amid the thicket of ideologies, institutional rules and regulations, and market forces, to play the game they played for a living *and* in the ways they loved to play it. What Leonard Koppett once wrote about the tactical essence of the sport might thus acquire a broader resonance: "Basketball players measure the quality of their play by the success they have in 'getting free.'"[41] And as they have done on the court, so have they done in relation to the institutions of the modern basketball state.

By experimenting with and inventing new forms of play, they attracted spectators willing to pay to watch games—first at YMCAs; then in a variety of venues, from dancehalls to armories; then in high school and college gymnasiums; and, finally, in large commercial arenas. Basketball players played and—by playing—made the game. The modern basketball state thus grew like a pyramid, building up from a broad base of youth interest stoked at YMCAs, on playgrounds, in amateur clubs, and eventually from high schools to the colleges and universities to the narrower ranks of professionals. Each successive level of the pyramid parasitically capitalized on the energy generated at the previous level, even as the promise of play at the higher levels fed the lower levels. As the numbers, revenues, and stakes increased, administrative organizations, educational institutions, and financial agents (or groups of any of these united by a recognition of common interest) invested more and more heavily in basketball play. In exchange for that investment, they sought and gained a much greater measure of control over the game and those who played it. As this control expanded—as in other sectors of American society—these basketball corporations virtually monopolized the sport, constituting the modern basketball state.

High schools developed masses of young players and then promoted and fed the best of them to the colleges, which developed, promoted, and then, in turn, fed their best players to professional franchises that—especially when linked to commercial interests such as equipment manufacturers and the mass media—shaped the desires, ambitions, and visions of a new crop of young players entering at the bottom. Institutional regulators (high school athletic associations, the National Collegiate Athletic Association, and league commissioners) and corporate owners of the means of production (high schools, colleges, and professional franchise and arena owners) determined who could play, controlled the production process, and sought to homogenize the product for consumers—and, of course, secured and collected profits. In the process, barnstorming teams, micro-leagues, and player-controlled operations were squeezed out of existence. Given the slow but steady consolidation of this arrangement, a young person who aspired to play basketball for a living must abide by the laws—in each domain—of the basketball state or be exiled to a kind of uncharted wasteland of recreational ball: economically and culturally marginal minor leagues, sideshow traveling teams, the neighborhood playground, or some combination of these.[42] For within its territories, the modern basketball state, backed ultimately by federal and state law in the United States, monopolized—vis-à-vis *basketball players*—two different kinds of power: the power to determine participation and the power to make and enforce the rules of the game.

Through a complex array of eligibility requirements, the institutions that make up the modern basketball state arrogated the power to determine whether an individual player could participate in basketball games sanctioned by those institutions. This power grew as their sanctioned competitions came (because of the talent level involved) to enjoy greater prestige among players and to occupy a larger and larger share of the market in basketball production and consumption. At every level, the modern basketball state has certainly sought—usually successfully—

to exercise its power to exclude from participation players who, for one reason or another, its agents have determined to be a threat to its integrity and stability.

Section 2 of the NBA Constitution—"Eligibility of Players"—begins by establishing, "All Players shall be of good moral character and possess qualities which will make them proper members of their respective Teams. The Commissioner shall have the right to disqualify a Player if the Commissioner finds that the Player does not possess the requisite qualities of character and morality."[43] Those against whom this power has been exercised have suffered hardship, as occurred with Connie Hawkins, a heavily recruited high school player from New York City who was unjustly implicated in a college gambling scandal in the early 1960s and blackballed by the NBA for nearly a decade. By the time his successful litigation forced the league to admit him, Hawkins's knees were shot from years of substandard playing conditions, and his earning power and window were dramatically reduced.[44] More recently, NBA regulations require that players be one year removed from their high school graduation date to be eligible for the NBA draft. Aspiring professional players, who are usually African American, must then either attend a U.S. college for a year or play abroad. While such experiences may or may not (as in the case of injuries) benefit players in the long run, the regulations clearly constitute a limitation on the young player's freedom—a limitation that is all the more disturbing when the racial aspects of the arrangement are taken into account.[45]

In addition to the power to determine what we might call "citizenship" (i.e., the right to play) in the basketball state, and concomitant with their monopolization of the basketball market, the institutions that make up the modern basketball state exercise sole legislative power with respect to the rules of the game itself.[46] The concentration of this power in the hands of agents of the modern basketball state implies, in effect, the power to designate technical innovations in the game introduced informally by players as legitimate or illegitimate. In this way, the modern basketball state insures that sanctioned basketball takes particular forms (and excludes others). In other words, the agents of the modern basketball state seek to wrest from the players control over the technical, tactical, and stylistic development of the sport.

The NCAA, for example, outlawed the dunk shot prior to the junior season of the dominating, seven-foot-two-inch sensation Lew Alcindor (later Kareem Abdul-Jabbar). The dunk, as we see in more detail in Chapters 3 and 4, loomed large in the imagination of the citizen of the modern basketball state around mid-century. It was, first of all, an unstoppable offensive tool. As such, it threatened with obsolescence any number of traditional patterns and scoring plays, especially those executed from below the rim. But perhaps most of all, first popularized in the 1950s by the superstar African American centers Bill Russell and Wilt Chamberlain, the dunk shot signified the rising domination of the game by black players. In this way, banning the dunk can be seen as an attempt not only to homogenize the game by eliminating a key scoring tactic but also, more nefariously, to curtail the ascendant power of African Americans to shape the game. Abdul-Jabbar was among those who saw it that way. "The dunk is one of basketball's great crowd pleasers," he said, "and there is no good reason to give it up except that this and other niggers were running away with the sport."[47]

As the examples of Connie Hawkins's blacklisting and the banning of the dunk suggest, the regulatory functions of the modern basketball state frequently operate to safeguard the fantasies of the white basketball unconscious—referring, recall, to *collective* cultural fears and fantasies—by restricting the access of players of color to the game or by "criminalizing" elements of their technical or stylistic repertoire, either making them illegal or, when this is impossible, disparaging them as morally suspect. It then justifies these exclusions through appeals to the sorts of myths we have already encountered (and to others we have yet to encounter). Thus, the myth of creation might serve to justify the elimination of the dunk shot since Naismith, in devising the horizontal, elevated goal to deemphasize sheer force in goal scoring, clearly did not envision that the ball might remain in a player's hand throughout its trajectory up and over the rim and into the basket. Indeed, all of the myths in the cultures of basketball—whatever their specific content, whatever their provenance or their contemporary points of circulation, and whenever they emerged or resurfaced—find their roots in the emergence of the basketball state. And it is basketball as it was organized and played under the auspices of this state that they hypostasize as the timeless essence of the game.

But imaginatively posing the modern basketball state as a posterior, reactive, and parasitic encroachment on the autonomous creative agency of the basketball player allows us to denaturalize the institutions that constitute it. We may be led to wonder whether state high school athletic associations or the NCAA, the AAU, or the NBA present us with the best models for producing basketball play. We may question the capitalist ownership model in professional (and "amateur") sports. We may simply begin to recognize the persisting divergent, often antagonistic interests and forces that the modern basketball state pretends to have reconciled forever more. And we may begin to look for and to cultivate those forces, in the past and present of basketball, that destabilize the modern basketball state, unsettle its myths, and thereby help basketball players (and those of us who love them and their play) do what they have always sought to do: get free.

MYTHS OF THE MODERN BASKETBALL STATE

(1949–1991)

THE MYTH OF THE RIVALRY

November 7, 1959

Almost any argument people wanted to have could
be carried on in the Russell v[ersus] Chamberlain
Debate, and almost any virtue and sin was imagined
to be at stake.—**Bill Russell**

A friend of mine expressed the feeling driving this chapter as an informal rhetorical question: "You see a man with 31,000 points. Another
has eleven rings. You think: I have to choose. What the hell is wrong
with you?"[1] The first man is Wilt Chamberlain, who amassed more than
31,000 points in the course of his NBA career—fifth best in history. (His
30.4 points per game career average is second in history.) The second is
Bill Russell, whose Boston Celtics teams won eleven NBA championships
between 1957 and 1969, including a record eight in a row. And what "you
think [you] have to choose" is who was better. My friend concisely depict-
ed a two-step perceptual ("you see") and psychological ("you think") process while challenging it with a pathologizing rhetorical question ("What
the hell is wrong with you?"). This simple two-step process, perceiving
two players and then believing one is compelled to judge which was
greater, has fueled basketball's oldest and most enduring, and among its
most highly charged, debates. The body of discourse that constitutes this
debate—the depictions, assertions, arguments, structures of thought,
metaphors, and narratives employed within it, all taken together—form
what I call the myth of the rivalry.

It may seem strange to refer to a *real* debate concerning a *real* rivalry as
a myth. The myth of the rivalry refers to *a way* to portray their competition that lays the basis for *a form of arguing* one particular position. The
myth of the rivalry presents the actual competition between Russell and

Chamberlain as not so much between two individual basketball players as between representatives of two opposed and mutually exclusive approaches to the game, styles of play, off-court demeanor, and, indeed, types of character and sets of moral values. Having assigned, as pseudo-fact, these attributes to each player, the myth of the rivalry relies on anecdote, metaphor, repetition, circular logic, and selective statistical reference to assert the objective superiority of Bill Russell over Wilt Chamberlain.[2] In this sense, the myth of the rivalry entails not merely the claim that Russell was greater than Chamberlain, but a particular way to frame, assert, and justify that claim.

The myth of the rivalry emerged (and continues today) to vent and contain powerful anxieties and desires, whether harbored by whites or blacks, stirred in that collective cultural repository I have called the white basketball unconscious by the rise to preeminence of African American men at basketball's highest and most visible level. In the face of the integration of basketball and the undeniable fact that the league's best players were disproportionately African American, adherents of the myth of the rivalry appeared to accept these realities while in fact denying them. This myth thus protected the imagined whiteness of the static, idealized form of the game postulated by the myth of creation and consolidated in the modern basketball state. Understanding this can help to counter its misrepresentations and to shed light on how the myth serves agendas that pertain to but extend far beyond basketball. But loosening the grip of the myth requires more than simply laying bare its inner working and hidden purposes. It requires inventing an alternative narrative grounded in what the myth obscures. In this case, that is the diverse skill sets and styles of play of Russell and Chamberlain—not isolated dichotomously from one another but as evolving in relationship together—as well as their connections to that history of race, in basketball and in America, that the myth's adherents prefer to ignore.

The Myth of the Rivalry

In his magnum opus *The Book of Basketball*, Bill Simmons summarizes the "Chamberlain-Russell debate":

> Wilt was more talented; Russ gave his teams a better chance to win. Wilt had a greater statistical impact; Russ had a greater impact on his teammates. Wilt peaked in the regular season; Russ peaked in the playoffs. Wilt shrank from the clutch; Russ thrived in the

clutch. Wilt lost nearly every big game; Russ won nearly every big game. Wilt averaged 50 points for one season; Russell was voted Most Valuable Player that same season. Wilt was traded twice in his career; Russ never would have been traded in a million years. Wilt was obsessed with statistics; Russ was obsessed with winning. Wilt cared about what fans, writers, and critics thought; Russ only cared what his teammates thought. Wilt never won a title in high school or college and won only two as a pro; Russ won two in college and eleven in the NBA.[3]

Although he devotes a chapter to debunking what he calls the "myths" on which rest any claims to Chamberlain's superiority, Simmons also explicitly claims that this paragraph alone stands as an irrefutable argument for Russell's superiority.

His certainty notwithstanding, Simmons charitably seeks out the sportswriter Chuck Klosterman to offer "a dissenting opinion about Wilt." Describing Chamberlain as "the greatest tangible basketball player of all time," Klosterman acknowledges that "the problem is my use of the word 'tangible.' Anything described as 'tangibly good' is inferred to mean 'intangibly flawed.' This is why Chamberlain always loses in any comparison with Bill Russell. Russell possessed intangible greatness, which means sportswriters can make him into whatever metaphor they desire."[4] In Klosterman's account, the categories of "tangible" and "intangible" pertain primarily to statistics and what we might call amateur moral psychology, respectively. Used in basketball, statistics offer scientifically objective measurements of physical achievements. By contrast, amateur moral psychology offers subjective descriptions of putative mental states—hence, the formulation of a Boston fan Simmons cites who contrasts Chamberlain's (physical) "talent" with Russell's "wanting it more."[5] One speaks to what the body has done, the other to a guess of what the mind may be doing.

We have in Western civilization a long tradition of similarly separating our human nature into two parts—body and mind—and then establishing a hierarchy between them. The tradition stretches backward from the seventeenth-century French philosopher René Descartes through medieval Christian theologians to the Greek philosopher Plato.[6] Within that tradition, the dominant position has been to consider the mind more important than the body. This influential tradition bears on Chamberlain and Russell within the myth of the rivalry. Chamberlain's greatness is associated with the tangible and with statistics, while Russell's greatness is associated with the intangible and with amateur psychology. Chamberlain is the body; Russell, the mind.[7] Once the psychological has been separated from the physical and established as the most important aspect of human nature, as Klosterman writes, Chamberlain "always loses in comparison to Russell." In this way, the myth of the rivalry deploys a powerful habit of Western thought to structure its assessment of these two players.

With this in mind, we can also understand better the operation of several other elements of the myth of the rivalry. We can understand why, for example, descriptions of Chamberlain dwell on his physical stature. Although Russell was an unusually large man (even among the basketball players of his day) with exceptional athletic ability, nearly from Chamberlain's first appearance within the culture of basketball and certainly down to the present day purveyors of the myth of the rivalry have fixated on his size, strength, and athletic ability. If someone encountering the myth of the rivalry had never seen the two men side by side, they might imagine Chamberlain as a hulking giant and Russell as stooped, skinny, and frail.[8]

This exaggerated contrast between the two players' physical stature then feeds a dichotomous account of their skill sets and styles of play. Chamberlain's size (and supposedly *natural* physical talent) makes him an offensive juggernaut. The apparent ease with which he could dominate a game offensively, the myth's purveyors speculate, led to a lack of interest in defense and rebounding. Russell, by contrast, appears as an overachieving defensive innovator (crucially, the myth dwells on Russell having *mentally* conceived his defensive style before trying it out on the court) with limited offensive skills who was happy, in any case, to sacrifice his offensive production for the good of the team.[9]

This dichotomous presentation conforms to (and so seems to be reinforced by) a couple of truisms within basketball culture: that defense depends on hard work and that defense wins championships. A syllogism results whereby if one "wants it" badly enough, one will put in the effort on defense, and if one puts in the effort on defense, one will win championships. By reverse engineering this logic, winning championships comes to be seen as indicative of competitive desire (and the lack of championships, conversely, as indicating a lack of desire). Defense, within this logic, becomes the primary site of moral virtue in basketball, the place where differences in putatively natural talent can be leveled by the virtues of hustle, effort, and hard work (or where evenness in natural talent can be differentiated).

Having contrasted Chamberlain and Russell as body and mind, offense and defense, talent and effort, respectively, the myth of the rivalry then presents a further set of contrasts that fall entirely within the moral domain. Russell appears, as we have seen, as physically vulnerable when contrasted with Chamberlain's dominating physical invincibility.[10] This opposition then gives rise to characterizations of Chamberlain's arrogance and Russell's humility. From there, Chamberlain's physical superiority and his confidence support characterizations of his laziness, since, after all, with his "natural" gifts he need not work to excel and, with his arrogance, he did not believe he had to. Meanwhile, Russell's comparatively meager physical abilities and his humility supposedly led him to develop a tremendous work ethic.[11] These putative personality traits then generate a further moral contrast when the two players are considered in the team context: Chamberlain (already physically gifted, confident, and lazy) becomes selfish and Russell (physically handicapped, humble, and hardworking) becomes unselfish.[12] At this point, we can begin to see how—given the values embedded in the culture of basketball by the myth of creation—Chamberlain is doomed to lose in comparisons with Russell, now cast as the embodiment of the sport's essential values of hard work, self-sacrifice, and cooperation.[13]

For the most part, the myth of the rivalry objectifies Chamberlain while to some degree "subjectifying" or humanizing Russell. But when the myth of the rivalry does imagine the world through Chamberlain's eyes, it depicts extreme emotional sensitivity to the views of others. Viewed in relation to his gargantuan physical being and his supposed narcissism, Chamberlain's "thin skin" comes to appear as a peevish lack of integrity or self-direction.[14] Unwilling to work and to work with others, the story suggests, Chamberlain forfeits his right to claim injury, and his expectations of others appear unreasonable. By contrast, nearly all of Russell's behavior reflects his integrity. For example, Russell's unwillingness ever to sign autographs becomes a sign, even for those who disapprove, of his defensible steadfast insistence that he be respected as a full human being and not just consumed as a basketball star.[15] In nearly every area in which the myth of the rivalry makes assertions about Chamberlain or Russell—especially, but not only, about their personalities—it regularly relies on the anecdotal views of their contemporaries, which it then circulates as empirical facts.[16]

But it is not only the content—body versus mind, strong versus weak, arrogant versus humble, offense versus defense, individual versus team, natural talent versus hard work, laziness versus effort, lack of interest versus desire, selfishness versus unselfishness—of this dichotomous presentation that is meaningful within the culture of basketball. The very dichotomous structure itself—the "versus," as it were—also signifies in important ways and offers a better grasp of the work the myth of the rivalry accomplishes for its adherents. This binary structuring is evident in the rhythmic contrasting beat of the names "Wilt/Russ" in Simmons's summary of the debate. And indeed, as Bethlehem Shoals puts it, "The Russell/Wilt binaries have since become staples of NBA discourse."[17] We might amplify Shoals's observation and say that those binaries had long been part of the discourse of the game and were certainly commonplace by the time the modern basketball state emerged around the middle of the century. But it is true, as Shoals suggests, that Russell and Chamberlain came to embody them.

David O'Connor sees in the debate the continuation of a philosophical conversation—going back to Aristotle—about excellence, how to achieve it, and the role of heroes in our efforts to do so. Although O'Connor refrains from deciding the issue, in the course of elucidating the stakes (by what ideal standards should we judge, and so strive for, excellence), he reproduces one of the most basic binary oppositions of the myth of the rivalry when he casts the argument as one between the "ideals of domination [Chamberlain] and the ideals of teamwork [Russell]." He then maps these ideals onto the figures of the "Romantic Hero" (Chamberlain) and the "Consummate Executive" (Russell).[18] If so, and recalling my analysis of basketball's genealogy of morals in Chapter 1, then to choose Chamberlain is to choose against the game itself, which may partly explain why so much of the basketball world in Chamberlain's time shared Jimmy Breslin's anxious question, "Can basketball survive Wilt Chamberlain?"

But perhaps there was even more than basketball at stake. "Binary structuring" forms one of the defining features of what Kieran Egan calls "mythical understanding" in young children. Egan explains that "organizing one's conceptual grasp on the physical world by initially forming binary structures—hot/cold, big/little, soft/hard, crooked/straight, sweet/sour—allows an initial orientation over a range of otherwise bewildering complex phenomena. . . . These oppositions are not necessarily, or even often, made up from genuine logical or empirical opposites; rather they are set up as opposites for conceptual purposes of orientation to complex phenomena, bringing them under some kind of initial conceptual control."[19]

We might apply Egan's work to anyone experiencing a complex, bewildering, unfamiliar situation as potentially threatening. Given a powerful enough sense of disorientation or a sufficiently dramatic change in a familiar setting, any adult might regress to the binary thinking that originates in and is most commonly found in early childhood. This may be more likely

THE MYTH OF THE RIVALRY · 61

in competitive and dramatic contexts—such as the culture of sports—that already lend themselves to binary structuring and mythic thinking.

Such a series of shocking changes occurred in the modern basketball state (and in American society) in the decade that led up to the first head-to-head meeting of Russell and Chamberlain on November 7, 1959. These changes entailed the desegregation of the sport at every level and, with it, a tactical and aesthetic revolution in basketball. By the time Russell and Chamberlain first squared off, Russell was already considered one of the most valuable players in the league. A decade later, by the time they played their final game against each other, basketball would be, in fact and in the American imagination, a sport dominated by black men. That this occurred in the context of desegregation in society, the rise of the Civil Rights Movement, and increasing racial violence served only to heighten the stakes. Perhaps Breslin meant to ask, "Can white privilege in America survive Wilt Chamberlain?" In any event, deeply frightened by and resentful of the changing territory of basketball, the white basketball unconscious of America was primed to create, propagate, and cling to the myth of the rivalry.

A Genealogy of Basketball Desegregation

In Chapter 2, I focused on the formation of the NBA as a symbolic and material watershed in the consolidation of the modern basketball state. But many in the basketball world considered another event in 1949 of even greater importance: the first ever national high school all-star game. If the NBA's formation represented the stabilization of the professional game, the First North-South National High School Championship (also known as the Converse Classic) in 1949 represented to many the breadth, stability, and promise of the base of the modern basketball state's pyramid of interlocking institutions.[20] The North-South Cage Commission selected final rosters from a list, supplied by sportswriters, of the best one thousand players in the country. After the game, Chuck Taylor himself (of Converse shoe fame) presented awards to five "All-Americans" and named as "Mr. Basketball" the best high school player in the country.[21]

Despite the apparent rigor of the selection process, it is unlikely you have ever heard of the vast majority of players who took part in the Converse Classic over the eight years the contest was staged (1949–1956) because few of them went on to have successful basketball careers. Given NBA draft rules at the time, Converse Classic alumni were eligible for NBA drafts from 1953 to 1960. In fact, only in 1954 did Classic alumni (from the 1950 game) appear among the top picks in the NBA draft. Moreover, of the nearly two hundred Converse Classic veterans, only three appear on lists of the NBA's all-time top 250 players as measured by two common metrics.[22] By comparison, those same eight NBA draft cohorts between 1953 and 1960 produced *nine other players* who were not Converse Classic All-Stars and yet still appear on those lists. Among these nine: Bill Russell and Wilt Chamberlain.

How is it possible that two of the best, most famous basketball players of all time could have failed to make a National High School All-Star game? Russell, it is true, bloomed late and so was little known as a high school player. But Chamberlain was the subject of the first mass recruitment in history, sought after by more than two hundred colleges and featured in national news media articles even as a senior. He certainly was known and could have played in the 1955 Converse Classic. So why did he not? What about Bob Boozer, Tom Hawkins, Dick Barnett, and Johnny Green, who along with Chamberlain were the top five picks in the 1959 NBA draft? Why were they not Converse Classic All-Stars in 1955? And why were Oscar Robertson, Ray Felix, Elgin Baylor, and Lenny Wilkens not? Besides being considered among the NBA's all-time top 250 players, all of these players—and Bill Russell—had one other thing in common: they were black. The Converse Classic All-Star game, one of the most symbolically significant events in the consolidation of the modern basketball state, was segregated, excluding black players.

The twenty-year period of American history stretching from that first Converse Classic in 1949 through to the last game Chamberlain and Russell played against each other in 1969 saw desegregation grow—despite considerable violent segregationist backlash—thanks to the persistent pressure of the black freedom struggle. This dynamic played out within the culture of basketball, as well, where a vibrant but long-marginalized tradition of African American basketball play made its way to center stage at the game's highest levels. By 1969, most NBA players—and a greater majority of its best and biggest stars—were black. Not only did the racial makeup of the game change; the increased prevalence of black players also changed the game itself, as they brought with them individual and team playing styles hitherto unseen in the all-white culture of the modern basketball state.

Before World War I, in addition to a tiny handful of black players on white college teams, numerous all African American teams (called "Black Fives") formed in northern cities.[23] The Black Fives in this period were amateurs, competing for fitness, recreation, camaraderie, and bragging rights. The early squads, originating in schools, athletic clubs, and other organizations, stimulated interest in the sport. In some cases, their players went on to organize or coach teams once their own playing days were done, thus influencing a subsequent generation of ballplayers. For example, in the early 1920s, Caribbean-born Bob Douglas, who played for the Alpha Club's all-black squad, founded the "Harlem Renaissance," which originally debuted on November 30, 1923, and became, over the course of nearly two decades of barnstorming, the New York Renaissance Five, one of the most successful professional basketball teams of all times.[24]

In the interwar period, the formation of athletic conferences by representatives of historically black colleges and universities, especially in the South, fomented interest in the sport and established regional and even interregional networks of affiliation and competition. This institutional development combined with rules and equipment changes to spark a transformation of the sport.[25] The elimination of the center jump after every basket in 1937 accelerated the game. It also created the possibility for the fast break, exploited (with encouragement by his mentor, James Naismith) by Coach John McLendon of the North Carolina College for Negroes (now North Carolina Central University). McLendon's squads, which also employed a full-court pressing defense, dominated the Central Interscholastic Athletic Association throughout the 1940s.[26] Meanwhile, the reduction of the size of the ball and the elimination of its laces made dribbling easier and reduced the emphasis on ball movement through passing. Together, these changes fostered the development of tactics and styles based in speed, leaping ability, and individual skills, and this changed version of the sport then developed on public playgrounds in both northern and southern cities by newly arrived black migrants beginning in the 1940s.[27]

The racial integration of the modern basketball state was uneven, occurring at different times and in different places depending on one's benchmark. For their part, Basketball Association of America (BAA) owners, whatever their individual racial attitudes, appear to have been afraid that integration would alienate Abe Saperstein, the owner of the Harlem Globetrotters, who enjoyed a virtual monopoly on the top black professional basketball talent.[28] Appearing in doubleheaders with BAA teams, the Globetrotters—at that time "basketball's biggest attraction"—helped keep the new league afloat.[29] Early discussions of the color line by BAA (and, initially, NBA) owners were strongly shaped by an awareness that luring talented African American players away from the Globetrotters could endanger the NBA's critical relationship with Saperstein.[30] At the same time, owners realized that the success of their venture would depend on putting the best product on the floor, and this meant integrating the league. Thus, in the 1950 player draft that followed the NBA's first season, the first three African American players—Chuck Cooper, Earl Lloyd, and the former Globetrotter and Ren Nat Clifton—were added to NBA rosters.[31]

Over the next few seasons, a trickle of African American players entered the NBA, and some had outstanding success. Still, it would not be until the 1958–1959 season that all eight NBA franchises would have at least one African American player on their rosters, and even that year only two teams would have as many as three. Despite (or perhaps because of) the effectiveness of pioneering players, it appears that owners imposed unofficial quotas that limited both the number and the roles of black players.[32] Indeed, Commissioner Maurice Podoloff actually suggested a formal racial quota at a board of governors meeting as late as the early 1960s.[33] Russell himself, with grim irony, recalled that the rule of thumb was to "put two black athletes in the game at home, put three on the road, and put five in when you get behind."[34] In addition to quotas and, in some cases, patronizing (or worse) attitudes from owners, coaches, and teammates, players frequently faced segregated traveling, dining, and lodging arrangements and insults, hostility, and violence from racist fans.[35]

Understanding the modern basketball state's racial history helps explains the emergence and persistence of the myth of the rivalry. Apart from major political leaders such as Dr. Martin Luther King Jr. and Malcolm X, and alongside the boxer Muhammad Ali, arguably no cultural figures in America better emblematized the growing power and assertiveness of African Americans than Russell and Chamberlain.[36] Not only were they the dominant players in the game; they were also physically imposing, outspoken public figures who together forever changed the way the game of basketball would be played. Patterned offenses, passive defenses, and floor-level play gave way to pressing, aggressive defenses, fast-breaking offenses, and above-the-rim play on both ends of the court, including what might be, for the white basketball unconscious, the most terrifying symbol of African American ascendance in basketball: the slam dunk, called by one writer of the time, describing Chamberlain, "the most devastating method yet found to score two points."[37]

This may explain why the writer John McPhee found that by 1962 his feeling for basketball "had faded almost to nothing." He wrote, "The game seemed to me to have lost its balance, as players became taller and more powerful . . . with few patterns of attack and almost no defense any more.

The players, in a sense, had gotten better than the game [by taking] the skill out of basketball."[38] In his sensationally titled article "Can Basketball Survive Wilt Chamberlain?" published in 1956, Jimmy Breslin described a play that made Nebraska's Coach Jerry Bush "feel sick": Chamberlain, driving near the top of the key, "went up for what appeared to be a one-handed jump shot. But he didn't come down. He kept floating through the air, did a complete twist, so that his back was to the basket, shoved his arm behind him, rotated it in helicopter style and dunked the ball in the net."[39] This may not be a factual description of anything Chamberlain ever did. In fact, the description strikes me as difficult even to visualize. But for this very reason, it captures well the fantastic quality of not only the fears but also the perceptions of many whites in the modern basketball state. As Gary Pomerantz puts it, Chamberlain "proved his physical superiority night after night and made a mockery of the league and its racial quotas and the notion that his white opponents were the best players in the world. He reduced to rubble the white-defined ideas of *fair play* and *sportsmanship*, which he knew as lies. Whites didn't want fair play; they feared it."[40] This is what the historian Michael Novak calls the persistent "cultural resistance to the domination of blacks within the game."[41]

The myth of the rivalry expresses an anxious response on the part of the white basketball unconscious to these events. It may now be easier to see, in view of this history, why the dichotomies I noted above took the particular form they did and were applied as they were. Adherents of the myth of the rivalry *appear* to accept that basketball has become a black-dominated sport (since, after all, the question they pose is which of two black men is the greatest) but then undo that acceptance by reductively characterizing Russell as a paragon of all the styles, tactics, and virtues associated with whiteness in the days of the segregated modern basketball state: unselfishness, cooperation, hard work, intelligence, and defense. Chamberlain, by contrast, can come to embody all that the white basketball unconscious believed or feared to be the case about black basketball players and (it is not too much to add) black men more generally: physical prowess, natural talent, selfishness, laziness, and egotism. In this, of course, it reflects a broader historical tendency on the part of the "white imaginary," which, as Glyn Hughes succinctly puts it, "manages race through a choreography of proximity and distance to White norms and expectations. Good Blacks are welcomed into the center of American cultural life, bad Blacks are condemned, and, at the same time, proximate Blacks are always haunted by the condemned because they are defined by what they are not."[42]

Strikingly, this occurs even when the myth of the rivalry addresses the very racial politics (in and out of the NBA) that it exists to erase or, at least, contain. Thus, Russell's outspoken activism comes to be seen—as, of course, it should be—as a humanizing expression of his integrity and unselfish, communitarian sensibility, although it is worth noting this would occur especially retroactively, after his playing days ended and the intensity of the antiracism movement had peaked. Meanwhile, Chamberlain's responses to racism appear to indicate either moody sensitivity or aloof narcissism.[43] At the same time, the myth of the rivalry suppresses the investments they shared as politically aware and active black men in America in the 1960s. The myth of the rivalry ignores, for example, that Russell and Chamberlain talked on the phone in the wake of King's assassination in 1968 about whether or not to hold their imminent playoff game. It ignores that both preferred not to play, though both ultimately yielded to their teammates. It ignores that both attended King's funeral in Atlanta.[44]

This is not to say that Russell and Chamberlain held identical political positions or were somehow regular partners in political activism. Far from it. But whatever the real differences in how the two players experienced and combatted racism, the myth of the rivalry incorporates this material first to safely vent and thereby contain some of the racialist energy driving it in the first place (as if it were saying, "I can *so* talk about race and politics") and then to confirm its dichotomous division of the two players. It grinds down the edge of Russell's often angry, radical, and controversial activism to bland expressions of a vaguely universal humanity and team spirit while chalking up Chamberlain's political activity to his thin skin and selfishness. In this way, the myth of the rivalry simultaneously exaggerates their differences and oversimplifies their positions, reductively reading everything back to its foundational, dichotomous matrix of moral oppositions.

Inventing a Basketball Revolution

Wilt Chamberlain himself once tried to account for the selective logic of the myth of the rivalry: "The white media was always building up blacks to go against each other—a sort of 'OK, niggers, let you and him fight.' . . . In basketball and other sports in those days, they did much the same thing; they set it up so that one of the blacks constantly had to demonstrate his superiority against the other, and that left only one black superstar to challenge the white superstars."[45] Chamberlain's description captures the *fundamental* racial logic of the myth of the rivalry, whereby the white basketball unconscious "selected" the two most dominant black players of the time, pitted them against each other, and then polarized them: mapping onto one (Russell) all the mythic qualities associated with (white) basketball during the rise of the modern basketball state and onto the other (Chamberlain) all the stereotypical qualities associated with black masculinity. In this way, the myth of the rivalry allowed the white basketball unconscious simultaneously to accept and to deny that a racial, stylistic, and tactical revolution had taken place in basketball. Because the racial significance of the myth emerged only in view of its *dichotomous way* of narrating the rivalry, I wish to counter this myth by presenting a non-dichotomous approach to the competition between Russell and Chamberlain and their teams.

To begin with, let me simply complicate the myth's misleading, over-simplifying characterizations of the two players. Russell was an extremely capable offensive player, and Chamberlain was an intimidating, effective force on defense who, despite his lauded physical strength, never once fouled out of an NBA game.[46] Although Russell's teams indeed won more championships, Chamberlain's teams won a great number of games in their own right and, moreover, Chamberlain, by most advanced statistical measurements, contributed to more victories over the course of his career.[47] Over the course of the nearly 150 games their teams played against each other, the overall average margin of victory for Russell's teams was two points—a single field goal. Contrary to images of his lack of interest, Chamberlain played a higher percentage of the minutes available to him than any player in history, and Russell, by his own admission, shirked practices. Finally, each player's supposed areas of weakness appear so only when compared with the unprecedented and often still unmatched strength of the other in that area.[48]

But we can do more than simply correct the *content* of the myth of the rivalry. We can imagine a richer and more inventive *way* to see, understand, and narrate what is happening when two individuals from opposing teams meet on a basketball court. Consider, for example, the maverick art critic Dave Hickey's description of one such encounter: "Julius [Erving] is driving to the basket from the right side of the lane against Kareem Abdul-Jabbar. Julius takes the ball in one hand and elevates, leaves the floor. Kareem goes up to block his path, arms above his head. Julius ducks, passes under Kareem's outside arm and then under the backboard. He looks like he's flying out of bounds. But no! Somehow, Erving turns his body in the air, reaches *back* under the backboard from behind, and lays the ball up into the basket from the *left* side!"⁴⁹ After the game, Abdul-Jab-bar expressed his admiration for Erving's creative talent. But "Kareem's remark," Hickey contends, "clouds the issue because the play was as much his as it was Erving's, since it was Kareem's perfect defense that made Erving's instantaneous, pluperfect response to it both necessary and pos-sible—thus the joy, because everyone behaved perfectly, eloquently, with mutual respect, and something magic happened."⁵⁰

The breathtaking genius of Chamberlain-Russell lies in the fact that their matchups demonstrated this and provoked this joy not just in a single play but many times per game in 142 games over a ten-year period. Julius Erving, as Chapter 4 shows, revolutionized the forward position with his aerial improvisations in the 1970s and 1980s. Indeed, the play Hickey describes could be read as emblematic of this revolution because Erving's creative innovation eludes the considerable obstacle presented by the best that conventional basketball wisdom could possibly imagine in the consummately skilled, seven-foot-two-inch Abdul-Jabbar. But it must be said that, in revolutionizing the center position, what Russell and Chamberlain *together* created the conditions for what Abdul-Jabbar and Erving would later do.

If we must see Russell and Chamberlain as rivals, then we must expand and complicate our understanding of rivalry so that we may see not merely a zero-sum contest from which one must emerge labeled a winner and the other a loser, one a success and the other a failure. We must see the fluid interaction of two agents competing freely, certainly, but also symbiotically bound up in a joint creative endeavor in which the perfection of one is a condition for the perfection of the other. The combi-nation of the two perfections completely transforms a sport and a culture, terraforming the existing ground and laying it open to possibilities—like those Hickey describes—that, I daresay, neither Chamberlain nor Russell would have imagined when he first jumped center against the other on November 7, 1959.

Of course, a basketball game results in an outcome in which one team scores more points than another at the conclusion of a predetermined period of play, and, although neither "win" nor "lose" appears anywhere in the rules, everything in athletic culture tells us to call the team that scores fewer points the loser. It seems natural and even unavoidable, and certainly understandable, to view a basketball game through the lens of the binary opposition between winning and losing. From there, it is just a short step to casting the most important and visible individuals on each team as winners and losers. But even a moderately attentive observer knows that the outcome of basketball games is determined by the interaction of a multitude of factors. It is, after all, a team sport and an extremely dynamic one in which all players are regularly involved in the flow of the action. From that standpoint, the outcome of the game no longer reflects directly on any single individual.[51]

There is no need to choose between Russell and Chamberlain. One can note the differences between the two players, and even have a preference for one over the other, without perpetuating the pernicious discourses of the myth of the rivalry. Indeed, even seen through the lens of what Stephen Mumford calls "competitive perception" (meaning with a powerful emotional investment in final outcomes), the exceptionally high level of competition between Chamberlain and Russell only intensifies affective experiences of hope and dread—the accelerators of fandom's fire.[52] Rather than the boredom ensuing if either player easily dominated a game, the competition between the two of them would not only bring out the best in each but also leave fans of each excruciatingly and delightedly uncertain as to the outcome of any individual play, let alone the game. But their competition is also a valuable phenomenon in its own right in which the contested outcome operates as a heuristic, a kind of enabling fiction whereby fans and players all agree to participate as though winning were the most important thing to maximize the competitive intensity and, with that, the excellence of the athletic performance and the affective and intellectual appreciation of the event. Russell himself seemed to understand this when, mourning Chamberlain's death in 1999, he said, "We didn't have a rivalry; we had a genuinely fierce competition that was based on friendship and respect. We just loved playing against each other."[53]

In that case, the importance and, indeed, excitement of Russell-Chamberlain stems from the number of times the two most dominant players of their age faced each other directly on the court with so much at stake and thereby spurred each other to peerless levels of basketball excellence. But the greater significance of their competition emerges only by restoring the context that the myth of the rivalry suppresses or distorts: racism and the struggle for freedom in America and in basketball. In pursuing excellence on the basketball court, they simultaneously revolutionized the sport for generations to follow and both exposed and demolished racist barriers in the game and in society, which should only make us appreciate them more: each of them as individuals, I mean, but also *them*—their relationship. There is virtually no aspect of basketball as millions around the world play and enjoy watching it today that cannot be traced back, more or less directly, to the tactical and cultural revolution that Bill Russell and Wilt Chamberlain, together, ushered in.

Seen from this vantage point, it strikes me as either childish or petty to insist that a choice must be made simply because they played on opposing teams in a sport in which one team wins and another loses. That the choice should be accompanied by pseudo-explanations recurring to dubiously backed and, in any event, certainly reductive characterizations of moral character, simplistically mapped onto likewise oversimplified stylistic and tactical differences, intimates something more harmful. But when this insistence, with its moralizing overtones, subtly attaches itself to powerful racial stereotypes, as the myth of the rivalry does, it becomes much more than petty. It devolves into the dangerous demand that we suppress a history of oppression and struggle and diminish the accomplishments of two human beings to pacify our unexamined anxiety over perceived threats to our privilege. If so, then by rejecting the myth of the rivalry we refuse complicity with a shameful legacy of racism in basketball and in society and ally ourselves instead with innovative forms of relationship pursued for the sake of freedom, on and off the court.

THE MYTH OF THE GARDEN

May 8, 1970

The Knicks are about the possibility of shared
values even after the whole world seems to have
broken wide open.—**Bethlehem Shoals**

Shortly before retiring after the 1969 season, Bill Russell led the Boston
Celtics to their eleventh championship in thirteen seasons. En route,
they defeated the New York Knicks in the Eastern Division finals.
But neither Knicks fans nor journalists covering the team nor players
despaired.[1] On the contrary, they eagerly looked forward to next season.
The series had been close, and several key Knicks players were either out
with injuries or ailing. What is more, many predicted that with Russell's
retirement the Celtics dynasty would finally come to an end, so the road
to the NBA title appeared wide open. Meanwhile, the Knicks had improved
steadily in each of the previous few seasons. With a healthy roster of young
players, the right coach, and the full support of New York City basketball
fans, the Knicks seemed set to take the next step and assume what many
saw as their rightful place atop the basketball world. And so they did: just
a little over a year after bowing out to Russell's Celtics, the Knicks cruised
through the regular season and knocked off the Los Angeles Lakers to win
the team's first NBA championship on May 8, 1970. More than a few in
the galvanized "Mecca" of basketball believed the team was making good
on the forward Dave DeBusschere's hopeful proclamation, made after Boston's loss of the previous year: "We're in the process of building a dynasty."[2]

Already in the wake of the title, numerous books heralded the team
and its individual players, lauding, in particular, their unselfish style of
play.[3] As recently as 2011, the columnist Harvey Araton of the *New York*

Times described the squad as "the most democratic team in professional basketball history."[4] This phrase is representative of what I call the myth of the garden (after Madison Square Garden, the legendary venue that was home to the Knicks). The myth of the garden consists of a celebratory narrative that combines praise for the Knicks' style of play and an emphasis on the racial and socioeconomic diversity of the team's roster, all lightly contextualized in reference to the American social, cultural, and political landscape of the time and set atop a nostalgic prehistory of basketball in New York City.

This myth emerged and has operated such that the Knicks of the early 1970s are remembered as among the greatest basketball teams ever assembled, alongside other teams that sustained similar levels of success over longer periods of time (the Celtics of the 1960s and 1980s, the Lakers of the 1980s and 2000s, and the Bulls of the 1990s). The myth of the garden advances the gratifying fantasy not only that the so-called purist style of play is superior in competitive terms but also that its ostensible values of unselfishness and hard work resolve both racial and class conflict.[5] Whether or not this may be the case in specific instances, the coherence of this particular fantasy rests on marginalizing racially stigmatized elements and styles of play eschewed by the Knicks but thriving at the time in the newly formed, rival American Basketball Association (ABA). These elements and styles would endure, shape the NBA through to the present day, and, finally, offer a more inclusive avenue by which basketball play may respond to issues of racial injustice.

The Myth of the Garden

The myth of the garden is, to paraphrase Pete Axthelm, who in 1970 wrote what is perhaps the canonical work on the Knicks, "the story of the city game, as it is experienced in the city that knows and loves it best."[6] It goes something like this: once upon a time, New York City and, in particular, its landmark arena, Madison Square Garden, was the Mecca of the basketball universe, the source from which some of the best basketball talent emerged and the center to which all great basketball talent, whatever its provenance, gravitated to prove itself on the biggest and brightest stage. Local boys transformed street smarts and basketball skills honed on the tough and crowded playgrounds of the city into careers with barnstorming teams such as the Original Celtics; went on to star for or coach local college powerhouses such as St. John's, Long Island University, and City College of New York in prestigious national tournaments played under the lights of the Garden; and set their sights on a spot with the hometown Knicks of the newly formed NBA.

But somehow the unthinkable occurred; a snake made its way into the garden. In 1950, just after City College, with a racially integrated roster consisting mainly of local boys, achieved the unprecedented and since unduplicated feat of winning both of the major college tournaments—the National Collegiate Athletic Association (NCAA) and National Invitational Tournament (NIT)—in a single season, an investigation into gambling in college sports revealed that some of the squad's players had accepted bribes to fix the outcome of games. As the scandal spread, many of the major programs in college basketball would be implicated. But New York and Madison Square Garden, venue for the most important college games, emerged as the vile epicenter of the plague of corruption.[7] Madison Square Garden's NIT would be eclipsed by the NCAA tournament, which stopped holding its now more prestigious tournament in New York. Meanwhile, the Knicks, who had reached the NBA finals three years running, began to fade after the 1953 season. As the college game flourished in such locales as Kansas, Indiana, North Carolina, Kentucky, and even Los Angeles, a professional dynasty arose in Boston that would dominate the NBA from the mid-1950s to the late 1960s. Nor were the Knicks of this period—unlike Chamberlain's teams in Philadelphia or San Francisco, Oscar Robertson's Cincinnati Royals, or Jerry West and Elgin Baylor's Los Angeles Lakers—even able to play the role of great teams tragically caught in the shadow of Boston's invincibility. It was as if the Mecca of basketball had simply vanished from the basketball map, its previously exalted inhabitants banished and forgotten.[8]

Then! Then, a few individuals, loyal New Yorkers, like basketball Robinson Crusoes stranded on a desert island with the tattered remnants of great shipwreck, began in solitude and anonymity the thankless task of bringing great basketball back to the city.[9] No heroes or pie-eyed idealists, these men—Fuzzy Levane, Eddie Donavan, Dick McGuire, and, above all, Red Holzman—were, on the contrary, clear-eyed realists and dedicated basketball men, earning their bread by the sweat of their brows, willing to drive hundreds of miles to obscure gyms and playgrounds, scouting players they believed had the basic talent and personality to be molded into professional basketball players. Patiently, year after year, they built, ladling player after player into the mix—Willis Reed (1964), Dick Barnett (1965), Cazzie Russell (1966), Bill Bradley, Walt "Clyde" Frazier, Phil Jackson (all three in 1967), and others—like so many ingredients into a slowly simmering stew, a stew then stirred by the understated Holzman, a City Game lifer, who assumed the head coaching duties midway through the

1967–1968 season, guiding the squad from a mid-season mark of 15–22 to only its second playoff appearance in nine years.

Nor was theirs a bond formed in pursuit of vulgar lucre. Although the formation in 1967 of the upstart ABA created a competitive market for top basketball talent and began to drive up salaries, the Knicks players stayed true. Bradley may have earned a lavish salary (and the nickname "Dollar Bill"), but he and the rest of the Knicks surely could have made more money had they jumped to the new league. Yet the prestige of the NBA, the hunt for a title, loyalty to the franchise that had brought them together, and, above all, the priceless joy of playing team basketball proved more attractive to them the glittering riches promised by ABA clubs.[10]

In the 1968–1969 season, Holzman led the team to the brink of greatness. After an early-season trade brought the working-class Detroit hero Dave DeBusschere to the club, the team finished off the regular season on a 35–11 run, including an eleven-game winning streak. Although the team fell in the playoffs to Boston, hopes were high that all the elements of the dynasty were in place. Even in defeat, the team had demonstrated that it had what it took: unselfish, hardworking, intelligent players, expertly selected for chemistry and complementarity and capable of internalizing the principles of Holzman's simple but forceful directives to "move without the ball" and "hit the open man" on offense and to support one another in a trapping, harassing defense. As Lewis Cole has summed up the assessment of legions of fans and media observers of the squads, "They became the game's dream team, the instance of how basketball should be played and why it should be watched, the moment of superb mastery in the sport."[11]

Each player brought a distinctive and indispensable element to the mix. Frazier handled the ball and wreaked havoc on opposing guards with his defense, frequently triggering fast breaks with daring steals. Reed anchored the defense and opened up lanes to the basket by luring opposing centers out of the lane with his outside shooting prowess. DeBusschere hustled to shore up vulnerabilities created by the Knicks' defensive traps and gobbled up loose balls and rebounds. The heady Bradley moved tirelessly without the ball and unselfishly kept it moving on offense. And Barnett contributed scoring with his deadly fall-away jump shot. Off the bench, the former All-American Cazzie Russell provided instant scoring; lanky Phil Jackson contributed defense and rebounding; and Mike Riordan and John Stallworth offered hard-nosed defense and steady play. This was basketball as the Creator had intended, as it always had been played in the prelapsarian age of the City Game, before the dark years of scandal, shame, and mediocrity. Basketball innocence had been restored to the garden, and the basketball globe thus was once again properly centered on its axis.

By the time the 1969–1970 season began, with America and New York itself engulfed in violent waves of protest against the Vietnam War, intergenerational class struggle, the growing militancy of the Civil Rights Movement, and white supremacist backlash, the Knicks reeled off eighteen straight victories, then unprecedented in NBA history, en route to a 19–1 record. Assembled without regard to race, creed, or social class, the meritocratic Knicks were a diverse mix of race, class, and geographical provenance and in this way showed the city and the nation how the very same principles of unselfishness, cooperation, and hard work that made them successes on the court could help heal the nation and propel it peacefully forward into the new decade. Indeed, although a violent riot—known as the "hard hat incident"—broke out between antiwar protestors and construction workers on the very day, May 8, 1970, that the Knicks won the title, the columnist Frank Deford would still write, a week after the title, "If there was a common cause left in town, it was the Knicks."[12] From playgrounds in impoverished projects to the luxury brownstones of the Upper East Side, from Greenwich Village cafés to suburban estates, *everybody* came together in love for their team, which finally brought championship basketball back to the Mecca in May 1970: "Rich, middle class, or poor, there wasn't a Manhattan neighborhood that wouldn't welcome the Old Knicks."[13] Even as New Deal liberal alliances were falling apart, the myth of the garden could hail the Knicks as a symbol of the successes and continued promise of liberalism.

When the second title came in 1973 (after two near-misses in 1971 and 1972), the cast of characters had changed somewhat, but only in ways that eventually cemented the legacy of the team. Early in the 1971–1972 season, a trade with Baltimore (which had defeated the Knicks in the 1971 playoffs) brought the superstar guard Earl Monroe to the team to share backcourt duties with the steady defensive wizard Frazier. Known as "Black Jesus" and "Earl the Pearl," Monroe had been a playground and college legend before taking his dazzling array of spins and fakes to the NBA. There, Monroe led the Bullets to excellent seasons while polishing his reputation as the league's most unstoppable one-on-one player. When he was traded to the Knicks, the world wondered whether the team's understated style and emphasis on unselfishness, effort, and teamwork could assimilate Monroe's flashy, individualistic talents. Would Monroe spoil the chemistry of the perfect team?[14]

But according to myth of the garden, the seemingly infinite flexibility of the Knicks system proved up to the challenge and helped persuade Monroe to subordinate his ostentatious individualistic instincts so that, when the Knicks won the 1973 championship, the perfect superiority of the team was decisively demonstrated.[15] Except, of course, that the Knicks would never win another title—or, as the historian Nelson George put it, "In the great flow of basketball history, they never exerted dynastic control of their era."[16] But according to the myth of the garden, this "misses the larger point of what the Old Knicks represented to . . . many neutral basketball connoisseurs: the game distilled to near perfection."[17] Perhaps, indeed, this explains why the Old Knicks, with their two titles, are mentioned alongside such dynasties as the 1960s Celtics (eleven titles), the 1990s Chicago Bulls (six titles), and the 1980s and 2000s Lakers (five titles each) and certainly ahead of such teams as the late 1980s Detroit Pistons (two titles) and the mid-1990s Houston Rockets (two titles). Perhaps their celebrated unselfishness merits such accolades. But, in fact, among the sixty-five NBA championship teams since 1950, the 1973 Knicks squad ranks thirty-third and the 1970 squad ranks fortieth in the ratio of team assists to team field goals, a commonly used statistical measure of teams' unselfishness. Indeed, neither squad was even the most unselfish team in its championship season.

A Genealogy of Eden

The title of Araton's celebratory (and celebrated) compendium of Old Knicks tales—*When the Garden Was Eden*—suggests, with its allusion to the paradise of Judeo-Christian creation myths, that from the standpoint of literary forms, the myth of the garden is an instance of utopian literature. Literary utopias, some scholars argue, express political desires not fulfilled (or even, possibly, directly expressed or experienced as such) in daily life.[18] If so, perhaps Leonard Koppett named the desire expressed by the utopian myth of the garden when he wrote that the "triumph of the Knicks brought into focus all the original hopes of the BAA, and pointed more than ever to a prosperous future."[19] The original BAA owners, you may recall from Chapter 2, had hoped to capitalize on the popularity of college basketball—primarily showcased to large crowds in Madison Square Garden before 1950—by staging a professional version in the large arenas of the East Coast. According to Koppett, the 1970 Knicks indeed provided exactly this "'college-style' basketball raised to the highest professional level and played in a big-league setting."[20]

Koppett seems to be thinking of the "college style" that prevailed in the late 1940s, when college doubleheaders packed Madison Square Garden and sparked the imagination of the BAA owners. This style involved patient patterned play designed to lead either to open layups or long set shots and supposedly favored rosters whose players were not necessarily tall or particularly athletic but possessed sound fundamental skills and what is called "basketball IQ."[21] What Nelson George calls "Big Apple style" was "a series of tightly choreographed patterns that encouraged passing from the pivot man to perimeter shooters through and around the defense. Eastern teams on all levels ran through these patterns endlessly, seeking to lull opponents into mistakes, fatigue, and lassitude."[22] The players and then coaches who practiced and promoted the style included Red Holzman, who went on to become the celebrated mastermind of the Knicks' championship-winning style.[23]

Although such a lineage may support Koppett's comparison, it nonetheless collapses together two moments in New York basketball history separated by decades: the heyday of Madison Square Garden college doubleheaders in the 1930s and 1940s and the resurgence of the NBA's Knicks in the early 1970s. Equating the two moments in effect suppresses the events that separate them, including the point-shaving scandal. However, identifying mid-century New York college hoops with the early 1970s Knicks eclipses more than just that. The changes in the period that had the most impact included, as I showed in Chapter 3, the desegregation of the college and pro games and the appearance in the league of the first black superstars in the late 1950s and early 1960s until, finally, by the time the Knicks won their first title in 1970, African Americans easily made up the majority among NBA players. And desegregation entailed stylistic and tactical shifts away from slow, patterned play below the rim to a fast-breaking, improvisational style played above the rim. Koppett may not have wished to erase the advance and accomplishments of African American players in basketball. Yet his comparison implicitly (albeit perhaps unwittingly) conveys satisfaction that the styles such players inaugurated could be successfully challenged by the style they superseded and concomitantly expresses an underlying anxiety that the style prevalent at the time of the founding of the modern basketball state had been eclipsed forever.

To understand more fully how the myth of the garden deals with the changing interplay (on and off the court) of race, basketball style, and moral value, I find it useful to look at Araton's *When the Garden Was Eden*. It not only brings together the various textual fragments of the myth of the garden but also more extensively and explicitly discusses questions of race and politics. And as the basis for a widely seen documentary film, *When the Garden Was Eden* refurbishes the myth for a new generation. Araton acknowledges—indeed, emphasizes—the social strife escalating in American society around the time of the Knicks' ascendance as a means of celebrating the team's healing effects. He devotes an entire chapter to what he calls "the real world" and for the most part repeats the myth's central assertion regarding the intersection of the Knicks and politics: that they provided at once an escape and a healing promise of harmony.

However, the *way* that Araton does this reveals some of the anxiety that this central assertion helps to allay so that a closer examination exposes some of the sources of the myth's staying power. Araton notes that "the country was choosing sides, and many sportswriters were beginning to ask the players they covered, 'For or against?'"[24] Indeed, this period included numerous instances of athletes (especially black athletes) using the platform of their celebrity to speak or act forcefully on political issues.[25] Araton focuses on the response to these issues of the player he calls "the most political of all basketball players": Bill Bradley, who went on to become a U.S. senator from New Jersey. As a player, however, Bradley "chose to say nothing, skirting inquisitions with a skilled evasiveness."[26] Named the college player of the year in 1965 and drafted first by the Knicks, Bradley deferred entering the NBA while continuing his education with a Rhodes Scholarship. Having rediscovered his love for the game, Bradley then returned to the United States and signed a record $500,000 contract to play for the Knicks in the 1967–1968 season.

Considering these facts, Araton wonders whether Bradley's reticence might have been "a result of his own sensitivity to the commotion he had caused just by deciding to play in the NBA" and whether Bradley eschewed political involvement because he "intuitively" understood "that to become part of a truly committed team meant that his personal ambitions beyond basketball could not become part of any public locker-room discussion."[27] Yet being "part of a truly committed team" never stopped Bill Russell from speaking out publicly on issues of racial justice. Moreover, speaking publicly on political issues can harm personal ambitions only if those ambitions include—as turned out to be Bradley's case—an individual career in American politics. By already having narrowly reduced "politics" to ambitions for a career in public office (in pronouncing Bradley "the most political of all basketball players"), Araton can safely characterize Bradley's refusal to speak on urgent political issues as an expression of a key value of the myth of the garden: unselfishness and teamwork.

And lest the silence this unselfishness imposed on Bradley lead us to suspect he was callous or apathetic, Araton reassures us that at the end of his rookie season, in the wake of Dr. Martin Luther King Jr.'s assassination in April 1968, Bradley, "without fanfare," found "his way uptown to Harlem, to work with kids who were trying to manage their own escape—from the cycle of poverty and drugs—and salvage an education in Urban League street academies, which were considered early versions of charter schools."[28] The myth portrays (white) liberal volunteering first as an adequate response to social crisis, and second, and equally important, as driven by the same moral values (unselfishness, humility) it uses to characterize the Knicks' on-court play and explain their success. In this way, Araton creates an associative chain whereby Bradley stands for the Knicks and, through his unselfishness and humility on and off the court, becomes a moral and political exemplar.

Then, as if this were not enough to secure the credibility of the Old Knicks with respect to racism, Araton offers a superfluous personal anecdote. Meeting Araton for the first time nearly forty years after the Knicks won their last title, Bradley says, upon greeting him, "You know, I've read your column for years. I would have sworn you were black." Araton takes the remark as a "compliment," meaning that he "had come across as an empathetic analyst of the NBA's majority African American player base."[29] Araton may well be such an analyst, but in this context the remark seems also to anxiously ward off an underlying concern that the on- and off-court moral and political values of the myth of the garden champions may appear as insufficiently empathetic to blacks or (it appears to be the same thing here) as too white.

Even a story Araton recounts acknowledging some racial tension on the ball club ultimately serves to defuse its potential disruption of the message of racial harmony conveyed by the myth of the garden. During the 1969–1970 season, following an injury to the starting forward Cazzie Russell (who is African American), Holzman made the decision to keep Bradley in the starting lineup, relegating Russell to the role of sixth man. Russell was incensed and, one day in practice, his resentment boiled over. He was, as Araton recalls, "playing like he wanted to hurt everyone around him." The team's captain, Willis Reed, confronted him, saying, "What the hell are you doing, throwing elbows at your teammates?" to which Russell snapped, "Be quiet, Uncle Tom." According to Araton, Reed looked Russell in the eye and said, "This Uncle Tom is gonna be whuppin' some ass in a minute if you don't keep quiet." Araton glosses Reed's reply with a two-sentence, bold print, italicized paragraph: *"If I'm an Uncle Tom for calling you out for abusing a white teammate, so be it. We play basketball here and we play it together."*[30]

I am less interested here in the exchange than in what Araton makes of it and of the role he assigns to Reed in the myth of the garden. Araton opens his book with a visit to Reed's home in rural Louisiana that prompts a biographical sketch emphasizing Reed's upbringing in rural Jim Crow–era Louisiana and, in particular, the lessons he learned about how to deal with racial prejudice and injustice. Reed appears in Araton's portrait as a paragon of dignity, rising above the temptations of militancy through a firmly grounded sense of self-worth and a belief that the best response to racism was the demonstration of excellence, on and off the basketball court.[31] This image then gives a kind of unimpeachable authority to Reed in the face of Russell's challenge. It is as if the myth of the garden was reprimanding Russell for his selfish, violent anger and petulant, extremist provocation by confronting it with the image of a black man who had overcome the worst of racism—emblematized by the rural South—through a modest commitment to interracial cooperation and to the basketball values that echo that. The effect is to assert that the values of the Old Knicks could properly contain the racial tensions of the time.

Perhaps they could. But perhaps, as with the story of Bradley's politics, this tale betrays an anxiety about race and a fear that basketball could *not* resolve racial conflict. This anxiety manifests also in the role played by the legendary NBA guard Oscar Robertson (who was African American but never a Knick) in the same chapter on "the real world." Araton suggests that Robertson raised the "metaphorical curtain" on "the infusion of black talent" that was "lifting the game to higher athletic and cultural levels" (as explicitly compared with the 1940s) with an exhibition game he organized in August 1968 to memorialize King and to raise money for the organization he had led, the Southern Christian Leadership Conference. Citing Robertson's role as the head of the NBA Players' Association in organizing a threatened boycott of the 1964 All-Star Game, Araton concludes that he "had made it his life's calling to speak his piece, whether people wanted to hear it or not, on subjects related to what happened inside the lines or out."[32] Indeed he had, but why spotlight Robertson and not other African American players of the era who also spoke out. Why not, for example, spotlight Bill Russell or Elgin Baylor?

The reason is that Robertson, uniquely among these players, allows the myth of the garden to yoke a specific, narrow definition of blackness—on and off the court—to the moral ethos of the Knicks. Consider Araton's offhand remark that Robertson "never once slammed a ball through the hoop" and never had to be "prodded to belittle the diminished state of fundamentals in the modern game." Araton continues: "Robertson rightly linked the lack of movement and teamwork to the dunk-and-pony shows that were seemingly designed to suit the pyrotechnic NBA experience."[33] These remarks associate an African American player Araton has already characterized as politically active but moderate with the same on-court values the myth of the garden lauds, thereby identifying him with both Bradley and the Knicks in general.

Meanwhile, although Russell also espoused fundamentals and team-work on the court, he took far more controversial public stances than Robertson on issues of racial injustice.[34] As for Baylor, who had already refused to play a game in 1959 because of segregated accommodations in Charleston, West Virginia, and who, as Araton notes, supported Robertson in the threatened boycott in 1964, his style of play is usually described as a progenitor to the improvisational, high-flying modern NBA game that Araton seems here, through Robertson, to criticize and contrast with the Knicks' style. Indeed, Baylor, as much as any other NBA player of the era, emblematizes the "infusion of black talent" that took the game above the rim.[35]

Robertson, then, who eschewed both extreme political views and threatening basketball styles, may be summoned as a kind of honorary Knick. But because he was black and spoke openly of the experience of being black in basketball and in America, Robertson can simultaneously mitigate the impression that the myth views the white Bill Bradley or the soft-spoken Reed as the sole embodiments of its on- and off-court values. The myth of the garden thus unites Bradley and Reed with Robertson (and with Araton himself, representing New Yorkers and, for that matter, fans of the Old Knicks) in the service of a liberal politics that conflates on-court style and tactics with moral values (cohesion, humility, unselfishness) and in the process implicitly defines the appropriate ways to be black, both as players on the court (not dunking, like Baylor) and as citizens off the court, acting to support racial justice in the United States (not taking extreme positions, like Russell).

Claims that the Knicks were the most "democratic" or the most "perfect" teams of all time and that they embodied racial and social harmony, when viewed in the wider context of both basketball and racial politics in the United States at the time, serve to set narrow limits within which change threatening to white supremacy in both spheres would be accepted. In this respect, like other kinds of utopian fiction, the myth of the garden constitutes its perfect world in part by establishing firmly exclusive boundaries. In society, calls for change must be made peacefully and humbly and with an eye on the benefits for all society. In basketball, too, black players would be accepted as long as they hewed to traditional values of unselfishness, humility, and effort; did not seek "extravagant" financial compensation; and, symbolic of all of these, did not dunk.

Inventing the Dunk

The dunk offers its greatest *tactical* value as a scoring play in the face of defensive obstacles near or above the rim. In such situations, where a conventional layup might be blocked, both the elevated height from which the dunk is released and its greater downward force give a greater likelihood of scoring. Obviously, the dunk requires height or leaping ability, body control, and strength. Through the dunk, an individual player who possesses these can score, even in the face of defensive obstacles, without the aid of teammates or the intricate patterns of movement designed by coaches to get players free for open shots. The dunk thus advances two values—individuality and physical force—that the white basketball unconscious disdains, grounding its attitude, through the myth of creation, in the invention of the game.[36] Considering the moral values supposedly baked into basketball by Naismith—unselfishness, cooperation, social cohesion, nonviolence—it becomes easier to understand how dunks violate the ethos the myth of the garden associates with the Knicks.[37]

But as we have seen, in the basketball universe (as perhaps in American society at large) normative moral values frequently entail racial connotations. The ostensibly universally applicable and therefore neutral language of morals becomes a way to vent attitudes about race without ever speaking about race directly. There may be no more striking instance of this than the dunk, especially when it evolved from a disturbingly unstoppable tactical weapon in Wilt Chamberlain's offensive repertoire to a creative, crowd-pleasing aesthetic expression of individual style, which occurred—in less revered settings than Madison Square Garden, such as playgrounds and half-empty arenas—around the time the Knicks were working their gravity-bound, 1940s-era "college-style" game to two NBA titles. In that evolution, dunking—primarily practiced by and, in any event, almost exclusively associated with African American players—came to be seen as a gratuitous and ostentatious exhibition of narcissism, revealing a dangerous disregard and disrespect for the game itself, including its moral values.[38]

Perhaps nowhere was this threat more unapologetically paraded than in the ABA, whose original franchise owners formed the league in 1967 to force a merger with the NBA. In fact, initial attempts to merge the two leagues were stymied by a successful antitrust lawsuit filed by none other than Oscar Robertson, then head of the players' union, in the 1970s. Competition for talent between franchises in the two leagues had driven up players' salaries and presented a de facto challenge to the NBA's longtime "option clause" that bound a player to a single team in perpetuity. When the NBA agreed to allow free agency for its players in 1976, the suit was settled, and the merger went forward with the ABA's Indiana Pacers, San Antonio Spurs, Denver Nuggets, and New York Nets (as the New Jersey Nets) entering the NBA.[39]

In contrast to the NBA of the era, which showcased imposing centers and crafty guards, ABA rosters featured forwards whose combination of size, athletic ability, and skills permitted them to take an active role in more facets of the game.[40] Whereas positional responsibilities in the NBA of the early 1970s remained strongly specialized, the combination of particular player talent and rules in the ABA allowed for more positional freedom. With few talented centers defending the rim and the three-point shot opening up defenses, these ABA forwards could easily snatch a defensive rebound and, rather than passing off to a point guard (as was the convention), just take off on a full-court fast break. Often enough, these fast breaks would culminate in a variety of creative dunks.

This helps explain why, in the words of Dan Issel, who played in the upstart league, "the dunk was so important to the ABA that the pregame warm-ups became a show."[41] Perhaps nothing demonstrated this with greater impact than the first-ever dunk contest, staged during halftime of the ABA All-Star Game in 1976. Although the ABA may be best known for such formal departures from the NBA as its red, white, and blue ball; the three-point shot; and gaudy marketing tactics, as Issel puts it, "the Slam Dunk Contest went right to the heart of the old ABA." The ABA was in serious financial trouble at that point, and obstacles to the merger had not yet been resolved. With the game scheduled to be shown on national television, producers discussed "what the ABA was known for—its athletes and its dunking"—and came up with the idea of a halftime slam dunk contest.[42]

Julius Erving of the ABA's New York Nets, known as "Dr. J," won the contest in spectacular fashion. Just before his final turn in the contest, he stood at the free throw line facing the basket. Then, dramatically, palming the ball in one hand, he turned and in loping strides measured his steps to the free-throw area at the opposite end of the court. Erving turned back to face up-court, paused, and then, with the ball still held firmly in his right hand, sprinted toward the opposite basket. When his left foot hit the free throw line, Erving took off, soaring toward the hoop. Raising the ball up and back with his right arm, he jammed it down through the basket as flashbulbs popped and onlookers jumped to their feet in joy and wonder. Recalling the play, Erving imagined himself "palming the ball up over my head, outstretched, like Lady Liberty holding her torch."[43] The image is striking, especially when combined with what stands out in other observers' memories: Erving's high blowout Afro shifting slightly backward in the wind generated by his liftoff.[44] This is Erving, native of New York's playground circuit and star of New York's *other* professional basketball team, as an African American Statue of Liberty, expressing the creative joy and power of freedom through this single dunk.

Not only striking, the image is also fitting, since in very real terms the ABA created jobs (and, through the bidding war for talent, higher salaries) for black basketball players, including great players such as Connie Hawkins, Moses Malone, and Spencer Haywood, who for various reasons were prohibited from entering the NBA.[45] In this sense, the ABA challenged the hegemony of the modern basketball state. But beyond this, the ABA created a cultural space, free of the moralizing basketball conventions of the NBA and the NCAA, in which the creative, improvisational, fast and fluid style popular among African Americans on urban playgrounds—Erving drew inspiration for the dunk from Jumping Jackie Jackson, a friend and New York City playground legend—could enjoy at least some measure of the attention, and recompense, it deserved.[46]

Erving's dunk, which stands as a metonym for his game overall, embodied the spirit, style, and unconventional and unconstrained talent of ABA players, playing (and experimenting and innovating freely) in the shadow of their more established, and conventional, NBA counterparts. Meanwhile, Assistant Coach Robert Bownes of Hunter College shed light on the cultural stakes when he explained that the NCAA's 1967 no-dunk rule was really not about stopping Kareem Abdul-Jabbar but, rather, about stopping "the six-foot-two brothers who could dazzle the crowd and embarrass much bigger white kids by dunking. The white establishment has an uncomfortable feeling that blacks are dominating too many areas of sports. So they're setting up all kinds of restrictions and barriers. Everyone knows that dunking is a trademark of great playground black athletes. And so they took it away. It is as simple as that."[47] Bownes not only echoes Abdul-Jabbar's explanation for the rule ("This and other niggers were running away with the sport"); he elaborates on it, reminding us that not everyone was equally welcome in the modern basketball state.

While the Knicks might well stake a claim to embodying a liberal version of racial harmony in terms of basketball style, morality, and politics, the myth of the garden simultaneously suppresses more radical claims of African American autonomy, such as might have been voiced by the Black Panthers or Bill Russell or exemplified by the City Game's soaring other son, that Statue of Basketball Liberty, Julius Erving.

But if Erving emblematized the ABA, then by the time he led the NBA's Philadelphia 76ers to that league's title in 1983, the ABA itself—no less than the NBL had thirty years before—was transforming the NBA. Erving himself observed, "Every night I watch an NBA game I see the ABA. When you watch the up-tempo game and the three-point shot and much of what the strategy employed is, it is definitely an ABA game. There is no question about it. You see the flair. You see the innovation. You see the accent on the entertainment."[48] Or, in Jacob Weinstein's striking visual image, the ABA might be a petri dish in which flourished "a new style of play, one that would eventually kick in the doors to the establishment."[49] That might explain why, at the dunk contest held during the NBA All-Star Game in 2015, not only Dr. J but also the Old Knicks' Clyde Frazier sat side by side at the judges' table. Meanwhile, past complaints notwithstanding, Oscar Robertson sat laughing courtside, next to Bill Russell, clearly entertained by what Araton dismissed as "the dunk and pony show."

The ways in which the ABA, seen as a parasitic body, came in time to overtake its host did not necessarily sit well with all observers. The Knicks' Bill Bradley, for example, complained in *Values of the Game* that the three-point shot had the effect of diminishing "team movement and finesse."[50] And Terry Pluto, who assembled a colorful oral history of the ABA, draws a distinction between Erving's dunk (as a "statement of grace and athleticism") and its contemporary NBA descendant, which he views as "attached to the in-your-face, trash-talkin' style," "more violent, self-absorbed," and "a put-down play, too often followed by mean stares and finger pointing at the opponent, despite the NBA's efforts to crack down on such gestures."[51] Such remarks voice a purist desire to regulate black men's bodies by applying (dubious) moral judgments to black innovations in basketball style. It is as if, when the dunk is Erving's, now safely preserved in the past as in a museum diorama (not to mention in the carnivalesque ABA, where, after all, proper scruples had been suspended so that anything goes), it can be praised. But when that same dunk escapes the museum and takes living flight in the hallowed NBA, a line must be drawn.

When the Garden Was Eden features on its cover a widely reproduced photo taken just after the Knicks won the NBA Championship in 1973.

Call it the poster for the myth of the garden. It shows Bradley, Phil Jackson, Willis Reed, Walt Frazier, and Jerry Lucas, seated in front of lockers, extending their arms toward the camera and raising their index fingers in the "Number One" sign. The selection of this photo for the cover—which excludes Earl Monroe, perhaps, after Frazier, the player most crucial to the team's success—symbolizes what the myth can and cannot include in its story of basketball in the late 1960s and early 1970s. When Monroe joined the sacred Knicks, as Nelson George puts it, echoing the imagery others have applied to the ABA, "it was as if a deadly germ were being injected into a beautiful body."[52] From a poor urban background, legendary on playgrounds, known for a flashy improvisational style, and traded to the Knicks only after a contract holdout and a brief flirtation with jumping to the ABA for a larger contract, Monroe seems to embody much of what was new in the culture of basketball around the time the Knicks had their run—and not only what was new but also what was specifically a threat to those values of the white basketball unconscious as expressed in the myth of the garden.

Russell and Chamberlain inaugurated an unstoppable (racial) revolution within the modern basketball state; the myth of the garden offers a liberal, reformist response. It seeks to define the terms under which change may occur by presenting its values as natural, universal, and critical to the survival of the sport and, indeed, American society. In this way it seeks not so much to prevent change entirely as to control it: in particular, to control the participation and interpretation of black bodies in the modern basketball state. As the 1970s unfolded, basketball culture would be riven by the racialized tensions between, on the one hand, black basketball players, and, on the other, the primarily white partisans—including fans, the media, coaches and owners, and some players—of the basketball styles prevailing at the time of the consolidation of the modern basketball state.

No less than in Erving's high-flying dunks, the future success of the NBA—contrary to Koppett's opinion—lay not with the denizens of Madison Square Garden but in the whirling spins and double-pump improvisations in traffic of Black Jesus. As Monroe proudly noted, the scholar and writer John Edgar Wideman (who, Monroe pointedly reminds his readers, was a "Rhodes Scholar, like Bill Bradley and Jerry Lucas") described Monroe's style as "a paradigm shift in the pro game of basketball."[53] Not the Garden but the urban playground, not the college game but the pickup game would cultivate the stars and styles of basketball's future.

THE MYTH OF THE AMATEURS

March 26, 1979

[Our] lives had become intertwined, like vines
from an old tree that had crossed paths so many
times they were permanently entangled.
—Larry Bird and Earvin Magic Johnson

The most watched basketball game in the history of the sport took place in Salt Lake City on March 26, 1979. One-fourth of American television sets tuned to NBC, which broadcast the NCAA Men's Tournament final to forty million viewers.[1] About two months later, just twelve million viewers tuned in to watch the NBA finals—the fourth-lowest rated series of any between 1974 and 2014.[2] What accounts for the massive disparity in popularity? Historians claim that many fans complained that the league featured too much one-on-one play, violence, drug use, players only interested in contracts and individual statistics who did not really try, and too many African American players: 84 percent of National Basketball Association (NBA) players were black in the 1978–1979 season. So even Knicks fans, who in the early 1970s fell in love with what one writer calls the "healthy mix of white and black players," took to calling the 1978–1979 squad, composed entirely of black players, "the Niggerbockers."[3] These and other unhappy fans, the common explanation continues, turned away from the pro game and instead renewed their interest in college basketball, which in the late 1970s the television industry was beginning to supply in greater abundance.[4]

In 1979, unknown Indiana State enjoyed an undefeated season, was ranked number one, and featured the nation's top scorer, the senior forward Larry Bird. Michigan State, meanwhile, emerged as Big Ten champion, reaching the NCAA final by trouncing Penn by thirty-four points.

They were led by the versatile, six-foot-nine-inch sophomore point guard Earvin Johnson. Johnson's Spartans defeated Indiana State 75–64, and Johnson and Bird entered the NBA for the 1979–1980 season, joining the fabled Lakers and Celtics, respectively. Between them, they won eight of the ten championships during the 1980s. Along the way, the story goes, Bird and Magic saved pro basketball and set the stage for Michael Jordan and the NBA's global empire. Perhaps, but I am more interested in *how* that story gets told, via what I call here "the myth of the amateurs."

If Johnson and Bird "saved the NBA," they obviously did so in their capacity as *professional* basketball players, paid to play and so to make money for their employers and the league. Yet this myth's power stems from its association of the two with emotion, and through that with amateur values. Originating in their college championship duel, the myth of the amateurs emphasizes Johnson's and Bird's openly expressed love of the game for its own sake. Meanwhile, differences between the two allow them to function as a complementary unit containing racial antagonism. The lower-middle-class African American Johnson's unthreatening congeniality, at home in Hollywood, complements Bird's Boston-based, taciturn, white working-class toughness. These traits shape their emotional investments in basketball: Johnson's expressive joy and Bird's focused diligence. But the myth joins these variations as flip sides of a single coin: a shared unselfish will to win that would nourish both rivalry and loving friendship. Considering existing racial stereotypes and perceptions, the myth contrasts a league saved in the loving image of "the amateurs" with the narrowly escaped dangers posed by selfish black professionals cynically using the sport to garner undeserved riches. The myth of the amateurs, however, deemphasizes elements of their story to preserve its amateurist color-blind fantasy. Telling their story from the point of view of their innovative on-court styles, by contrast, helps situate them as heirs to the maligned era that preceded them and as clear predecessors of NBA stars who would follow them a generation later.

The Myth of the Amateurs

About seven months after winning the NCAA championship, Magic Johnson made his NBA debut. With just two seconds left, his Lakers were down a point. Receiving an inbounds pass at the free-throw line, the All-Star center Kareem Abdul-Jabbar wheeled to his left and, from eighteen feet away, put up a hook shot. The ball settled in the bottom of the net with no time remaining on the clock. Johnson leaped into the air with an upraised fist when the shot went in and then sprinted to half-court, where he jumped into Kareem's arms "in a move," as one columnist put it, "that seemed almost incongruously joyous in the staid NBA."[5] It certainly seemed so to Abdul-Jabbar, who recalled feeling "shocked" and "a little embarrassed—such a public display, so little cools."[6] As for Johnson, he was surprised that Abdul-Jabbar did not share his excitement: "'What's the big deal?' [Kareem] seemed to be saying. 'Hitting shots like that is my *job*.' . . . But I wasn't about to change my style. I'd always played with passion."[7]

Across the country, Bird's debut in Boston's victory over Houston would be less dramatic. Playing with an injured finger and in foul trouble, Bird still managed to contribute fourteen points, ten rebounds, and four assists in just twenty-eight minutes of play. The very next night, Bird made twelve of seventeen shots to net twenty-eight points in a Boston rout of Cleveland. Although Bird, shy and reserved with the media, did not display joy like Magic Johnson's, he was praised—even when he was not scoring effectively—for his effort, concentration, guts, and unselfishness. "Bird," as one columnist's headline put it, "does job."[8]

But this superficial contrast between Magic's exuberance and Bird's workmanlike reserve did not prevent the media from recognizing that both players brought levels of "heart" and "passion" to the court every night, even in meaningless games during the long NBA regular season. If Magic's joy was evident and Bird's a bit harder to identify as such, it was nonetheless the case that his creativity and all-around effort led Celtics fans to compare the team to the fast-breaking teams of the Russell-era dynasty. And the emotional intensity of Bird's hustling play led some to see the Celtics as "a college team going for its first-ever NCAA championship."[9] Bird himself emphasized the pleasure in his work, noting that he was doing what he had wanted to do "for many years. I was playing and thinking about basketball twenty-four hours a day," and that he, and his teammates, were having fun.[10] NBA executives were having fun, too. For a league that had been steadily losing fans (and viewers and advertisers) to the college game, nothing could be better than that Magic's and Bird's emotional styles of play were leading some to see the popular NCAA in the NBA. That they were doing so on two of the league's fabled teams (and larger media markets) was just icing on the cake.[11]

Moreover, not only were the two in the game at the same time and not only were their respective *teams* historical rivals, but Bird and Johnson themselves had also established at least the potential for a marketable, long-term individual rivalry with their NCAA championship matchup in March 1979. Bob Logan of the *Chicago Tribune*, for example, led off his

NBA preview column, which featured photos of the two stars in action for their college teams, both sporting jerseys with the word "State"—iconic metonym for intercollegiate athletics—emblazoned across the front, by asking, "Will Earvin 'Magic' Johnson and Larry Bird stage a rematch in the 1980 National Basketball Association Finals?"[12] Influential columnists such as Boston's Bob Ryan previewed their first NBA matchup as "the single most awaited regular-season game in Laker history."[13] By the beginning of their second seasons, the NBA had put illustrations of the two on the cover of its *Official 1980–1981 NBA Guide*, and with good reason: that first *regular season* game between the two in 1979 garnered higher television ratings than any NBA finals game of the 1970s.

The framing of the rivalry between Bird and Johnson, like the myth of the rivalry but via different means, first vented and contained the anxieties of the white basketball unconscious over the effects of the desegregation of the modern basketball state—five out of six NBA players were black—by exaggerating the contrast between the two players. As Ryan described them, "Magic, from the big school famous for its sports teams, was outgoing and perpetually smiling, the media's darling. Bird, from the little school with no reputation for athletics, was introverted and suspicious of the press. Magic seemed to be everybody's friend; Bird picked his friends carefully." Once the pair entered the NBA, these differences were extended so that "theirs became a bicoastal rivalry, even a cultural rivalry": "Magic became the embodiment of Showtime with his behind-the-back wizardry, his look-away passes and his million-dollar smile. . . . Bird became the favorite of knowledgeable Celtic fans mostly because of the effort he expended. Bostonians applauded him as much for diving to the floor as for draining three-pointers or throwing no-look passes."[14] This contrast catalogues exactly the cultural and moral values—entertainment and hard work, affability and seriousness—that the conventional wisdom perceived to be lacking in the NBA.

Unlike the myth of the rivalry, however, the myth of the amateurs also acknowledged *similarities* between the two players and allocated positive skill sets and moral attributes to *both* players. Both were said to lack exceptional athletic ability, and both were said to have successfully compensated for this through their intelligence, competitive intensity, and commitment to teamwork, as demonstrated by their "obsession" with passing.[15] The two appeared as mirror images of each other, so that the myth of the amateurs created a complementary *pair* out of the two players, an image of their rivalry in which each was incomplete without the other, just as their respective, supposed skill sets were incomplete without the other. *As a pair*, "Magic-Bird" was unathletic and competitively intense (like the stereotypical white player) and entertaining and creative (like the stereotypical black player). In this constructed combination, we see a fantasy of racial harmony. Any fan looking into the mirror that was Magic-Bird could find an embodiment of their preferred values—and skin tone—gazing back.

The myth of the amateurs bears a resemblance to romance novels published in many nations in Latin America in the wake of political independence in the nineteenth century, when these newly formed countries were often fractured by civil war. In that context, popular romance novels served to galvanize diverse populations around national identities by portraying star-crossed lovers as representative of contending races, classes, regions, or ethnicities.[16] By prompting readers to invest emotionally in the marriage of these protagonists, the novelists prepared the emotional ground for the possibility of a harmoniously unified nation. The myth of the amateurs functioned similarly with respect to racial divisions that had the modern basketball state on the brink of disaster when Johnson and Bird arrived on the scene in 1979. And like Latin America's "foundational fictions," it did so by emphasizing emotion.

The importance of the emotional dimension of the Bird-Johnson pairing had already been underscored symbolically by the point of origin of their rivalry, in a college basketball championship game whose emotional intensity could be contrasted with the perceived flatness of the NBA in the late 1970s. True amateurs, Bird and Johnson shared a *love* of the sport and its competitive aspects. But as their careers and lives progressed, this component came to take on added dimensions to the point that, by the time they retired from the league, their *mutual* love, despite—even because of—their differences, appeared as the most profoundly enduring legacy of their rivalry.

A key episode in constituting the centrality of emotion to the myth, included in almost every version, recounts the first time that Bird and Johnson actually spent time together off the court, in the course of shooting a television commercial for Converse basketball shoes in the summer of 1984. The Celtics had just defeated the Lakers in a seven-game finals series, and Bird had corralled the league's MVP award. The commercial itself aimed to profit from their divergent images by staging a one-on-one game between them. "The Bird shoe, the Magic shoe," its narrator sternly commanded. "Choose your weapon!"

However, the dramatization of an armed duel notwithstanding, what endures from this commercial in the myth of the amateurs is that it represents the moment that an off-court friendship added dimension to their on-court rivalry.[17] During downtime during the commercial shoot, the story goes, Magic and Bird, aided by the folksy hospitality of Bird's mother and grandmother, discovered how much they had in common. This discovery required both men to lower their guards, allowing each other to see what is characterized as their deeper personalities. Magic discovered Bird's sense of humor. Bird discovered "Earvin," the midwestern boy hidden beneath the glitzy persona of "Magic." As Johnson put it, despite the superficial appearance of contrasts, "we're both a couple of small-town boys. We're still close to our families, our teachers, our former coaches, and the people we grew up with."[18] If, as Magic claims, the new friendship added a layer of "warmth that made our competition fun," it is also true that it allowed for the consummation of the foundational romance plot required by the myth of the amateurs. Now we could see that the differences of outward personality, franchises, and—literally superficially—skin color were just that: surface differences whose sharply contrasting edges were blunted by the deeper, human similarities revealed through vulnerability. And these similarities were themselves firmly rooted in emotion—specifically, in the warmth of shared love of home, love of family (especially of mothers), love of basketball, and, eventually, love of each other.

This love story persisted—indeed, deepened—through Johnson's shocking HIV diagnosis in 1991.[19] But it would climax in 1992, near the end of their careers, when the two would lead the U.S. men's national team in competition at the Summer Olympics in Barcelona, where the so-called Dream Team captured the gold medal in dominating fashion. More important from the vantage point of the myth of the amateurs, although Michael Jordan was already by then the best and most famous member of the team, Bird and Johnson were its most agreeable, not least because their association with amateur values helped mitigate whatever discomfort the first ever participation by American professional players might have occasioned. The duo presided over a goodwill ambassadorship for the modern basketball state, sparking desire for the game in youngsters from Germany to Argentina and China. As the final buzzer of the gold medal game sounded, Bird and Johnson embraced.[20] The next year, Johnson made an emotional appearance at Bird's retirement ceremony in Boston, and nearly a decade later, Bird would officially induct Johnson into the Naismith Memorial Basketball Hall of Fame.

The term "amateur" derives from the Latin word *amator* (lover). And it was, the myth of the amateurs maintains, as "lovers," amateurs in a deep and encompassing sense of the word, that Bird and Magic saved the NBA through what one documentarian referred to as "a courtship of rivals" and Magic himself described as a "marriage." Through their love, Bird-Magic stoked our desire to get close to them by setting aside our shameful attachment to irrelevant, superficial racial differences and tapping instead into our own deep love, our investment in the deep values of the game, that the duo embodied. Their emotional bond helped to cement the superficial contrasts into the image of a single, perfect, multiracial basketball persona capable of healing the stylistic, cultural, and racial tensions that had riven the modern basketball state over the course of the preceding three decades. Of course, we might still have preferences, even strong ones: darker or lighter skin, West Coast or East Coast, cheerful or grouchy. But within the regime of the myth of the amateurs, the differences between them did not threaten the unity of the modern basketball state. Either way, the myth reassured us, we would be getting competitive intensity, a reliable winner, unselfishness, team play, effort, and stylistic flair. And in all of this, "the amateurs" not only saved the game but also prepared us (and primed the pump) for Michael Jordan's basketball empire.

A Genealogy of Basketball Amateurism

Although Johnson led the team to a title in his rookie season, the Lakers had failed even to make the finals in his second year. So as Magic's third season got under way, Coach Paul Westhead introduced a tactical change. Instead of the fast-breaking style the Lakers had employed in Johnson's first two seasons, the team would now use a slower-paced half-court offense aimed to get the ball to Abdul-Jabbar. The Lakers struggled to a 2–4 record through mid-November, and Johnson, at least, blamed the new system. Although the Lakers won their next five games, Johnson's frustration with Westhead continued to simmer. On November 18, after a narrow three-point win over the Utah Jazz, Johnson, "citing differences with Coach Paul Westhead," explained that he was not "having any fun" and told reporters, "I can't play here anymore. I want to leave. I want to be traded."[21] Less than twenty-fours later, Jerry Buss, the Lakers' owner, fired Westhead and replaced him with Assistant Coach Pat Riley. The next night, as the Lakers took the floor in Los Angeles, Magic Johnson was loudly booed by his own fans perhaps for the first time in his life.

A disapproving chorus of journalists echoed the fans' boos. They pointed to the new contract Johnson had signed during the off-season—

$25 million over twenty-five years, unprecedented in NBA history at the time—as evidence that he had grown narcissistic, arrogant, and, perhaps worst of all, cynically professional. Johnson was vilified as a "spoiled brat" and a "spoiled punk," "an infidel," a "traitor," "un-American" and a "Bolshevik," a "monster," a "villain," and a "pariah."[22] But beyond the name calling, what emerged in the firestorm of criticism was that Johnson had ruined the story, violating the constitutive values of the myth of the amateurs.

The ideology of amateurism originated in England, where it was a "product of the nineteenth-century leisure class, whose ideal of the patrician sportsman . . . was part of their pursuit of conspicuous leisure."[23] Referring to the athlete who plays for the love of the sport, the concept came to imply a number of corollary qualities, including that the amateur derives pleasure from the contest, participation is freely chosen, the process of competition is as important as its outcome, the amateur is motivated by rewards intrinsic to the sport rather than by extrinsic rewards such as fame or money, and, finally, sportsmanship—a valuation of the sport itself above all else—is paramount. This effectively kept working-class athletes, who had neither the resources nor the leisure time, from challenging upper-class domination of sport so that, in effect, amateurism "established a system of 'sports apartheid' with white males from the upper classes enjoying the advantages."[24] Allen Guttman puts it more bluntly: "The amateur rule was an instrument of class warfare."[25]

Within the culture of basketball, amateur ideals have been applied selectively toward similar ends. During the period of the consolidation of the modern basketball state, it was amateur basketball—particularly intercollegiate competition—that established a national market for the game and affirmed the core values that, from the time of its creation, basketball was supposed to convey: unselfishness, cooperation, sportsmanship, effort. At the same time, the growth of the college game and the institutionalization of coaching as a profession forced the amateur ideal to accommodate two additional values: respect for the authority of the coach (as an expression of humility and unselfishness) and competitive intensity (not winning for its own sake, of course, which was seen as unseemly, but the desire to win as a mechanism for spurring the passion and excellence that would reflect positively on the larger body—such as a college—one represented). Because the amateur ideal took root in basketball culture while the sport was still segregated, the values came unconsciously to be associated with whiteness.

Returning to Johnson, criticism by the media and fans betrays a rage that he violated these ideals first by failing to respect his coach, and second by getting paid *and* insisting that he have fun playing the game. Red Auerbach, Russell's former coach, was marshaled to explain the perils awaiting franchises "when a player is bigger than the organization," and Coach Larry Brown of New Jersey (later inducted into the Hall of Fame) criticized Johnson for a selfish unwillingness to make sacrifices for the good of the team.[26] Another column reminded readers that even as a college player Johnson had led a group of Michigan State players who confronted Coach Jud Heathcote, insisting that he allow them to implement a more up-tempo style of play.[27] As Johnson was judged to have violated the (amateur) ideals of the sport, sportswriters and fans alike—in perhaps the most telling trope of the backlash—determined that he was no longer magic (or "Magic"); he was now just "Earvin." Thus, one *Los Angeles Times* columnist, under the headline "Just Call Him Earvin Johnson; Magic Is Gone," quoted another: "For the rest of his days, he won't be Magic anymore. He will be the spoiled brat who couldn't wait until he owned a team of his own to show his power, the infidel who had to have a coach's scalp to go with his millions, the traitor who hid behind a false, happy face, and he was someone we loved. That's the frightening thing."[28]

Johnson's popularity among writers and fans apparently depended more on his ebullient on- and off-court personality than on his exceptional individual talents or his contributions to his team's successes. Johnson could be "loved"—and recall the importance of love to the amateur ideal—insofar as he joyfully brought amateur ideals into the professional game. By mixing the professional (through the power of his long-term contract and relationship with Jerry Buss) with the amateur (his insistence on having fun), Johnson had unwittingly exposed the myth of the amateurs as a ruse and betrayed fans' love for him. The purveyors of this myth disciplined him accordingly. Although none of his critics explicitly invoked race, their invective nonetheless bears a racializing subtext, since criticism of the NBA at the time yoked complaints about players' apathy and excessive salaries with the perception that the league was too black. In this sense, perhaps, fans and media observers were unconsciously enraged because Magic "robbed" them of something they desperately needed: the image of an entertaining black basketball player who played just for the fun of it and loved everyone while doing so. Or, to put it another way, it was as though Magic had betrayed fans by turning out to be "black" after all.

The racializing dimension of the myth of the amateurs may have remained subtext in the controversy of 1981. However, it burst to the surface later in the decade, as a result of comments made by Dennis Rodman, then a rookie with the Detroit Pistons, and the veteran star Isiah Thomas following a loss to Bird's Celtics in the decisive seventh game of the 1987 Eastern Conference finals. Rodman told reporters that Magic had gotten "screwed out of the MVP award last year," explaining that Bird, whom Rodman characterized as "slow," had won it instead only because he was white. Thomas endorsed Rodman's view, saying, "I think Larry is a very, very good basketball player. An exceptional talent. But I have to agree with Rodman. If he were black, he'd be just another good guy."[29]

Rodman and Thomas expressed a belief, by no means theirs alone, that Bird—like the white stars Pete Maravich, Bill Bradley, and Jerry West before him, and with due acknowledgment of his "exceptional talent"— was nonetheless the beneficiary of the white basketball unconscious's desire for a great white hope who could singlehandedly turn back the tide of black dominance of basketball at the sport's highest levels. Although Bird was a "phenomenal basketball player" with "undeniable" talent, his *popularity* was in part the effect of an "impulse that is probably inside of all white fans. It is simultaneously a frantic desire to be included and a patronizing belief that the white athlete can restore the sanctity that has been traditional to sports and reverse the damage caused by black irreverence. This is the motivation behind the long-lasting phenomenon in sports of rooting for the white guy: it combines a nostalgic remembrance of how sports used to be with anger over what's become of them."[30] That accounts for the media firestorm that ensued as columnists across the country tripped over themselves to condemn the remarks as everything from "unnecessary" to "sour grapes," from "unsportsmanlike" to "racist."[31] Meanwhile, Bird's characteristically understated response redounded to his established reputation for caring little for distractions that did not directly relate to playing and winning basketball games.

But from the point of view of the myth of the amateurs, what is most striking about both controversies is their threatening potential to divide the unity of the couple, centered on the loving core of amateur values on which their role as saviors of the game depends. After all, the working-class Bird played the game for its own sake and might have been expected to be critical of Magic for his large contract and, especially, for getting mixed up in the business of the Lakers' organization. But in fact, the myth of the amateurs reassures us, "Bird was puzzled by the national furor" generated by Johnson's remarks, saying, "I felt kind of bad for him." After all, "Magic was averaging double-figures in assists. How could anyone call him selfish or spoiled?"[32] Not only does the detail reestablish the bond—even prior to the Converse commercial that would establish their friendship—between the two players; it also reminds us that what was important to both of them was playing ball, and playing it unselfishly, and that, in accord with the oldest ideas of the game, to play the game unselfishly was *to be unselfish.*

Similarly, in the case of the race controversy surrounding Bird, the most important among the many voices criticizing Rodman and Thomas was Magic's. "Johnson," the myth of the amateurs informs us, "was angry with Thomas," although the two were close friends. And more telling still, when the news broke, "Johnson did not call his friend [Thomas] to find out [what he was thinking]. The call he placed instead was to Bird. 'Isiah does not speak for me,' Magic said."[33] In this way, Magic, *because* he is African American, a Laker, the ostensible beneficiary by comparison of the negative comments, and Bird's great rival may authoritatively put to rest the notion, so threatening to the white basketball unconscious, that Bird is just another good player. And once again, the growing affective bond between the two players allows them to stand united to safeguard the amateur values of competition, sportsmanship, and love of the game against the intrusive, inappropriate, and potentially divisive issue of race.

From the genealogical point of view, the myth of the amateurs pacifies the white basketball unconscious in an era (and at particular moments within it) when its belief in the capacity of basketball values, putatively universal but long unconsciously associated with whiteness, to cement social unity comes to be shaken—and shaken no less, at least in part, by the disorienting fact of its own desire for black basketball. As we see in the next section, however much Bird and Johnson may genuinely have espoused values that may be cast in the terms of amateurism and therefore made palatable to the white basketball unconscious, their *style on the court* undeniably echoed the American Basketball Association (ABA) and the playground game that it resembled and *in this* prefigured the basketball empire first presided over by Michael Jordan.

Inventing the Basketball Empire

In 1978–1979, the year before Johnson and Bird entered the league, former ABA players were already making their mark on the NBA. The league's leading scorer, George Gervin of the Spurs, and leading rebounder and MVP, Moses Malone, both had their starts in the ABA. Meanwhile, Julius Erving, who had joined the Philadelphia 76ers, averaged twenty-three points, seven rebounds, and nearly five assists per game. By Johnson's and Bird's first season in the league, Erving would improve on those numbers in leading his team to the NBA finals against Johnson and the

Lakers. In that same year, the NBA introduced the three-point line, adopt-ed from the ABA. And in 1983, Erving and Malone would join forces to win the only NBA title between 1980 and 1988 *not* won by Bird's Celtics or Magic's Lakers. Magic and Bird, writes Bethlehem Shoals, "were sons of the ABA," adding that "they had been rendered palatable (or compre-hensible) to mainstream fans"—thanks in part, I would add, to the myth of the amateurs.[34] Conversely, Bird and Johnson both, despite the myth's emphasis on their non-athleticism, unselfishness, effort, and fundamen-tal skills, routinely flouted the conventions of fundamental basketball associated with whiteness and employed instead a variety of maneuvers and skills derived from African American innovations in the game—or, at the very least, from styles primarily emphasized by and therefore associ-ated with African American basketball players.

According to conventional wisdom, a fundamentally sound pass requires a player, well balanced with both feet on the floor, to face his target squarely and deliver the ball with two hands.[35] Like most of the tru-isms concerning sound fundamentals in basketball this one assumes that the team is the fundamental creative unit. Confronted with an intractable defensive arrangement, the principles of fundamental basketball permit only those solutions predicated on team play. Thus, screens or movement without the ball should allow a trapped player to find an angle for a fun-damentally sound pass to an open teammate. Likewise, team play is the privileged means by which players may get free for uncontested shots. Prohibitions against leaving the floor with the ball in a crowd of defenders or passing without facing your target amount to prohibitions against indi-vidually asserted creativity in the sport. The team, of course, is overseen and directed by the coach, who embodies the intelligence and creative initiative that players then simply enact by following direction. In this way, the fundamental principles of the sport express moral principles of unselfishness, humility, and cooperation.

But these principles reflect more than mere tactical and moral prefer-ences. Because many of the proscribed maneuvers, and the ethos of indi-vidual creativity they express, emerged and predominated among African American players on urban playgrounds, these principles carry racial implications. Moreover, because at the most visible levels, and until very recently, most basketball coaches were white, the conventional prejudice against player prerogative implies the subordination of African Ameri-can players to their white coaches.[36] In this way, to describe Bird's and Johnson's style of play within the framework of values—as teamwork, as creativity expressing nothing more than sheer love of the game—purveyed by the myth of the amateurs serves, in effect, to diminish, perhaps to contain, the African American influence on their play. Considering the context of Bird's and Johnson's appearance in the league—the declining popularity of the professional game, the recent merger, the perception that it was "too black"—the myth of the amateurs appears to safeguard the sport for the consumption of white fans.

But Johnson and Bird distinguished themselves by the dazzling variety of ways they both found to defy these norms: passes thrown backward over their heads, while in the air, or underhand the length of the court; tap passes off a dribble; or bounce passes thrown from the floor. In addition to their passing, both employed elaborate ball fakes, complex footwork, and off-balance shots in heavy traffic. Moreover, two apparently contradictory elements of the situations in which the two made such plays—either when the offense had broken down completely or when the maneuver was unnecessary—underscore the individualism their creativity expressed. In the first case, both Bird and Johnson seemed to employ playground maneuvers to create possibilities for themselves or teammates when the conventions of the modern basketball state offered no solutions to a defensive challenge. In this respect, their deceptiveness recalls the elusive cunning of Athena I described in Chapter 1.

Moreover, Bird and Johnson also employed these tactics when they were unnecessary. While we can only guess at motivations, in such instances the maneuvers appeared to serve to humiliate an opponent, to amuse themselves, to entertain fans, or, most likely, all of the above. The strategically superfluous ostentation involved in the latter instances might appear at first glance to be the opposite of the pragmatic solution to urgent on-court puzzles evident in the former. But as Leonard Koppett has argued, in basketball individual style is not opposed to but simply an extension of the practical imperative to deceive: "Style *is* deception, made visible."[37] So Johnson employed no-look passes not only with an eye toward misdirecting defenders on a fast break but also with what seemed like an awareness of the cameras situated on the baseline ready to capture his smile as he looked to one side and shoveled a one-handed pass across his body in the opposite direction. Or a Larry Bird ball fake might be employed as a practical means to shake a tenacious defender in one case and, in the next instance, to simply make another defender look foolish. In the latter case, Bird is simply, as Koppett would put it, making the deception inherent in the first play *visible* in the second. In doing so, of course, he also humiliates the opponent, amuses himself, and entertains the fans.

Bird, moreover, employed another tactical element even more directly derived from the informal culture of playground basketball: he was considered one of the most notorious trash talkers of his time. In one case, the Indiana Pacers rookie Chuck "The Rifleman" Person announced before facing the Celtics on Christmas Day that he was going "Bird hunting." Bird approached Person before the game to tell the rookie he had gotten him a Christmas gift. Then, on Boston's first possession, he spotted up right in front of Person (who was on the Pacers' bench), drained the three pointer, and then turned to Person and said, "Merry Fucking Christmas."[38] Bird taunted opponents almost continuously throughout games, often telling defenders what he was going to do on offense before going on to do just that or, on defense, leaving players open for jump shots and verbally challenging them to make it. Bird even taunted Johnson when Johnson would cover Bird on a defensive switch, calling to his teammates, "Give me the ball. I got a little one on me!"

The myth of the amateurs notes Bird's trash talking with head-shaking bemusement, as an expression of his indomitable drive to win. But whatever the basis for such views, they *effectively* deemphasize the historical links that connect Bird's and Johnson's on-court style with the African American–dominated basketball venues in which elements of that style originated. Trash talking first emerged as the distinctive cultural expression of black men on urban playgrounds in the second half of the twentieth century, where it evolved out of existing African American traditions of verbal sparring such as "sounding" and "playing the dozens."[39] By eliding the history of trash talking, interpreters of Bird facilitated a double standard whereby black trash talkers could still be considered unsportsmanlike. At the same time, such interpretations confine Bird to the stereotypical image of the hard-nosed, competitive white player. But it is possible to see in Bird's trash talking his adoption of certain African American cultural practices as the best means available for expressing his confidence and competitive zeal.[40]

In one other respect, too, Bird and Johnson adopted ABA styles, inflected them, and in this way paved the way for a transformation of the NBA: they carried forward a flexibility with respect to traditional positions first inaugurated by skilled athletic ABA forwards such as Erving and Denver's David Thompson. "In playground ball," writes Todd Boyd, "positions are irrelevant. The best players simply control the flow of the game" so that Michael Jordan could, as he puts it, "be a small forward and a shooting guard all at once."[41] But we should also observe that Bird regularly performed the functions traditionally associated with four of the five positions, and Johnson at times performed all five. This is what Bethlehem Shoals first called the "positional revolution," rightly citing Bird and Johnson as the prototypes for succeeding generations of big, mobile, skilled, athletic basketball players—from Derrick Coleman and Penny Hardaway to Kevin Durant and LeBron James—who could shape the outcome of games from any position on the floor.[42]

Bird and Johnson, when freed from the confining parameters of the myth of the amateurs, can thus be seen as critical relay nodes in the story of inventive basketball. Although it may be true that they "saved the NBA" and even that they each believed in traditional values such as unselfishness, competitive intensity, and fundamental skills, the myth of the amateurs' exclusive emphasis on these elements and its deracination of those elements of their on-court play that bespeak the pervasive influence of styles of African American derivation obscure the most important contributions they made to saving the league. Moreover, the myth's emphasis on their love of the game suppresses the critical ways in which Bird's and Johnson's entertaining styles of play were (and were calculated to be) indispensable to *selling* the game as a commodity. Bird and Johnson saved the league (and paved the way for Jordan) as much by injecting what Nelson George calls the "black basketball aesthetic"—deceptive flair, individual creativity, positional versatility—into the NBA and making it seem safe for white fans to consume.

It is a question of emphasis, of course. The myth of the amateurs emphasizes the aspects of Bird and Johnson that were amenable to threatened white fans, which, unsurprisingly, are the very values that the myths of basketball culture, from the beginning, have hypostasized as fixed, essential, and perpetually under siege, especially by African American innovations. It is not that Bird and Johnson did not espouse such values. It is that, given the normative force of such values, they were the marketing sugar that made the stylistic medicine of ABA basketball go down for alienated white fans. In the decade between their NCAA Championship matchup and their decisive victory in the 1992 Barcelona Olympics, the two effectively persuaded white fans that while the path to the future *need not* entail the sacrifice of their cherished traditional values, it *could not* dispense with the creative contributions of the black basketball aesthetic. It was their success in doing so that laid the foundation for the rise of the basketball empire, emblematized by Michael Jordan; presided over by a new commissioner, David Stern; funded by Nike; and telecast by ESPN.

III

MYTHS OF THE
BASKETBALL EMPIRE

(1991–Present)

6

THE MYTH OF THE
GREATEST OF ALL TIME

June 13, 1991

By acclamation, Michael Jordan is the
greatest player of all time.—**NBA**

hree different college player of the year awards, an NBA Rookie of
the Year award, five NBA MVP awards, six NBA finals MVP awards,
fourteen NBA All-Star Game appearances, ten All-NBA first team
appearances, nine All-NBA defensive first team appearances, one NCAA
championship, two Olympic gold medals, six NBA championships, ten-
time NBA leader in points per game, career NBA leader in points per game,
three-time NBA leader in steals per game, seven-time NBA leader in player
efficiency rating, career NBA leader in player efficiency rating, eight-time
NBA leader in win shares per forty-eight minutes, career NBA leader in
win shares per forty-eight minutes. Michael Jordan is the greatest of all
time: if there were such a thing as a safely indisputable subjective claim
in the basketball universe, surely this must be it.

But the very consensus surrounding this claim means also that it is
perhaps the most potent myth in basketball history: the myth of the greatest of all time. I am not interested in debating Jordan's greatness relative
to other great players; instead, I am interested in understanding the workings of the narrative elements by which the belief that Jordan is the greatest of all time is conveyed and consumed. Jordan's status as the greatest
of all time would not be sealed until his retirement in 1998. But arguably
the pivotal moment in the myth of the greatest of all time occurred on
June 13, 1991, when Jordan's Chicago Bulls won the first of the six NBA
championships they would win over an eight-season span. With that vic-

tory, Jordan went from being an outlandishly talented individual athlete to a winning team player, permitting the myth of the greatest of all time to crystallize as a morality tale in which Jordan's ascent coincides with the subordination of his ego and his mature internalization of the timeless values of basketball under the guidance of his head coach and guru, Phil Jackson, who was a figure in the myth of the garden.[1] The view that took shape then would be written in stone—literally—a few years later, when a one-ton bronze statue of Jordan was dedicated outside the Bulls' lavish new United Center arena. Called "The Spirit," that statue's inscription reads, "The best there ever was. The best there ever will be."

The myth of the greatest of all time took shape amid a profound, interconnected series of changes in the business of basketball, American politics, the media, manufacturing, and the global economy. These forces—new Commissioner David Stern, a conservative shift in American politics, the rise of telecommunications satellites and cable television, and the relocation of multinational manufacturing to the Third World, as well as the penetration of overseas markets—helped (along with his talent, of course) to make Jordan an internationally recognized icon and the NBA a global brand, all in the context of America's apparent material and ideological triumph in the Cold War. Grasping the force, intensity, and broader import of the myth of the greatest of all time requires reconnecting it to the conditions in which it emerged, crystallized, and came to be accepted as self-evident. One of the casualties of the myth is our ability to perceive, and appreciate fully, Jordan as a basketball player, independently of our assessments of his relative (or incomparable) greatness, and despite our investments in him as a commodity. Inventing Jordan in the face of the myth of the greatest and in the wake of a genealogy of his canonicity frees up a Jordan who carries forward an image of basketball as an improvisatory creative art ever proliferating new forms.

The Myth of the Greatest of All Time

"What," Michael Jordan asked the audience during his Hall of Fame induction speech in 2009, "don't you guys know about me?"[2] Indeed, the story of his career has been recited so often that even many casual fans of the sport can repeat it. Cut from his high school varsity team, Jordan rebounded to earn a scholarship to the University of North Carolina, where as a freshman he hit the winning shot in the 1982 NCAA championship game. Entering the NBA in 1984, Jordan set the pro league ablaze, averaging 37.1 points per game in his third season, the highest single-season scoring average since Wilt Chamberlain's rookie year in 1959–1960. Meanwhile, Jordan's thrilling, airborne improvisations and likable persona garnered him massive endorsement contracts, making him the wealthiest and most recognizable basketball player in history. Still, Jordan's Bulls, though improving, failed to become serious contenders for the NBA title. The pattern of extraordinary individual accomplishment coupled with the modest success of his team would continue for the next few years. Jordan would lead the league in scoring and win the MVP award in 1988, 1989, and 1990, but in each of those years his team would fall in the playoffs.

In the 1989–1990 season, Jackson installed a system—known colloquially as "the triangle"—designed to incorporate Jordan's teammates into the offense, making it more difficult for opponents to focus exclusively on Jordan. The system paid off in 1991, when the Bulls captured the NBA title, defeating Magic Johnson and the Los Angeles Lakers. Two more titles would follow in 1992 and 1993 (with an Olympic Gold medal as a member of the 1992 Dream Team in between), and Jordan's already remarkable celebrity escalated to unparalleled new heights the world over. Then came Jordan's shocking announcement that he was retiring from basketball to follow his—and his recently murdered father's—dream of playing professional baseball. Two years later, Jordan returned and regained top form for the 1995–1996 campaign, in which the Bulls posted an all-time NBA best record of 72–10 on their way to another title, his fourth and the first of the Bulls' "three-peats." After the 1998 championship, Jordan's sixth in eight years, he once again announced his retirement from basketball. This time, it was understandable: Jordan was the most prolific scorer the league had seen since Chamberlain and had led the most dominant dynasty since Bill Russell's Celtics. There seemed to be little, if anything, left for Jordan to achieve. A league that had used Jordan's fame to transform itself into a highly profitable global brand bade him a grateful, if anxious, farewell.

For a story narrating unparalleled achievement in basketball, the myth of the greatest of all time's most striking feature may be the prominent role played by failure and setback. From being passed over for his high school's varsity to being passed over by two teams in the 1984 NBA draft, from the recurrent bitter defeats at the hands of the Pistons to the murder of his father and the indignity of his baseball mediocrity, the myth of the greatest of all time emphasizes the depths of Jordan's lows. Doing so not only sets Jordan's accomplishments in greater relief; it also permits the myth to emphasize—in explaining the source of Jordan's unsurpassable greatness—the intangible personal qualities that, much more than mere natural talent, led Jordan to his achievements: competitive intensity and hard work. Indeed, in that same Hall of Fame induction speech, Jordan himself emphasized this aspect of the myth by enumerating the slights he had suffered, fueling the competitive fire that drove him to work tirelessly to improve his game. To cap and confirm this extreme version of the myth of the greatest of all time, as Jordan concluded his litany of complaint, an audience member shouted, "You're the greatest ever, Michael!" eliciting warm applause from the rest of the assembled guests, a number of whom had just been on the wrong end of Jordan's insults.

But of all the valleys in the myth of the greatest of all time, the single most important one is his period of isolated, Sisyphean failure to win, torching the league and creating dazzling new shapes and lines of flight with his body while rolling the stone of a mediocre team and a limited coaching staff up the mountain of the playoffs, only to have it tumble back down year after year. Here, the myth throws two crucial narrative elements into relief: a nemesis and a mentor. As nemesis, the Detroit Pistons (who beat the Bulls in the 1988, 1989, and 1990 playoffs) were not only self-styled "Bad Boys" proudly intimidating opponents with a rough style of play; they were also, as I explain in Chapter 7, representatives of the city that at the time symbolized everything that terrified white America about blackness: defiance, inscrutable violence; unapologetic disregard for common decency—in short, incorrigible chaos. But however distasteful the Bad Boys may have been to the white basketball unconscious (and although their principal villain, Bill Laimbeer, was in fact white), they were—and won as—a team. So however likeable and extraordinary Jordan may have been, and however despised the Pistons were for having dethroned both Bird's Celtics and Magic's Lakers, the white basketball unconscious would not cast Jordan in the title role of the myth of the greatest of all time until he avenged his predecessors by unseating the Pistons as a member of a functioning team.

Enter Jordan's tactical mentor and spiritual guide through this underworld of adversity: Phil Jackson. "The triangle offense," writes Roland Lazenby, "provided a format that allowed Jordan to relate to his less talented teammates."[3] As the myth has it, Jackson's triangle offense expressed tactically the core values of Jackson's psychological and spiritual beliefs. Jackson adopted the offense because "it empowered everybody on the team by making them more involved in the offense, and demanded that they put their individual needs second to those of the group."[4] Previously, Jordan's assertiveness and individual effectiveness had led his teammates to become passive spectators, allowing defenses to double and triple team Jordan. But the triangle activated these passive teammates, putting them in positions to score and giving them the responsibility to do so when the opportunity presented itself. If defenses ignore one offensive player to double team another, "the structure of the triangle," as Lazenby explains, "demands that the ball be passed to the open man."[5] In this way, the defense must, as the cliché has it, pick its poison.

Of course, an offensive system by itself does not do anything. It is the players who make it work and, the myth reminds us, the coach who must, one way or another, get the players to do so. Challenged with persuading the superstar to accept what Jordan called, in a metaphor that is tellingly dismissive of affirmative action policies under fire at the time, an "equal opportunity offense," Jackson, rather than heavy-handedly imposing his authority, drew on Jordan's own qualities, especially his competitive intensity, to convince him that the new system would allow him to elude the tragic dichotomy between asserting himself individually and winning. Fueled by the team's frustrating failures, Jordan accepted that giving his teammates more opportunities was the only way to get defenders to play the Bulls honestly and thus, seemingly paradoxically, would offer him greater freedom within which to operate as an individual.

By Jackson's second season at the helm, in 1990–1991, the Bulls had broken their old habits and mastered the triangle. A four-game sweep of the Pistons confirmed their new identity (and when the Pistons stalked off the court without shaking hands, it confirmed for many fans that something in fact had been truly bad about them all along). From there, the Bulls' 4–1 finals win over Magic's Lakers was almost anticlimactic, but not so much so that the myth does not dwell on a key, morally edifying turning point. Ahead in the series three games to one, the Bulls were struggling to close the series out on the experienced Lakers' home floor. Midway through the fourth quarter, the Lakers had taken a lead, and Jackson noted that Jordan was reverting to his old, individualistic habits, forcing shots against double and triple teams. During a timeout, Jackson "kneeled in the huddle and stared into Jordan's blazing eyes," according to Roland Lazenby. "'MJ, who's open?' Jackson demanded. When Jordan did not reply, Jackson insisted, asking again, 'Who's open?' Jordan then relented and says, 'Pax!' [the Bulls' sharpshooting guard John Paxson]. Jackson then asserts the golden rule, 'Well, throw him the fuckin' ball!'" Paxson went on to make five long-range jump shots in the final four minutes to help seal the Bulls' victory.[6]

Bethlehem Shoals astutely observes, "We're now supposed to see [Jordan's] first years in the league as an NBA bildungsroman."[7] A German word that literally means "formation novel," "bildungsroman" refers to a novel "that follows the development of the hero or heroine from childhood or adolescence into adulthood, through a troubled quest for identity."[8] The myth of the greatest of all time indeed strikingly resembles the form.[9] Scholars tend to view the arc of the traditional bildungsroman as symbolically supporting the social status quo of industrial capitalism, for if its hero is to succeed in this world, he must learn to subordinate his understandable, but ultimately selfish and immature, romantic aspirations of transcendent individual greatness and accept instead the values of the bourgeoisie.

And if Jackson played an instrumental role in Jordan's growth and ascendance, it was at least as crucial that Jackson provided continuity with the myth of the garden and the Knicks of the early 1970s, whose coach, Red Holzman, Jackson credited with the basic tenets of the tactical and moral approach to the game he had then imparted to the greatest of all time. Jordan seemed thus to embody all of basketball history effortlessly, combining Chamberlain's superlative individual excellence with Russell's indomitable will to win, Johnson's entertaining stylishness with Bird's gritty work ethic, Erving's aerial acrobatics with Oscar Robertson's completeness, all under the auspices of the Old Knicks and as a global ambassador turning the modern basketball state into basketball empire. In this way, Jordan seemed to have resolved, for the first and last time, the mythic tactical and moral antinomies of basketball history.

These antinomies, however, had always been racialized in the white basketball unconscious, born of deep-seated fears and anxieties about the destruction of the sport's core tactical, stylistic, and moral essence through changes spurred by racial integration. In this sense, by appearing to resolve the tactical and moral conflicts of basketball history Jordan appeared also to resolve the suppressed racial conflicts for which the former were made to stand in myth.

Here, the myth of the greatest of all time marshaled visual, media accompaniments to seal the deal. The first Nike Air Jordan ads, in which Jordan did not speak, fetishized his black physicality. In the first, the camera pans down the length of his silent body before pausing to dwell on his shoes, banned by the NBA, offering consumers the vicarious thrill of antiestablishment rebellion. In the second, he appears on a deteriorating urban playground, soaring for a dunk on a basket with a chain net, before intoning in a voiceover, "Who said man was not meant to fly?"—again suggesting, but more broadly and less pointedly, defiance. But as the myth gathered force, the ads came to swathe Jordan's black body with the aura

THE MYTH OF THE GREATEST OF ALL TIME · 111

of an amenable, likeable, even funny personality, which many white consumers could contrast with the menacing black men of their fantasies and with which therefore they could identify all the more strongly. In the mid-1980s, the white basketball unconscious might have chosen Magic's weapon, but by the end of the decade those governed by it—whether black or white—longed to *be like* Mike, whose super-powers could protect them not only from alien invaders, as in the animated movie *Space Jams* of 1996, but also from the frightening specter of unapologetic, undiluted blackness. Jordan had literally saved the(ir) world.

No wonder, then, that by 1993, the cover of a special issue of not a sports publication but of the mainstream *Newsweek* was proclaiming Jordan "the greatest ever," a pronouncement that has now become consensus.[10] The issue featured an "in-depth" article by Jordan's handpicked sycophantic biographer Bob Greene, on the cover of whose first Jordan biography, *Hang Time*, the star appears, standing behind the author, resting his elbows on Greene's shoulders, face frozen in that inviting trademark half-smile, expressing perhaps bemused tolerance for our need to be that close to him.[11] No wonder, then, that by 1994, the specially commissioned "The Spirit" statue ("The best there ever was. The best there ever will be") would be unveiled at the Bulls' arena in Chicago.

With this affirmation of disembodied perfection, the myth of the greatest of all time, in effect, proclaims the end of basketball history. If Jordan is truly the greatest there ever was and the greatest there ever will be, then henceforth basketball can produce only lesser iterations of all the hitherto incompatible elements of the game that Jordan's singular basketball body gathered together and blended so incomparably. Ultimately, perhaps Jordan himself revealed the end game of the myth of the greatest all time when he pondered the question, "How would I have done against me?" Where every other player in the game must be compared with someone else, Jordan knows well what his myth proclaims: for the greatest ever there can be neither comparison nor competition, only an endless imaginary game of one-on-one played in a hall of mirrors.[12]

A Genealogy of All Time

Beyond what it might really tell us about Michael Jordan's abilities as a player, the myth of the greatest of all time occupies a special place in the collection of myths I am examining. It marks the historical transition from the basketball state to the basketball empire. It can do so in part because it incorporates and resolves elements of all of the myths that preceded it.

For example, Jordan appears as the synthesis of terms established as irreconcilable dichotomies in the myth of the rivalry and the myth of the amateurs.[13] It offers a direct vindication of the values purveyed by the myth of the garden and appears to confirm the validity of the myth of foundation in that Jordan's greatness is inseparable from the guiding wisdom of NBA Commissioner David Stern and from the league's own ascent, more generally. Finally, it reaffirms the message of the myth of creation with respect not only to the core values supposedly embodied in the sport but also to the timeless insulation of those values beyond historical vicissitudes and material change. In this respect, the myth of the greatest of all time offers a culminating image of Jordan as the immortal, time-ending essence of the sport created by Naismith, an image as frozen and immobile as the statue—called "The Spirit," do not forget—erected in his honor.

Over the past decade and a half, numerous scholars have analyzed the political, social, and cultural conditions in the United States within which what David Andrews called "Michael Jordan, Inc." took on particular characteristics and became a globally recognized image and brand. The so-called Reagan Revolution included political and economic policies that led to a sharp decline in industrial manufacturing jobs in major U.S. cities, especially in the North, even as legislation during the same period rolled back a number of social welfare programs.[14] The loss of manufacturing and of jobs eroded local tax bases, which further diminished social services available to the mostly African American residents of urban cores. As a result, poverty, drug use, and crime rates rose in these areas throughout the 1980s, which in turn appeared to justify the need for anticrime legislation that promoted aggressive policing tactics and harsher sentencing guidelines.[15] These policies created "ever more deteriorating, and increasingly isolated, economic, social, and physical environments," termed by some scholars "hyperghettos." Social and economic isolation within these spaces thus resulted in "increased poverty, crime and incarceration rates and decreasing education, employment, and health outcomes for what was an already vulnerable community."[16]

This neoliberal evisceration of African American communities in America's urban centers was accompanied by a resurgent affirmation, on the cultural front, of the American dream of individual freedom, rights, and responsibility, offering the promise of equal opportunity for all individuals as long as they were willing to sacrifice and work hard.[17] Within this cultural accompaniment, a new discourse pertaining to race emerged wherein the legacies of slavery and segregation were declared overcome. Affirmative action therefore was seen not only as superfluous but also as victimizing, "reverse racist," and un-American. Poverty, crime, drug use, and welfare dependence among African American populations were framed as symptoms of dysfunction essentially rooted in black culture. And as if to demonstrate the fact, individual black celebrities such as Michael Jackson, Bill Cosby, and Oprah Winfrey were marshaled as examples of what African Americans could accomplish if they possessed sufficient determination, work ethic, and positive attitude.[18]

As Walter LaFeber argued in a now classic study, related transformations in the behavior of multinational corporations and the rise of new telecommunications technology (both facilitated by Reagan administration deregulation) combined with shifts in marketing strategies to set the stage for Jordan and Nike.[19] But although these material transformations were certainly indispensable, by themselves they could not make Jordan appealing and meaningful without the racist cultural accompaniment provided by the Reagan Revolution. In that context, Jordan's carefully managed persona combined qualities designed to appeal simultaneously to stereotypical notions of racial difference (e.g., the naturally gifted black athlete) and to putatively American values (e.g., hardworking, determined, competitive, trans-racial).[20] This combination of qualities proved tremendously attractive to a consuming public whose perceptions and preferences were primed by the new racial discourse prevailing during the 1980s. However, understanding why assessments of Jordan's basketball legacy took the specific narrative shape they did—as the myth that he is the greatest *of all time*—requires, I believe, that one more component be added to the portrait of Jordan's time and place: the end of the Cold War.

As important as domestic deregulation policies were to facilitating deindustrialization and the globalization of economic production, two other factors helped make the world "safe" for multinational corporations: American military intervention abroad, both covert and overt, and a massive buildup in military expenditures at home. Together these two factors helped to push the Soviet Union to and over the edge of collapse, ushering in the end of the Cold War and a so-called new global order in which the United States reigned as the world's only military and economic superpower, the self-appointed guarantor of economic and political freedom the world over. Of course, the economic and political freedoms thus "safeguarded" primarily benefited upper-middle-class consumers, multinational corporations, and those foreign elites who were allied with them. Nevertheless, despite these very real limitations of the U.S. victory in the Cold War, its end had a powerful impact on cultural and political discourse in the United States.

Among the most revealing expressions of this impact was the political scientist Francis Fukuyama's best-selling *The End of History and the Last Man*. Surveying events marking the breakup of the Soviet bloc, such as the fall of the Berlin Wall, Fukuyama wrote that we might be witnessing "the end of history as such." Fukuyama meant that history, as a flow of events driven by a contest of ideologies, had come to an end with the triumph of the United States in the Cold War. Western liberal democracy, he argued, was "the final form of human government" for which there were no longer any viable competing visions.[21] Fukuyama believed that "we are now at a point where we cannot imagine a world substantially different from our own, in which there is no apparent or obvious way in which the future will represent a fundamental improvement over our current order."[22] Fukuyama's vision, in short, was that the new world order of neoliberalism, of which the Reagan Revolution was both an agent and an emblem, was the horizon beyond which our social imagination could not reach—the greatest of all possible social orders.

Fukuyama became a media sensation, and although his argument prompted critical responses from both left and right, his essay and book evidently voiced a broad, deeply felt sentiment—or, at least, wish—that we had indeed produced the ideal social order and therefore could stop imagining alternatives, stop trying to do better.[23] As Fukuyama put it in his book, evoking a figure to emblematize our condition, "The last man at the end of history *knows* better than to risk his life for a cause."[24] While it is certainly unlikely that most people who have subscribed to and purveyed the myth that Michael Jordan is the greatest of all time have ever heard of Fukuyama (let alone read his writings), I do not think it is too much to claim that in its form this myth echoed and partook of the broader cultural sentiment that Fukuyama's argument expressed. After all, as a Google Ngram Viewer search for the terms "greatest basketball player ever" shows, basketball culture did not really have much interest in the category until this era.[25]

Consider how this myth fits into the narrative of the NBA's rise from its late 1970s ashes. We know already that Magic Johnson and Larry Bird "saved" the league by providing an infectious image of a professionally competitive but joyful, racially harmonious love of basketball play. But the fact is that—"choose your weapon" notwithstanding—Magic and Bird did not succeed in parlaying their popularity among basketball fans into broad commercial success through endorsements; nor was the NBA able to use the duo as a lever to financial stability, let alone global preeminence as a brand. For that, the story goes, it took Jordan, Nike, and the far-seeing vision of David Stern. In 1979, average attendance at an NBA game was 9,295. By 1984, Magic and Larry, the myth of the amateurs might say, had increased that number by about 20 percent, to 10,983. Five years into Jordan's career, in 1989, however, average attendance had increased by 50 percent more, to 15,649.[26] Only through the combined efforts of this trio could the NBA overcome the central contradiction bedeviling its past: that a primarily white audience was resistant to purchasing a primarily black product.

The complex racial positioning of Jordan within the context of the socioeconomic and cultural transformations of the Reagan Revolution allowed white consumers to invest in Jordan, both as a player and as an appealing racially transcendent emblem of the American dream. For such consumers, to affirm Jordan as the greatest of all time was simultaneously to affirm the unsurpassable greatness of this moment in American history and, indeed, the unsurpassable greatness of ourselves as agents of the end of history. As with Fukuyama's vision of the triumph of Western liberal democracy, it was impossible to imagine basketball play (or the league, for that matter) beyond Jordan. This is why, by the way, as I discuss in more detail in the next chapter, the 1990s were marked by a growing parade—heralded equally by hopeful excitement and panicked anxiety—of "new Jordans," players such as Harold Minor and Grant Hill who, we prayed, would guarantee us a future of endless Jordans. In these ways, the myth of the greatest of all time not only announces the end of basketball history and the advent of an eternal basketball empire but also echoes the prevailing ideology of its day, which announced the end of social history and the advent of an eternal American empire.

Inventing Time

On the day in 2011 that we were to discuss Jordan in my Cultures of Basketball course, I showed my students four minutes and thirty-five seconds of NBA-sponsored, pre-1990 Michael Jordan highlights.[27] I felt like I was at a fireworks show. As we watched, each of us in our own private world, we emerged periodically, briefly, to exchange a collective "ooh." It was as though we were staging a skit about the birth of language and society. Perhaps it would be more accurate to say that in these sporadic, exchanged exhalations we were spontaneously living a moment like the ones from which language first emerged. After flipping on the lights, we adjusted our eyes and minds and eased our way out of amazement and into analysis. With the aid of the essay "The Invention of Air: The Brash, Brilliant

Doodles of Young Jordan," by Bethlehem Shoals, we were able to tease out the cultural and political value of letting this "Young Jordan" stand on his own rather than as a prequel necessarily overcome to facilitate the emergence of the greatest of all time.

Speaking of the transition in which Jordan began to give up the dunk for the jump shot Shoals offers a fascinating observation: "The dunk takes an instant and an eternity; it's both completely frivolous and totally domineering, a flash of light so blinding and brief that it might as well have never happened. A shot was the stuff of narrative; it was itself a story with a built-in arc, climax, and resolution. It also served as the perfect punctuation to any possession, game, season, or career."[28] Shoals argues that Jordan made a choice to alter his game, and his image, not only to win titles but also to become the stuff of official NBA history. It is to say that his transition from the high-flying solo dunker that we watched in class— all run outs and isolations, twisting layups and dunks—to the triangle-playing, Phil-obeying, jump-shooting team player capable of winning six titles in eight years not only effectively made his team more successful but also cemented his place as the consensus greatest of all time. It also (if unintentionally) became an effective poetic tactic rendering his game more amenable to narrative, which, after all, is essential to the circulation of myth and its transmutation into the concrete forms of official history.

There is, indeed, no way to build a history out of the "oohs" and "aahs" provoked by Jordan's early highlights. They are little more than a baby's first words—significant as such but with little staying power, like leftover pieces of a puzzle we have lost or the screws left over after assembling some piece of furniture. According to the bildungsroman purveyed by the myth of the greatest of all time, Michael, the brutally talented individual, eventually works hard, learns (from the Zen master Phil Jackson, no less) how "less is more," subordinates himself for the team, and in the end wins titles and the eternal admiration of all.[29] Obi-Wan Kenobi says to Darth Vader, "If you strike me down, I will become more powerful than you can possibly imagine." Something like that is the deal the young Jordan strikes with the old Jordan: "If you agree not to score thirty-seven points per game for your whole career (which is an abomination to the game), then you can win titles with obscene ease, drain a few legendary game-winning jumpers, and we will never, ever forget you." Young Michael lowers his light saber, folds his hands across his chest, and is launched into hoops immortality. In this way, Jordan, like so few others, gets to have it both ways: to have died young and so become immortal *and* to have lived out and fulfilled his promise in the established world and so to have that immortality narrated. Jordan is James Dean and Laurence Olivier, John F. Kennedy and Ronald Reagan, Maurice Stokes and Kareem Abdul-Jabbar. Maybe that is what it is to be the greatest of all time: to dunk and shoot the jumper.

But I would like to take this logic one step further. My students and I counted twenty-four different baskets, of which the most striking, certainly, were the fourteen dunks (the young Jordan's trademarks) and the two jump shots (tantalizing promises of the Jordan to come). If the dunk is the monosyllabic exclamation and the smooth, inevitable jump shot is the narrative of ineluctable triumphant conformity, what about the other eight baskets Jordan made in the video? What is their discursive equivalent? Jordan takes off somewhere within the general vicinity of the basket, leaving behind some earthbound defenders; encountering other, rising, obstacles in mid-flight, fragments of bodies—arms, and hands—floating into his space. He responds: beginning to turn his body away from the basket and the defender, or else drawing his knees up and extending the ball in one hand, he may begin to float beneath the basket. In either case, he designs and creates a physical space that he occupies alone, as he designs and creates it, to get the clear shot. Really, it is a space just for his left or right hand and the ball, since that is all he needed to have cleared.

These plays—which are what I, having seen Jordan in person in just his second professional game, most remember of his career—seem to me to carry the power of unfinished, unfolding narrative, like a jumper but without the foregone, prewritten character of that more predictable and repeatable shot. If these are part of what Shoals means by the "brash, brilliant doodles" of the chapter's title, they might also be seen, in poetic terms, as Surrealist exquisite corpse prose exercises in which the story begun by one individual is continued blindly by another and finished, again blindly, by yet another so that nobody really knows how it will end until it has ended and then, and only then, if at all, will it have looked inevitable. And *even* then, it will look strange and unfinished.

Whatever their tactical and poetic differences, the early Jordan dunk and the late Jordan jump shot share a sense of inevitability. But before one of the myriad variations on a layup that he improvised bounces around and drops in, before Jordan lands like a cat in a thieving crouch, surrounded by defenders shaking their heads befuddled, before space once again becomes one, and grounded, and shared by us all—before all that, there is the dilated moment of extended exclamation, and wonder, and invested uncertainty. We do not know how it will end, but it does not matter, because we already care. It is already amazing, just as it is—a perfect slice of pure invention in process.

A key term in the classical Greek art of rhetoric was *kairos*. The *kairos* was "the right moment" or "the opportune." In archery, *kairos* is "an opening or opportunity . . . a long tunnel-like aperture through which the archer's arrow has to pass." This requires timing and force. In weaving, Eric White explains, *kairos* is "'the critical time' when the weaver must draw the yarn through a gap that momentarily opens in the warp of the cloth being woven." White goes on to offer the implications for creativity in thought and action:

> *Kairos* therefore counsels thought to act always, as it were, on the spur of the moment. Such an activity of invention would renew itself and be transformed from moment to moment as it evolves and adapts itself to newly emergent contexts. The fluid and relative moments of the immediate situation would be constitutively involved in the invention process, which would become an improvisational one, a more or less successful attempt to "make do" with whatever is conveniently at hand. *Kairos* thus establishes the living present as point of departure or inspiration for a purely circumstantial activity of "invention."[30]

It is not hard, I think, to see the applicability of White's description to Jordan's midair improvisations, and this has important implications for history and time.

Fukuyama's argument about the end of history rested on a particular understanding of history. From that perspective, history moves as a result of a tension between the contradicting impulses of opposing forces. These forces might be seen, among other ways, as feudal lord and serf, colonizer and colonized, mind and matter, proletariat and bourgeoisie, or self and other. The end of history, on this view, occurs when these contradictions and the movement to which they give rise are resolved—or, to put it more concretely in Fukuyama's terms, when there is no longer an "outside" to Western liberal democracy.[31]

But history can be seen in other ways. In a work published a few years after Fukuyama's, Michael Hardt and Antonio Negri offered a very different account of the world as it stood in the wake of the Cold War, after the collapse of the Soviet bloc. They acknowledged the facts of globalization under the aegis of neoliberalism, a global condition they termed

"Empire."[32] But they also argued that, far from eradicating real or imagined alternatives to this condition, Empire had in fact proliferated the extent and variety of such alternatives. Where Fukuyama saw the course of history as a predictable, linear development, Hardt and Negri suggested that the so-called new world order offered us an opportunity to see history as radically unstable and uncertain, driven forward by multiple, varied assertions of autonomy around the world. Such assertions might or might not become the bases for sustained, mass social movements, let alone revolutions capable of seizing state power. But they should be seen, Hardt and Negri argued, as no less politically and historically significant because of this.

In short, Hardt and Negri encouraged their readers to see new opportunities for imagining, recognizing, and realizing multiple futures that, contrary to Fukuyama's claim, would be "substantially different from our own."[33] The word that Negri used to designate these "opportunities"—or, rather, ways to see the present as opportunity, as "singular and open"— was, strikingly, *kairos*.[34] An aperture in the supposed end of history, the *kairos* presents a flickering opportunity creatively to change the future in ways we may not, even in acting, fully foresee. *Kairos* offers an opening through which potential may express itself without ever fulfilling itself and in this way counter the apparent eternity of constituted power.

In the film *Goodbye, Lenin!* Christiane, who has devoted her life to the publicly professed ideals of East German communism, lapses into a coma as a result of a heart attack just before the fall of the Berlin Wall. Anxious to protect her from further shock as she convalesces amid the collapse of her beloved East Germany, her son conjures excuses to prevent her from leaving the house and manufactures an alternative reality via fabricated newscasts that he plays for her nightly. In this way, he seeks to preserve for her an illusion that time has stopped.

One day, she wanders outside their building to discover garish billboards hawking Western products and luxury sports cars tearing down the road in front of her. As she gapes at the signs of change whirling around her, we see a helicopter in the distance. It turns toward her, low in the sky, at the far end of the busy street. A figure dangles below it. As the helicopter nears, Christiane looks up to make out the dangling object: a statue of Lenin, right arm stiffly extended in front of him, palm open, as though in the midst of a speech. However, the statue is tilted downward at an angle so that, as it passes in front of her, Lenin's arm beckons not skyward toward the abstract ideals of communism, but earthward, offering Christiane his outstretched palm.

Like the statue of Lenin, which reveals its fragile beauty and full humanity only after it has been toppled, Jordan reveals his fragile beauty and full humanity—and, indeed, his inventive greatness—only when we have let go of the myth and toppled the statue. These instants of Jordan at play, in motion, neither exclamatory dunks nor smooth narrative jumpers, serve as apertures in the closed narrative universe of the myth of the greatest of all time. These instants enable us to see Jordan not frozen in a ton of bronze as the greatest of all time, but alive, actively inventing himself and the game. Moreover, to the degree that this myth within the basketball universe expresses and echoes those declarations of the end of history that serve nothing so much as to foreclose the possibility of imagining, let alone realizing, alternative futures, then I believe these moments set history back in motion. Or, rather, they remind us that history has never stopped; it is still unfolding, full of uncertainty and wild potential for surprise. What was truly great about Jordan, which is also what is great about basketball, which is also what is great about history and our present moment in it, is actually that you never know what might happen next.

7

THE MYTH OF BLACKNESS

March 12, 1997

People don't want to pay $200 a night
to see jail culture.—**Michael Wilbon**

L ate in the 1996–1997 season, Michael Jordan and the defending champion Chicago Bulls came into Philadelphia to play the lowly 76ers. The
Bulls, at 54–8, were winning at a clip just behind the record-breaking
72–10 regular season win-loss mark they had set the year before. The 76ers
were struggling at 16–46. And yet in the third quarter, with the Bulls ahead
by two, the hard-to-please Philly crowd suddenly rose to its feet in cheers.
The rookie guard Allen "The Answer" Iverson had just caught a short flip
pass from his teammate Clarence Weatherspoon beyond the three-point
line near the left sideline. As Iverson caught his pass, Weatherspoon set a
screen on Iverson's defender. The Bulls switched on the screen so that as
Iverson dribbled to his right, toward the top of the key, he was picked up
by Weatherspoon's man: Michael Jordan, NBA All-Defensive First Team,
former Defensive Player of the Year, and, of course, greatest of all time.

Iverson dribbled back and forth a couple of times in place, before leaning to his left and allowing the ball to rise a bit higher toward his left
hand. Jordan lunged to his right to cut off the anticipated drive, but Iverson quickly crossed the ball back over to his right hand. Jordan recovered
his defensive position in front of Iverson as the Philly guard dribbled the
ball back from his right hand to his left between his legs. Again, the ball
rose high toward Iverson's left hand, and just as Jordan again lunged to
his right, Iverson crossed the ball back over to his right in a flash, taking
one hard dribble in that direction before stopping and rising—as Jordan

regained his balance and attempted to catch up—for a jump shot. Jordan leaped to block the shot, but the ball had already left Iverson's hand and was on its way toward the basket, where it settled cleanly through for two points and a tie game.

This play symbolizes a struggle over the direction of the league and the face of the sport, for even as Jordan appeared to have permanently resolved the challenges presented by the league's blackness, a new generation of African American players—none better known or more popular than Iverson—appeared, listening, talking about, and even recording hip-hop music and unapologetically displaying tattoos, cornrows, and other cultural markers of their upbringing in the urban ruins of the Reagan Revolution while building on and raising to new levels technical and tactical innovations first developed in urban playgrounds in the 1950s and 1960s. In the words of one historian, "For [NBA executives] the challenge of managing the infusion of hip-hop . . . was akin to playing with fire: handle it right and it would power the NBA into the new millennium: manage it wrong and it would burn down the house that Stern, Magic, Bird, and Jordan had built."[1]

The NBA sought to capitalize on the new markets this "hip-hop invasion" helped it penetrate while simultaneously trafficking in the social and cultural stereotypes arising out of blackness in its attempt to regulate the presentation of these players to the league's traditional white male consumers. The moment that Iverson crossed Jordan with a tactic first developed on the playground signifies a contest between two contrasting marketing visions and futures for the league, two different experiences of being black in the NBA and in America, and two different ways to respond to experiences of blackness. The moment also helps us apprehend and critically reflect on blackness in the NBA as a myth that expresses and contains anxieties relating to race and change in the sport, suppresses its own social and historical origins, and may be countered by careful attention to the on-court styles it tends to oversimplify and disparage as aberrations contrary to the spirit of basketball.[2]

The Myth of Blackness

In 1907, William James offered the example of the "climate" to illustrate his pragmatist critique of metaphysical essentialism. "The low thermometer to-day," James wrote, "is supposed to come from something called the 'climate.'" However, he continued, although "climate is really only the name for a certain group of days . . . it is treated as if it lay behind the day, and in general we place the name, as if it were a being, behind the facts it is the name of."[3] The myth of blackness does something similar, though more pernicious. It groups together decontextualized descriptions of playing style, clothing, and on- and off-court behavior with stereotypes about urban black men and boys common in the 1980s and especially the 1990s. While this group of supposed attributes in fact constitutes the category "blackness," the myth reverses the order and portrays blackness as the underlying cause of all the attributes. It then uses blackness to characterize the "post-Jordan generation" of African American basketball players as a danger to the game, to themselves, and to society. In effect, it blames the blackness of players for what it describes as their distracting, divisive, and dangerous inability to forget their blackness.

Because the myth of blackness is so pervasive and naturalized within the culture of basketball, it can be difficult to isolate and describe without falling into generalizing summary. To counter this, I examine how the myth of blackness concretely manifested itself in the media coverage of the particular game I began with, between the 76ers and the Bulls. In Chicago and Philadelphia, beat writers reported two results: the Bulls won the game (or "the war"), but Iverson scored thirty-seven points (and won "the battle").[4] But most fans nationwide would have read instead the Associated Press (AP) recap, picked up and circulated by local newspapers, which ran under a variety of headlines, including "Bulls Overcome Iverson," "Bulls withstand Iverson Highlights," "Iverson Is the Star, but Bulls Win the Game," and "Iverson Has Flashy 37, but Bulls Stifle Sixers."

In sports journalism, the lead (or lede), as the opening lines of a story are called, "sets the tone for the story" and "establishes quickly and clearly what the story will be about." It is what you would tell a friend who has asked you what happened at the game last night.[5] Beneath the headlines above, the AP ran the following lead: "This time Allen Iverson kept his mouth shut against the Chicago Bulls and let his game do the talking."[6] This lead frames our perception of the game, recasting the teams' matchup as a contest between Iverson (since the 76ers are not mentioned) and the Bulls. But it also introduces a tension between Iverson's "mouth" (which he kept shut) and his "game" (which he let do the talking). This implies that Iverson struggles to keep his mouth shut and so metaphorically evokes an inner struggle for self-control on Iverson's part. So, in other words, if a friend called and asked what happened at last night's game, this writer would have answered, in effect, "Iverson for once controlled his impulse to talk in his one on five contest against the Bulls team."

The point here, however, is not merely that the lead distorts the image a reader might form of the game but also that this *particular* distortion succinctly mobilizes a powerful collection of basketball truisms that simultaneously carry a moralizing implication and play on racial stereotypes. To begin with, not only the lead but also the various headlines beneath which the story ran present the game, in a manner reminiscent of the myth of the rivalry's depictions of contests between Bill Russell's Celtics and Wilt Chamberlain, as between a team (the Bulls) and an individual (Iverson). Within the ethos of basketball's myths, this conveys a moral hierarchy in which Iverson, however talented or effective, falls short by comparison with the Bulls, who by playing as a team not only are able to overcome a great individual performance but also, by implication, better embody the essential spirit of the sport. But in the 1970s, this particular moral hierarchy had come to be racialized, as well, so that selfishness came to be one of the stereotypical attributes of African American players.

Then there is the portrayal of a contest between "mouth" and "game." Although the lead may initially appear complimentary to Iverson, it is so in a backhanded way that affirms a moral tenet of the sport: that the morally upright (and therefore effective) player eschews unsportsmanlike displays (such as taunting) and keeps his attention and his effort on excellent play. As far as Iverson is concerned, the lead merely admits that he conformed to this moral tenet on this occasion, and, what is more, did so only grudgingly, since its opening phrase "this time" sharply implies that Iverson's moral conformity was unusual, possibly a fluke, and therefore should not be taken as indicative of genuine moral virtue. Iverson, in this regard, is on probation.

But this particular characterization carries heavy racial freight, as well, since the particular form of behavior Iverson is supposed to have controlled is "trash talk." The article goes on to remind us that Iverson "was involved in a trash-talking battle with several Bulls the first time he played them."[7] Trash talk is a regular part of basketball in a variety of venues and in diverse communities. Within the myth of blackness, however, trash talk appears as a threat to the game, both on the court and commercially, and as *exclusively* associated with African American players. Thus, in the mid-1990s, Rod Thorn, then the NBA's director of operations, explained that the league had instituted rules to control trash talking because it could "kill the game in the eyes of the public." Trash talk "has become a sociological thing, how city kids are raised," Thorn went on to explain. "Trash talking is a part of their lives." A writer at the time linked these anxieties to earlier anxieties: "Taunting could be for the 1990s what drugs were to the NBA in the 1970s."[8]

The myth of blackness may here explicitly voice both sour disapproval and deeper anxieties about the possible catastrophes that trash talk could bring to the game. In addition, though, the myth's prohibition on trash talking implies that black athletes are to be seen and not heard—and seen performing in conformity with the technical, stylistic, tactical, and moral preferences of the white basketball unconscious. In this, the myth of blackness mobilizes long-standing prejudices that associate black men exclusively with the productive capacities of their bodies. Other forms of self-expression are censored (or censured), particularly when they may be construed, as is the case here, as interfering with a commanded performance.[9]

The AP recap encourages its readers to recognize the dangers implicit in Iverson's inability to keep his mouth shut by tying his earlier "trash-talking battle" to the potential for violence, reminding readers that in a previous game Iverson "almost got into a scuffle with Dennis Rodman."[10] Speaking of a "trash-talking *battle*" obviously characterizes trash talking in bellicose, violent terms. At the same time, the phrase helps sharpen the contrast between the violent brawls Iverson is supposed to resist (and that *this time* he did) and the healthy competition on the court in which he is supposed to invest his energy. The word "battle," specifically, also may evoke "hip-hop battles" and in this way bring to mind black urban culture and experience more generally—including, perhaps, the bowling alley brawl for which Iverson, while in high school, was unjustly imprisoned before he was pardoned by Virginia's Governor Douglas Wilder. Finally, the appearance of "trash-talking battle" in the same sentence with "almost [getting] into a scuffle" suggests not only an equivalence between the two but also, via the syntax, a cause-and-effect relation. In this way, simple verbal discourse on the court is equated with fighting. Finally, the mere invocation of Rodman (the white basketball unconscious's icon of frightening, unacceptable, or just weird behavior) moves Iverson into that domain.[11] All in all, it is as though—prefiguring the Reebok print advertising campaign that features side-by-side images of an angelic and a diabolical Iverson—a Jordan angel (grow up, shut up, and play ball) and a Rodman devil (behave badly) sit on Iverson's shoulders and, for "this time" at least or for this time only, Iverson listened to the Jordan angel.[12]

Except for one other thing: his play itself, which is where the myth of blackness lands to seal the connection among behavior, morality, race, and style of play. Reading the recap, readers might think that the Jordan angel on Iverson's shoulder was the unreformed, brash, ball-hogging, highlight-reel Jordan of 1985 whose teams could not win. But Iverson actually delivered a performance more like that of the acceptable post-racial champion Jordan of 1997. Iverson shot a blisteringly efficient fifteen for twenty-three from the field, including five for eight from three-point range, *and* led his team in assists on his way to thirty-seven points (while Jordan went nine for twenty four, one for four from three-point range, with three assists). What is emphasized in the article, however, is not Iverson's overall excellence and efficiency but the spectacular (and, as we have seen, individual) nature of his play. Thus, the Bulls "withstood several highlight-reel plays by Iverson," culminating in a description of "the highlight of Iverson's night . . . where he was isolated against Jordan at the foul line. He made several crossover dribbles and stutter steps, popped free and buried an 18 footer to tie the score."[13]

Running beneath headlines trumpeting Iverson as a "star" and the "flashy" nature of his performance, the emphasis on individual highlights in contrast with the Bulls' team success (and even Jordan's subpar individual performance) exemplifies a trope of the myth whereby blackness is associated with a morally suspect investment in style over substance. This concern had already appeared in the 1970s. But in this moment, with the rise of ESPN, the myth of blackness took on this preoccupation with renewed zeal, lamenting the "modern" player's lack of substantive skills and his exclusive focus on the types of plays that are likely to be featured in nightly highlight reels and recalling nostalgically the days when players were fundamentally sound and complete players and who, in any case, measured their abilities by the successes and failures of their teams.[14] From this vantage point, Iverson may have crossed Jordan, and that might be shown on highlight films the next day, but Jordan had the championships and Jordan had learned to harness his prodigious individual skills to the needs of his team, in the process becoming the greatest of all time.

A Genealogy of Ghettocentrism

The conditions for the emergence and pervasiveness of the myth of blackness lie partly within basketball's past and partly off the court, in contemporaneous conditions in American society. Stories that convey convictions about blackness that served various purposes for their adherents—myths of blackness—had circulated through the culture of basketball before this time and served to buttress some of the myths I have already examined.

Thus, within the myth of the rivalry, a story of the pure physicality of the black man served to support a dichotomous opposition between Bill Russell and Wilt Chamberlain. Within both the myth of the garden and the myth of the amateurs, a story of the gaudy, unprofessional selfishness of black men supported a celebration of the New York Knicks of the early 1970s and the duo of Magic Johnson and Larry Bird. In that sense, the myth of blackness poaches and recombines elements from these earlier stories.

However, it also performs distinctive work for its adherents by joining the attitudes and convictions conveyed through these stories to contemporaneous anxieties about a post-Jordan era and about urban black men more generally. The myth of blackness echoes the logic of what Bill Yousman, writing about white consumption of hip-hop, termed "blackophilia" and "blackophobia," arguing that the two modes together express "part of the same overall process of the crisis in White identity and the retrenchment to White control and domination."[15] In relation to race, as we have seen, the policies and cultural messages of the Reagan-Bush era included, on the one hand, declaring the "end of racism," promoting images of the universal accessibility of the "American dream," and demonizing urban black men and boys as pathologically dysfunctional to justify draconian law enforcement measures that led to their mass incarceration, and, on the other hand, implementing policies that aggressively rolled back gains in social welfare, education, housing, voting rights, and health care won during the era of the Civil Rights Movement.[16]

The NBA's success during the era depended partly on its alignment with these messages.[17] This took the form of what David Andrews and Michael Silk call the league's "ghettocentrism." On the one hand, the league mobilized "stereotypical understandings of black spaces, experiences and aesthetics" as marketing devices to stimulate consumer demand for the NBA and related products.[18] On the other hand, the NBA did not hesitate to capitalize on sensational media portrayals of frequently minor on- and off-court "crises" to justify publicly disciplining and controlling its players.[19] Viewed in this context, and despite the fact that most black (and white) NBA players of the era came from middle-class backgrounds, the myth of blackness stirred and capitalized on the anxieties of the white basketball unconscious concerning the future of the game's essence and of the place of "whiteness" in it.[20] In short, just as the myth of the greatest of all time could be thought of as the most exalted expression of the desires of the white basketball unconscious, so the myth of blackness may be thought of as the deepest expression of its terrors.

The myth of blackness first coalesced around targets in the college game, perhaps the last refuge of the white basketball unconscious by the early 1980s. First, Georgetown University, then the University of Nevada, Las Vegas (UNLV), and then the University of Michigan's Fab Five, in the decade between 1982 and 1995, would draw the moralizing ire of purveyors of the myth of blackness. Georgetown's program, headed by John Thompson, a six-foot-ten-inch, black former NBA player, was charged with relaxing academic standards to recruit black players from the inner city of Washington, DC (rather than the white, suburban parochial school graduates it had previously featured), with encouraging "thuggish" tactics and behavior on the court, and with taking an aggressively defiant attitude toward the media.[21] A few years later, UNLV, featuring players recruited from junior colleges, would likewise be charged with lax academic standards. These charges fed insinuations of lawlessness so that, combined with their dominance and their fast-paced style, they would be characterized as a pro team among college players and thus as having an unfair advantage.[22]

All of these characterizations and more would then converge on the Fab Five, Michigan's 1991 class of highly recruited freshman. The Fab Five—with their on-court exuberance and trash talk and their joyful off-court celebration of hip-hop and other elements of African American culture, as well as their frankness in addressing the exploitative economic structure of college sports—presented a different kind of threat: not only menace but also autonomous indifference to the cultural norms of the white basketball unconscious. Moreover, for the white basketball unconscious their youth and explicitly expressed collective identity may have augured a frightening future—both within basketball and off the court—of young African American men galvanizing around shared experiences, autonomous forms of cultural expressions, and independently articulated political aims.[23]

Meanwhile, in the NBA, which some of these college players (including Iverson) would soon join, the only hitch in the smooth and exhilarating transfer of power from the amateurs to the greatest of all time were the self-styled Bad Boys—the Detroit Pistons—who battled their way a little deeper into the playoffs every year, unseating first Bird's Celtics, then Magic's Lakers, while holding off the ascendance of Jordan's Bulls through the physically aggressive defensive tactics known as "the Jordan rules." In part, the Pistons offended through the figure of their leading player, the point guard Isiah Thomas, who had endeared himself to college fans by emerging from Chicago's tough South Side to lead the stern traditionalist Coach Bobby Knight's Indiana University Hoosiers to the National Collegiate Athletic Association (NCAA) title in 1981. Thomas's fearless play and cherubic smile landed him on the cover of *Sports Illustrated*, with the accompanying article's headline echoing the biblical prophecy "And a little child led them."[24]

But the Thomas who led the Bad Boys seemed transformed, regressed even—at least through the lens of the myth of blackness—to his raw urban roots. Adherents of the myth of blackness might imagine that Thomas had been contaminated by the city in which he now played, for Detroit, with its postindustrial detritus and Devil's Night incendiary mayhem, had itself become an offense to white America, which vastly preferred nostalgic images of Detroit of the 1950s, symbolizing American ingenuity, industrial might, and class cooperation.[25] In this sense, the Bad Boys and Thomas became the perfect repositories for the anxieties and resentments of the white basketball unconscious. When Thomas led the team off the court after Jordan's Bulls dethroned the Pistons in the 1991 Eastern Conference finals, refusing the traditional sportsmanlike postgame handshake, well, that just showed that what we always thought was true: these thugs were a disgrace to the ethos of the game, and Jordan's greatness was supercharged by the moral dimensions of his victory over the Pistons.[26]

Although Jordan would return for the 1995 NBA playoffs and go on to win three more titles with the Bulls, his first retirement primed league anxieties over the prospect of a post-Jordan NBA, anxieties manifest in repeated (and unsuccessful) attempts to anoint a "next Jordan" or "Air/heir apparent"—most notably, the Duke University alumnus and nemesis of UNLV and the Fab Five, Grant Hill—who could keep this new model afloat. But despite these efforts and in the face of these anxieties, the mid-1990s ushered in not a likeable "post-racial," crossover superstar like Jordan but this so-called hip-hop generation, headlined by Allen Iverson. Of course, as long as Jordan was still playing, the new generation's rough edges did not necessarily pose a threat to the NBA's broadening appeal. After all, these players drew in a younger demographic for whom Jordan, from an aesthetic and cultural standpoint, was a representative of a staid establishment. However, after Jordan's retirement in 1998 and as the hip-hop generation swelled the ranks of the NBA, the league began to fear alienating what was still its main audience: white men in their thirties and forties.

These concerns could be seen in the reaction to teams that represented the United States in international competition in the late 1990s and early 2000s. Although U.S. teams, like the original Dream Team of 1992, went undefeated en route to winning the FIBA World Championship in 1994 and Olympic gold medals in 1996 and 2000, mainstream fans and the media focused more on what they viewed as unsportsmanlike displays on the court and unseemly behavior off it. Unsurprisingly, the teams included players such as the UNLV alumnus Larry Johnson and the Georgetown alumnus Alonzo Mourning, who lamented the double standard. "It seems like we can't win," Mourning said. "If we don't win by a ton of points, everybody says we're not as good as the Dream Team. And if we do win by a lot, people say, 'Yeah, but it was more fun when the Dream Team did it.'"[27] By the time the United States won the gold medal at Sydney in 2000, including a two-point win over Lithuania in the semifinals and a ten-point win over France in the final, criticism began to mount, as I show in Chapter 8, that the current generation of players—characterized, like their African American NBA predecessors of the 1970s, as selfish, one-dimensional, lazy, and unfocused—had lost not only its tactical and competitive edge but also its moral compass.

But what David Leonard, referring to the array of administrative and economic policies that ranged from dress codes to age minimums and from restrictions on emotional expression during games to salary caps, has called the "assault on blackness" took on particular intensity when a brief shoving match between the Detroit Pistons' Ben Wallace and the Indiana Pacers' Ron Artest (Metta World Peace) escalated into a brawl between fans and players after a Pistons fan threw a drink on Artest, who had extricated himself from the fight and gone to lie down on the scorer's table.[28] The so-called Malice at the Palace became a popular touchstone, a symbol for media commentators and league officials of the catastrophes to which, in effect, insufficiently regulated blackness could lead.[29] Not since (black) Kermit Washington nearly killed (white) Rudy Tomjonavich with a single punch in a game in 1977 had NBA violence so fascinated and horrified the public and the league.[30] The NBA suspended Artest for the remaining seventy-one games of the season and the playoffs. Meanwhile, Harvey Araton of the *New York Times* (who would later literally write the book on the Old Knicks) used the event as an occasion for a book critical of the current crop of NBA players (and, to a lesser degree, league executives) who "have made a mess of their affairs, often in painfully public ways," by playing the role of "the jock reprobate and have been deserving of the scorn they received by the media and the fans."[31]

Inventing Basketball Autonomy

I saw Iverson cross Jordan on television when it first happened, and I have viewed it again since then to prepare for classes. But in drafting this chapter, I wanted to see it again. I found it mesmerizing and could not stop watching—again and again, clicking on different links to see the different angles and replays and commentaries and contexts. The whole play is so *quick*: from the time Iverson gets the ball to the time the shot drops through the net takes no more than twelve seconds, the actual cross no more than about four seconds. So my interest partly stems from cognitive thirst, as though I were watching a magician at work, replaying frame by frame to see how Iverson did it, to isolate *the moment* that sealed Jordan's fate. But I can see there's something more than detached intellectual curiosity about technique driving me there. There's also an affective investment at work, an emotional response—admiration? gratitude? even love?—that keeps me glued to the play.

Hans Gumbrecht rightly observes that "what we enjoy in the great moments of a ballgame is not just the goal, the touchdown, the home run, or the slam dunk" but "the beautiful individual play that takes form prior to the score." A "beautiful play," Gumbrecht writes, "is produced by the sudden, surprising convergence of several athletes' bodies in time and space."[32] Indeed, Leonard Koppett, decades earlier, had already noted the way in which, because baskets themselves are relatively routine, basketball draws attention to the play unfolding before the score and, in particular, to its style.[33] Perhaps obviously, this applies to the Iverson crossover. The pick and the flip pass prompt a switch in defensive assignments that suddenly put Jordan (the league's top player) on Iverson (the league's top rookie).

Even set plays, Gumbrecht continues, become surprising because they are achieved "against the unpredictable resistance of the other team's defense."[34] Ideally, a ball screen for the point guard that results in a defensive switch creates an advantage for the offensive team in that a larger and presumably slower player is now left alone to defend the smaller, quicker point guard (and at the same time, the smaller defensive guard is left alone to defend the larger offensive player who set the original screen and who may roll toward the basket where he can better exploit his height advantage). But in this case, although the expected size differentials did occur—the six-foot-six Jordan was left alone to defend Iverson, who was perhaps six feet tall, in the center of the floor—they do not lead to any obvious advantage for Philadelphia because Jordan was also quick and widely considered the best defensive player in the game at the time. So as Gumbrecht describes it, "The team in possession of the ball tries to create a play and avoid chaos[;] its opposing team in the defensive position tries to destroy the emerging form and precipitate chaos."[35]

In addition to this complex and unpredictable convergence of bodies, Gumbrecht argues, part of the fascination of plays as epiphanies lies in their temporality—that is, in the fact that they begin to end the moment they start. "No still photograph," Gumbrecht writes, "can ever capture the beauty of this temporalized reality." Indeed, my own repeated replays of even the video of the play testify to the elusive—because temporally finite—quality of the beautiful play. Moreover, considering the temporal aspect of the play suggests also another fascinating aspect of the cross-over: good timing, which Gumbrecht defines as "perfect fusion between a perception of space and the initiation of movement . . . the intuitive capacity to bring one's body to a specific place at the very moment when it matters to be there."[36] Violence for Gumbrecht is "the act of occupying spaces or blocking their occupation by others through the resistance of one's body." Timing, then, relates to violence because "the player will be in the right place" at the right time "either because the spot in question will not be occupied (not covered) by the body of another player at that moment, or precisely because the body of another player *will* occupy it."[37] The latter describes good defensive timing whereas the former describes good timing from the perspective of the offensive player trying to get free. Jordan tries to anticipate where Iverson will be in the next instant so he can be there instead, while Iverson, of course, tries to—and does—get to the spot where Jordan will *not* be.

Koppett, again, seems to have presaged the central point of Gumbrecht's comments on timing when he described the central task of the basketball player as "getting free," although he centered on deception and fakery (rather than timing) as the means by which basketball players do this.[38] Good timing, however, may also simply be a component of effective deception. At least, it is with Iverson's crossover, in which it is not simply a matter of leaning explosively in one direction to throw the defender off balance (the fake) but of intuitively grasping the perfect moment to yank the ball quickly back in the other direction (the cross) to get free. That precise moment might be thought of as the *kairos*, which, you may recall from the preceding chapter, was what the Greeks called the opportune moment for invention and, indeed, as the instant in which an opportunity presents itself to crack open the still tomb of the end of history.

Beautifully ephemeral and deceptively magical, Iverson's cross evokes the image of a jagged flash of lightning splitting the night sky. An epiphany of form, to be sure, the play reminds me of the position described by T. S. Eliot in the poem "The Dry Salvages."[39] Eliot might have had in mind something like a beautiful play, the illuminating arc that emerges and vanishes before you *know* it. Something's happened; it was beautiful and elevating and thrilling and it somehow left itself in you. But *what was it?* Eliot suggests that approaching the meaning (trying to read the play, to understand what it meant) can restore the experience. That restored experience may be in a different form, but it may still, like the original, deliver an illuminating affective shine that eludes confining meanings.

As an individual tactic, a crossover dribble means the attempt, via precisely timed deception, by a player to get free from a defender. As we saw at the end of Chapter 1, however, the dribble itself stands within the history of basketball as a kind of outlaw or rogue maneuver that simultaneously violates the putative timeless spirit of the sport and thereby embodies perfectly a fluid, antiessentialist view of the game. The dribble, as Koppett puts it, is at once the sport's "most identifying characteristic" and "one of the worst ailments of otherwise healthy basketball offenses."[40] Perhaps no particular form of the dribble exemplifies this better than the crossover. When Iverson executed the crossover early in his career, he was sometimes whistled for a violation as it appeared to officials that he was actually carrying the ball to gain an advantage. But in addition, the crossover dribble is a product of urban playground experimentation and its culture of joyful individual one-upmanship. Alexander Wolff approvingly describes it as "of a piece with hip-hop culture" with its "rat-tat-tat rhythm, the badinage and braggadocio, and the distinctly big-city yearning to break-free of the crowd by making one's mark."[41] In this way, like the dunk before it—but perhaps even more dangerous because, as Wolff puts it, the crossover is more "democratic" (since you do not have to be tall or an exceptional leaper to execute it; you just have to practice)— the crossover dribble may bring the white basketball unconscious a little closer than it would like to come to the urban raw materials off which it secretly feeds but whose contextual realities it prefers in sensationalized, fantasy form.

Wolff's comparison of the dunk and the crossover as different forms of individual self-expression, moreover, frames what might be the most evident and important symbolism of this particular crossover: Iverson (playground practitioner of the crossover par excellence) tries to get free of Jordan (the game's most renowned dunker). In addition, this crossover echoes—through a kind of wordplay reminiscent of free-style rap—Iverson's insistence on eluding Jordan's ability to execute a crossover of a different sort (racially, I mean, as a commercial pitchman). When he turned pro, Iverson famously rejected a shoe deal with Nike because he felt the company would require him to follow in Jordan's crossover footsteps.

Instead, Iverson signed with Reebok, making the sole demand that "the company not try to change him."[42] In this sense, in using the crossover to get free of Jordan, Iverson affirmed his independence and autonomy from the commercially tried-and-true, racial crossover model Jordan had established and, moreover, demonstrated the viability of his own path. Finally, this particular crossover, as an instance of perfect timing, evokes the *kairos* that reveals that—despite the myth of the greatest of all time— time has not stopped and that basketball (and other) history continues to march forward, as always, driven by the creativity of those with nothing to lose, for whom necessity is truly the mother of invention.

Now remember that Iverson scored on the play—two of the thirty-seven very efficient points he would put up on the defending champs that night. Recalling that the crossover is a means by which a point guard, usually the smallest man on the floor, can become a scoring threat draws Iverson's crossover dribble into yet another framework of meaning: Bethlehem Shoals's concept of a "positional revolution," which I described in Chapter 5.[43] Conventionally, basketball culture arranges players on the court and distributes their responsibilities in relation to size. That is to say, it presumes that being tall puts you vertically closer to the basket and therefore makes you more likely to be adept at scoring the ball near the hoop, as well as rebounding and blocking shots, both of which also tend to happen near the basket. At the other extreme, far from the basket, conventional positional dogma places the point guard, the smallest player on the floor and therefore deemed the least likely to score regularly or efficiently. The point guard traditionally has been assigned facilitating responsibilities such as spearheading the defensive pressure on opponents and stewarding the ball up court on offense before safely depositing it in the hands of a scoring teammate. Moreover, the point guard has been viewed as a coach on the floor, prized for emotional poise and intellectual acumen, somewhat like a quarterback in football.[44] And because of racist assumptions about the intellectual ability and self-control of African American athletes, like the quarterback in football, the point guard position in basketball was the last to be desegregated.

In the early to mid-1990s, the positional revolution was ushered in not only but also primarily by some of the very same players—heirs to Magic's and Bird's positional flexibility—who came to represent the hip-hop insurgency within the realm of the greatest of all time: the Fab Five's Chris Webber, a devastatingly effective passing center; Rasheed Wallace, six-foot-eleven but capable of deforming defenses with his efficiency as a three-point shooter; and Kevin Garnett, a "7 footer who handled and passed like a guard, soared with the best of them, could lock down every opponent on the floor, and do all the things that came with his height."[45] But Iverson and his crossover present a revolution at the other end of the positional spectrum: the emergence of the scoring point guard. Iverson led the league in scoring four times from the point guard position and, moreover, in a body deemed relatively small by NBA point guard standards. Iverson may nowadays be criticized for inefficiency by some on the basis of (a misuse of) advanced statistical analysis of his play (more on this in Chapter 8), but it is also true that he paved the way for the style of play that characterizes the best point guards in the league today, such as Derrick Rose, Tony Parker, and Russell Westbrook, who create more opportunities for teammates by having established themselves as viable scoring threats capable of getting free for scores by use of, among other weapons, the crossover dribble.

Although fans may view the positional revolution as a tactical advance, even as such it carries a broader cultural significance, for as a tactical advance it was initiated by the successful experimentation of players who refused to be chained to a limited set of functions by conventional wisdom and the authority of coaches. These new physical moves and forms and new tactics emerged first experimentally in informal play before being presented in their more refined form to coaches—sheer unstoppability providing a kind of irrefutable argument. Considering that the myth of blackness projects essentializing stereotypes concerning black Americans (especially black men) onto African American basketball players and so inhibits "their individuality, agency, and works toward curtailing any conception of black self-determination," the positional revolution restores the thrill of witnessing black self-determination on the court.[46]

In this sense, an emotionally expressive black player who effectively takes the game into his own hands by revolutionizing the point guard position appears as anathema to the conventional wisdom of the white basketball unconscious. The fact that even the most established of today's coaches embrace the positional revolution should not obscure the fact that the positional revolution, like the dribble itself, began as a creative bid for autonomy and self-determination by players and one inaugurated precisely by a generation stereotyped as undisciplined dangers to the game, even as the game at its highest levels, as it always has, happily absorbed and exploited the entertainment and commercial value of their inventions. Jorge Luis Borges once used the fiction of Franz Kafka as a lens through which to reconstruct a literary history of his "precursors."[47] Likewise, from the present vantage point, a player like Allen Iverson may serve as a lens through which we may retrospectively liberate other players—Jordan, Magic, Dr. J, Russell, and Chamberlain, to name just a few—from the hoops mausoleum in which the sport's dominant culture has immured them. To see them through the lens of Iverson is to see them as constituting a renegade tradition of creative, self-determining hoops inventors that stretches back to *both* James Naismith and the game's "incorrigible" first dribbler.

THE MYTH OF THE RIGHT WAY

June 15, 2004

Playing the Right Way is more than a way to win
basketball games. It's a way of life.—**Henry Abbott**

O n the eve of the 2004 NBA finals pitting the Los Angeles Lakers
against the Detroit Pistons, few in the media or in Las Vegas had any
doubts about the outcome of the upcoming series. Oddsmakers had
the Lakers as ten-point favorites to win the first game and for the series
as a whole listed Los Angeles as $6 favorites (meaning that a $6 bet on the
Lakers would net you just $1 if they won) and Detroit as $8 underdogs (so
that a $1 bet on the Pistons would get you $8 if they won).[1] The Lakers,
after all, had the better regular season record in the more challenging
Western Conference and so had the home court advantage in the playoffs.
But that, really, was the least of it. The Lakers had won three consecutive
titles in 2000–2002 and had only narrowly missed a chance at a fourth in
2003. In addition to a superstar coach, Phil Jackson, the team featured
the game's top big man in Shaquille O'Neal and its top perimeter scorer in
Kobe Bryant, each of whom had that very season been selected for the All-
NBA First Team. Moreover, the Lakers had added two veteran superstars:
the forward Karl Malone (number two on the NBA's all-time career scorer's
list) and the point guard Gary Payton (a multiple all-star and defensive
stalwart who was fourth on the league's all-time career steals list).

The Pistons, meanwhile, had finished second in their division during
the regular season and had struggled even to make it to the finals. Their
only all-star was the undrafted Ben Wallace, who, though an excellent
rebounder and defender, was deficient offensively and, at a mere six-

foot-nine, undersized for an NBA center, especially one about to face the enormous, athletic O'Neal. The rest of the Pistons' roster, including the other starters, included players who were young and unproven (Tayshaun Prince, Richard Hamilton), journeymen who had fallen short of early expectations (Chauncey Billups), or considered problematic (Rasheed Wallace, who joined the team with twenty games remaining in the regular season). As the television broadcaster Al Michaels observed, "The Lakers had Hall of Fame players, while the Pistons used players nobody wanted."

Yet despite the odds and the collective wisdom of the basketball world, less than ten days later, on June 15, the Pistons were crowned NBA champions. And it was not really even close. They won the best of seven series four games to one, by an average margin of victory of nine points per game. Indeed, the Lakers had to go to overtime to eke out their only victory, on their home court in game two, and thus narrowly avoid being swept. How had this team of castoffs so easily dispatched a star-studded roster of proven winners led by one of the most successful coaches of all time? The papers the next day told the story. The *New York Times* headline described the win as "striking a blow for the right way" and Pistons Coach Larry Brown himself confirmed, "This sport is about players playing the right way."[2] The phrase "playing the right way" became a kind of banner and a myth advanced by its adherents ostensibly to describe a set of effective tactical choices but carrying as well a set of moralizing, often racialized, connotations. In time, this myth of the right way would become a key cultural vehicle for a reaction against the perceived insurgency of blackness.

The Myth of the Right Way

In Chris Broussard's article in the *Times*, Brown reported that he had told his players before the clinching fifth game that "it would be a great statement if we had an opportunity to win because we do play the right way." Elsewhere in the same story, Stu Jackson, an executive with USA Basketball and the NBA, defined the right way: "playing excellent defense, playing unselfishly on offense, everybody committing themselves to rebounding the basketball and committing themselves to the team before themselves."[3] Brown elaborated, "Basketball is a team game[;] the object is to make your teammates better. To make sacrifices. To make the extra pass. Think about defending. Maybe sacrifice yourself a little bit for somebody else."[4] Or, as Brown summed it up more succinctly, "Play hard, play together, play smart, have fun, and try to guard."[5] Any player, coach, or fan can understand what sorts of on-court activities Brown is capturing with the phrase "play the right way." And anyone familiar with the rules of the game can comprehend why playing good defense, rebounding missed shots, and, on offense, moving the ball to get the highest-percentage shot would be good things to do if one wanted to win games. "Play the right way" seems as self-evidently true and natural an exhortation as there could be. And yet the exhortation came to be repeated frequently and with overwrought conviction.

Often in discussing Brown and playing the right way, writers mention his success as a coach. A Hall of Famer, he is the only coach to have won both an NCAA and an NBA championship and is viewed, by players and his peers, as someone who makes bad teams better, makes good teams contenders, and makes contenders champions.[6] In other words, Brown's approach to the game, when successfully imparted to his players, seems to maximize individual and team potential and thereby to increase the opportunity to win basketball games. Here we have, in other words, a pragmatic dimension of the word "right." Playing the right way means playing the way that gives you the best chance to play effectively and to win ball games.

The objective of a basketball game is to score more points than your opponent within a fixed period of time. Because teams alternate possessions after every basket made, each of the two teams in a game will have approximately the same number of possessions. This places a premium on tactics that maximize a team's chances of converting possessions into points. In fact, offensive efficiency in basketball is usually measured by calculating the number of points a team scores per one hundred possessions (and is closely correlated with winning).[7]

As Dean Oliver, who pioneered the advanced statistical analysis of basketball, concludes, the four most important factors to winning basketball games are all related to efficiency: (1) shooting a high field goal percentage, (2) not committing turnovers, (3) getting offensive rebounds, and (4) shooting a high number of free throws.[8] Teams that win, Oliver argues, regularly meet at least three of these four conditions. Clearly, the tactics emphasized by Brown contribute to meeting Oliver's conditions for winning basketball games, and that goes a long way toward explaining Brown's success as a coach—and, indeed, Brown's Pistons outpaced the Lakers in each of the four categories.

Brown indisputably advocated a very *good* way to play basketball if you want to win a lot of basketball games. But has he come up with *the right* way? The slippage from "good" to "right" suggests that the maxim "play the right way" confuses likely tactical effectiveness with absolute moral propriety. There is not much question that Brown advocates a pragmatically effective technique for winning basketball games. There are, however, all kinds of questions about whether that same pragmatically effective technique is also morally superior—not to mention questions about why such a moral claim would even be asserted, let alone asserted, as I mentioned above, with such vehemence.

Taken as a tactical recommendation, the exhortation to "play the right way" so self-evidently aims to satisfy the conditions that, most observers agree, lead to winning basketball that it would seem to speak for itself. Yet as a matter of fact, "playing the right way" seems not to be permitted—by coaches, many fans, and commentators in the media—to speak for itself. To say that playing the game the right way speaks for itself is to say that the results (in successes, presumably) of *just playing* the game the right way *speak for themselves* and require no further commentary. Yet the opposite is the case. It seems almost a requirement that playing the right way—however effective and whatever its results—be accompanied by a discursive supplement: the myth of playing the right way. Playing the right way clearly does *not* speak for itself since it is spoken *for* with such frequency. And playing the right way is spoken *for* so often and insistently that one begins to sense overcompensation, an almost panicked insistence on playing the right way. Discursively, with its insistence on and celebration of the mantra of "playing the right way," basketball culture in the United States seems in the curious position of obsessive compulsively arguing for what is both obvious and widely accepted.

The myth of playing the right way offers two kinds of appeals—to tradition and to moral virtue—in defense of its tactical recommendation. When once asked, "What does play the right way mean?" Brown replied, before defining the phrase, by citing what might be called his basketball lineage. Offering a capsule summary of his career as a coach and player, Brown traced his basketball family tree back to James Naismith.[9] As Henry Abbott put it, "If Coach Larry Brown is a little old school, it's with good reason. He learned the game from the guys who learned from the guys who learned from Dr. James Naismith who invented the game. Literally. 'This guy has possibly the finest basketball pedigree of any coach alive,' explains [the Philadelphia 76ers'] radio broadcaster Tom McGinnis."[10]

To this appeal to tradition is appended a moral dimension. Abbott explains that "the way Brown talks about it, it's clear that Playing the Right Way is more than a way to win basketball games. It's a way of life. He takes issues with players that don't try to follow it. In fact, he usually trades them."[11] The view Abbot paraphrases shows how a set of tactical elements with the ostensible aim of winning a basketball game begins to acquire an extra-athletic moral force—playing the right way vaguely becomes living the right way—and this rather more ambitious claim is tethered, via Brown's "pedigree," to the deepest roots of the game. As steward of this moral tradition, Brown has a quasi-sacred duty to pass it on—which is to say, to teach it to his players. This might seem unproblematic until you consider that his players are only his players in the first place—that is, only NBA players—because they have already proved themselves to be among the best 450 basketball players on the planet. I do not mean that professional basketball players cannot or do not learn. I mean to point out only that one of the elements of the myth of the right way entails assigning coaches the authority, right, and responsibility to *morally* edify their players, even when these players are professionals and grown adults.

The myth of the right way offers a version of basketball history whereby the game's creator taught his own crew of morally incorrigible pupils that the technically and morally superior way to play the game of basketball (and of life) was with hard defense, rebounding, unselfish offense, and an attitude of self-sacrifice for the sake of team interests. Brown has inherited and come to embody this spirit of basketball for our day. In the words of Stu Jackson, in the wake of the Pistons' 2004 championship, "[Brown] has always represented his profession admirably. He's an excellent teacher, he's an excellent tactician and strategist, and he's a good guy who represents the basketball world very well."[12] In other words, to those who advocate it, the phrase "playing the right way" means playing the game the way that it was intended to be played in a way that embodies the virtues of hard work, unselfishness, sacrifice for the common good, and humility. If the self-evident tactical advantages of playing defense, rebounding, and getting easy shots by sharing the ball need to be repeated so insistently these days, and to be harnessed to such a potent historical and moral narrative, perhaps it is because these values are—or seem to some to be—in jeopardy.

A Genealogy of the American (Right) Way

To get at what lies behind the persistence of this fantasy, consider one particular battle in the war over playing the right way. It occurred back in 2001, and Brown, then the head coach of the Philadelphia 76ers, was at the center of it, feuding with his superstar guard: none other than Allen Iverson. More than once during the years they shared in Philadelphia, either Brown or Iverson became so exasperated with the other's inflexibility that one or the other threatened (or actually initiated the steps necessary) to leave the team.[13] If the spats between a coach and his star player were so engrossing to the American media and its sports fans outside Philadelphia, it may be because in that case each had come to represent more than just a particular opinion about how the 76ers should play basketball. While Brown embodied the team-first mantra of "playing the right way," perhaps "no player before or since [Iverson] has so sincerely believed in one-on-one basketball as a means to victory."[14] Brown represented the traditional game, claiming its lineage back all the way to basketball's invention in 1891. For his part, Iverson, as we saw in Chapter 7, not only revolutionized the point guard position and so eroded the authority of the coach; he also embodied the experience of African American youths raised in urban ghettos amid poverty and violence. He assertively expressed the cultural signifiers of that experience: cornrows, baggy shorts, tattoos, gaudy jewelry, hip-hop music, and trash talk. In a word, Iverson was blackness.

Whatever their conflict may have meant to Brown and Iverson, to *the white basketball unconscious* their conflict was the most critical front in a racialized war—escalating with the prospect, and in the wake, of Michael Jordan's retirement—over the essence of basketball and its implications for the country's values.[15] From the vantage point of the white basketball unconscious, on Brown's side stood the liberal-minded supporters of hard work, self-sacrifice, and humility as the virtues leading to success, the virtues that had also led to the country's greatness over the course of the twentieth century, while on Iverson's side were the cynical—not to say, thuggish—supporters of selfish egotism, shortsighted expedience, and the triumph of style over substance, the vices at once causing and expressing the nation's precarious state in the global order at the turn of the century. In this context, within the fantasies of the white basketball unconscious, playing the right way means playing the (white) American way, and it must be safeguarded from constant attack from those (African American) individuals who selfishly seek an easy way to the top—individuals, in turn, who at best may be taught, at worst must be excluded, and most likely must be continually disciplined. That may be why, despite its obvious tactical benefits and its nearly universal acceptance as a style of basketball at the highest levels, both its proponents and the American media seem to feel compelled to obsessively defend "the right way" from the siege they imagine it to be continually under.

If Iverson's 2001 insurgency was one sign of the peril in which the white basketball unconscious found American hoops in the early twenty-first century, another, more ominous blow would soon follow, and in the cradle of Hoosier Nation, no less. On September 4, 2002, during the International Basketball Federation (FIBA) World Championships in Indianapolis, after fifty-eight consecutive wins, dating back a decade to the Barcelona Olympics of 1992, a U.S. team composed entirely of professional stars lost a game for the first time. By a score of 87–80, Argentina defeated the United States, which would go on to drop games to Spain and Yugoslavia and finish a shocking sixth. Those in the United States who were paying attention to the FIBA defeats in 2002 viewed them as the tipping point of a process in which the nation's basketball squad in a decade had declined from dominating to dismal. While some recognized that international opponents had improved vastly over the previous decade (in part because of the excitement caused by the first Dream Team) and that international teams frequently had years of experience playing together, most observers seemed, with almost gleeful schadenfreude, to characterize the United States as "the bully finally challenged, beaten and then shamed into submission" because of its disregard for "fundamentals and team principles."[16] Barely a year after the national trauma of 9/11, further challenges to America's place in the new world order—even if only in the realm of sports—were not to be taken lightly.

It was no surprise, then, that in the wake of the Pistons' 2004 NBA title, earned the "right way," who but Coach Larry Brown should be selected to lead the U.S. troops back into international battle at the Summer Olympic Games in Athens. More surprising—to adherents of the myth of the right way, at least—was that Coach Brown's squad failed to bring home the gold, settling instead for a disappointing bronze. Perhaps because the Olympics are far more significant for most American basketball fans than the FIBA World Championships, the Olympic debacle raised the stakes and the public panic still higher. American anxieties were perhaps intensified precisely because Brown, who had previously tamed the likes of Iverson and Wallace, proved unable to impart the wisdom of the right way to his own group of "incorrigibles." For purveyors of the myth of the right way, this most visible failure clearly demonstrated that all the tactical, stylistic, and moral deficiencies they had been cataloguing since the early 1990s had borne a gruesome, shameful fruit.

Some opined that the right way appeared to have up and left the United States, its native land, to settle down instead in the more hospitable foreign environs of America's international opponents, especially the Argentine team that first shamed the bully Americans in 2002 and then drove in the coffin nail by taking the gold medal in Athens in 2004. Thus,

Harvey Araton noted that when the Americans lost to Argentina in 2002, "they were beaten for the most part at a game they had long abandoned."[17] These claims that a style of basketball play—namely, "the right way"— had migrated to Argentina were accompanied by explicit assertions that a moral virtue had gone along with it. So R. Scott Kretchmar, in considering a debate between "basketball purists" and "modernists," claimed that it was not all that different "from traditional philosophic arguments over the nature of the good life."[18] And Araton himself referred, in the subtitle of his book *Crashing the Borders* (2005), to "basketball" losing "its soul at home."[19]

In an *Esquire* profile of the new face of basketball, Chris Jones described European basketball in terms of an "engineered beauty, economical, and drama-free . . . like the insides of a watch" and contrasted it with what he characterized simply as the "racehorse" that was American basketball.[20] Glossing the passage, Jeffrey Lane rightly points out that "if the European game is beautiful, efficient, and free of drama, the implication is that the opposite holds true of the American game. American ballplayers are ugly, bungling and high maintenance—more animal in the wild, as the second part of the quote suggests, than oiled machine."[21] The resonance of the terms with racial stereotypes, in and out of the culture of basketball, is noteworthy. But also noteworthy is the reference to "efficiency": a term that during this period migrated from the financial austerity handbooks of International Monetary Fund economists and cost-cutting chief executives to statistical analysts in the NBA.

Rising alongside lamentations of the demise of the right way in American basketball and the hailing of a coterie of international stars, a vogue in advanced statistical methods grew rapidly among NBA franchises, in the media, and among fans. These methods (also known as "advanced basketball metrics" or, simply, "analytics") entailed the micro-surveillance of players' on-court activity via multiple cameras and other tracking devices embedded in equipment that delivered vast quantities of data on the movement of players and the ball to private companies that sold it to teams, whose specialists in turn analyzed it and relayed it to coaches and general managers and, through them, sometimes, to players themselves. Traditional statistical categories such as points, assists, and rebounds gave way to new categories, sometimes derived from complex formulas, such as "usage percentage" and "player efficiency rating."[22]

Independently of the tactical advantages franchises (and, no doubt, many players) gain from the use of these methods, this movement came accompanied by an ideological agenda that celebrates what Michael Lewis (who literally wrote the book—*Moneyball*—on advanced statistics in baseball, where the methods originated) called "the no-stats all-star" in a profile of Shane Battier, the NBA role player and former Duke University national player of the year.[23] The ideology implicitly (and sometimes explicitly) critiques players—like Iverson—who excited fans with spectacular play and amassed traditional statistical totals but who, from the perspective of advanced methods, appeared as inefficient illusions: flashy superstars not truly earning their keep on the court. *Moneyball*, after all, is a story of how a frugal baseball franchise used such methods to avoid wasting money on overrated superstars and invested instead in under-the-radar players rated highly by statistical specialists.[24] In this sense, the scientific pretensions of advanced statistics echoed the pejorative views of disgruntled fans in the late 1970s who viewed NBA superstars as flashy, overpaid, and lacking substance.

Araton's book, apparently written at once out of disgust at the Malice at the Palace and disappointment at the debacles in international competition, features on its cover four photos. In the upper left, we see Ron Artest in the midst of the brawl in Auburn Hills. Mirroring Artest in the lower right is Rasheed Wallace, pictured during the same fight. Contrasting with these two images of blackness run amok—never mind that Wallace was attempting to break up the brawl—we find, in the lower left corner, none other than Coach Larry Brown and, mirroring *him* in the upper right corner, Manu Ginobili, the star of the victorious Argentine national team. Here and elsewhere, Ginobili comes to appear as the on-court hero of the myth of the right way, not only as a member of the Argentine national team but especially as a member of the San Antonio Spurs, a club that has come to be held as exemplary for discovering undervalued international players who will "play the right way." Indeed, the Spurs' Gregg Popovich, who was himself a protégé of Larry Brown, has said of Brown's penchant for international players, "They did it the right way [abroad] . . . and they did it longer and harder."[25]

In this context, it is perhaps understandable that, describing one of Ginobili's spectacular driving baskets over the American Jermaine O'Neal in 2002, Araton concluded, "From that moment on, the prototypical foreign player was no longer a mobility-challenged white boy in a crew cut. The story was no longer Hoosiers with subtitles."[26] Araton apparently meant to signal a stylistic diversification in the international game. With the phrase "mobility-challenged white boy in a crew cut," Araton evokes a stereotypical basketball image of the midwestern white farm boy basketball player. In the white basketball unconscious, this image is the basis of a narrative fantasy in which the white hero overcomes his lack of natural athletic ability by hewing closely to the game's traditional techniques, tactics, and morals. This permits him to triumph—as in the film *Hoosiers*—over his fantastic counterpart, the stereotyped African American player who is blessed with the natural athletic abilities of speed, strength, and leaping ability, which are perfectly suited to the game of basketball. Out of this fevered fantasy rises the apparition of the great white hope, who will be able to rival his African American counterparts on the hardwood and redeem whiteness and the attributes putatively associated with it. Araton thus implied that previously the "story" of international basketball was embodied in such players.

But if the story was no longer "Hoosiers with subtitles," then what was the new story? In *Crashing the Borders*, it was that Ginobili and players like him embody a kind of dialectical synthesis of the racialized stylistic antithesis between white and black.[27] Or, in the words of another observer, Ginobili is a new breed of superstar "who, while flashy and entertaining, brings a diverse set of team-oriented skills."[28] Like the stereotypical white player, they are heady and skilled, and they work hard. Like the stereotypical black player, they are athletic, creative, and exciting. Ginobili certainly combines a highly developed set of fundamental skills with athletic ability. But this does not set him apart from a number of other NBA players, past and present, such as Michael Jordan, Dwyane Wade, or LeBron James. One thing that *does* set him apart from that particular group of players is that his skin is comparatively light in tone.

This runs unfortunately close to the grooves of a logic I doubt Araton or others intended. First, the American game is divided into a white game and a black game, and these are set against each other as incomplete halves of a whole. Then, the American game is opposed to the international game—represented by Manu. This international game simultaneously heals the ills of basketball and the racial conflicts of American society. But it does so via the white body of Manu Ginobili. In this way, Ginobili becomes the greatest of the great white hopes because he is the great white hope who ends once and for all the need for a great white hope because he transcends the very antagonism—white game versus black game—that historically provoked white feelings of inferiority and engendered the desire for a great white hope in the first place. The distortions required to feature Ginobili as the poster boy for the right (natively American) way to play basketball suggest just how averse the white basketball unconscious is to accepting African American players—Wade, for example—as stewards and emblems of basketball values.

Inventing Other Ways

In the Argentine movie *Nine Queens*, the paths of two grifters collide when the younger of the two, Juan, botches a con at a convenience store, only to be rescued by the elder, Marcos, who rapidly ushers him out of the scene posing as an arresting undercover officer. From this seemingly random encounter, the two strangers form an uneasy alliance. Marcos will take Juan under his wing, show him some simple cons, and eventually reveal that he has a much bigger proposition for which he enlists Juan's assistance: the sale of some rare (and counterfeit) stamps to a corrupt Spanish businessman. Reluctantly, Juan, who is desperate to raise money to bribe a judge so his father (also a con artist) can be released from prison, agrees. The film then takes us through an unpredictable, dizzying, and often harrowing set of twists and turns during which it is never quite clear what is planned and what occurs by chance, what is an obstacle and what is an opportunity, what is real and what is mere appearance, and who has the upper hand. And even at the end, when it is all finally clear, there's this overwhelming urge to replay the whole thing to see what you missed the first time, how the whole thing got pulled off.

You could call it "That Manu Ginobili Feeling," for the sense of having been duped, or of having missed something, is not resolved but heightened by watching Ginobili play, which may be partly explained by what a friend on Twitter referred to as his "lumpenproletariat" style of play. The lumpenproletariat, for those unfamiliar with Karl Marx's classification of the margins of the industrial working class, include "swindlers, confidence tricksters, brothel keepers, rag-and-bone merchants, and beggars"—in other words, the heroes of *Nine Queens*.[29] On first impression, Ginobili appears chaotic on the court. Almost constantly moving, he is prone to changing speeds with frequency and without any obvious motivation, with and without the ball. With the ball, he may throw himself headlong, seemingly out of control and against all sense, into a crowd of taller defenders near the basket. He seems to initiate plays without knowing how his wild beginning will resolve itself. Sometimes the ball seems to slip from his control as he shifts from dribble to pass or shot. Indeed, this chaotic unpredictability is what a number of his coaches, teammates, and opponents signal as his standout characteristic: it is what makes him next to impossible to defend but also, sometimes, difficult to play with and to coach.

But beneath this presentation of chaotic complexity, Ginobili's most distinctively effective plays combine a fairly limited set of components that one might think of as the elements of his style: the deployment of mutability (of speed, direction, or size) to create a misleading impression of vulnerability (manifesting in the form of apparently bad judgment or awkwardness).[30] Ginobili seems almost to look for trouble, seeking out the tightest and least comfortable spots seemingly by some defective instinct, then wriggling out with a maximum of breakneck effort. He ignores or violates many of the time-honored tenets of basketball: throwing one-handed passes, leaving his feet without a clear path to shoot or pass, exposing the ball to the defender while dribbling, shooting without facing the basket, all of those and often. But he gets to the basket and finishes (or makes the right pass) with such persistent effectiveness that it eventually becomes clear that perhaps it only looked like trouble to us; that Ginobili himself saw something different and knew all along what he was going to do—or, at least, what it was possible for him to do. When he is at his mercurial best, Ginobili even inspires the thought that appearing to be in trouble is an integral part of his eventual, continued, sustained success.

Ginobili transforms what appears as inevitable constraint in the world around him—an opponent's dunk on a breakaway or a blocked path on offense—into the viral unstoppability of his own invention. "We have to see creation," Gilles Deleuze once said, "as tracing a path between impossibilities. Creation takes place in bottlenecks."[31] But this is in fact not quite enough for Ginobili, who does not just *transform* the constraints he confronts; he actually *creates* the impossibilities in the first place—or, at least, the appearance of them. This is how he disarms his defenders, how he pulls off heist after heist. He inspires the same baffled awe and confusion in those tasked with stopping him that he does in those of us watching him.

My wife introduced to me to a poem written in 1996 by the late Argentine poet Vicente Luy (1961–2012):

> ¿Por qué los secuestradores prosperan?
> ¿Por qué sonríen los diputados?
> Porque tienen plan.
> Vos no tenés plan.[32]

Here's my rough translation:

> Why're the kidnappers gettin' paid?
> Why're the politicians smilin'?
> They got a plan.
> You ain't got no plan.

It is a tricky poem to translate; there is nothing literally colloquial about the Spanish original, yet it conveys to my ear a sense of confiding, intimate informality. And it is at least as tricky to make sense of. It includes a simple riddle with an apparently simple answer in its first three lines. Then it offers, in its last line, a harsh description of modern reality and our place in it. It also appears, in a tough sort of way, to suggest a path.

But at the same time, that last line keeps switching back and forth in valence: should I be dismayed or relieved that I have no plan? If I have a plan—if I plan, if I calculate—it seems to say that, like kidnappers and politicians, I can prosper and be happy. But then, of course, the downside, at least to my way of thinking, is that I would be like kidnappers and politicians: as immoral, as craven and cruel and bad. But not having a plan would seem to leave me poor and sad. How to break this impasse? How can you, or I, or anyone slip this trap and get ahead? I think this ambiguity and confusion with respect to the value of planning, from a fellow Argentine, resonates well with my understanding of Ginobili's on-court play, which completely exceeds simplistic formulas promoting a single "right way."

Even if he does not always seem to, Ginobili knows how to slip the trap. He gets ahead, first, by dissolving simultaneously the seemingly fixed dichotomies between having a plan and not having a plan and between reality and appearance. Manu's play both responds to the tricks in Luy's poem and embodies the artful deceit of the characters in Nine Queens by appearing to have no plan when he really does have one and by appearing to have a plan when he really does not. And if that is so, then Ginobili is also, at the same time and at any given moment, pretending to pretend when he is not pretending and really being real when he is not being real and therefore both pretending and being real. Confused? Imagine guarding him.

The trick, Ginobili's play seems to say, lies neither in having a plan nor in not having a plan but in never letting your opponent know whether you have one or not. Yet as in any good con, the apparent revelation of the trick is really only the last trap for the mark. There is always another twist, another trick, a truth yet to be revealed. It took my heretic wife to point out that in the case of Ginobili's game, the final twist may be this: whether or not he really does or only appears to have or not have a plan, Ginobili really, really does know that you do have a plan, and he knows what your plan is. Oh, and you do not know that he knows. But it would not even matter if you did, because you are a planner, so you will always have a plan, and someone can always crack its code. For all of Ginobili's play with appearance and reality, with calculation and improvisation, to work he has to know—or, at least, have a pretty good idea of—what his defender's plan and reactions will be. If this were not true, all his crafty, chaotic sleight of hand would wind up looking like involuntary spasms: random and ineffective.

In that sense, like that of the hero of *Nine Queens*, Ginobili's plan involves playfully conjugating appearance and reality, planning and plan-lessness, all the while observing and anticipating your plan and using it against you. This may be a cause or effect of all of the time he has spent as a sixth man, taking in the flows and patterns of energy on the court in the opening minutes before stepping onto the floor. But whenever Gino-bili plays and however he's used, his chaotic non-plan consumes or cannibalizes any and all others. Ultimately, all of the calculating energy you invested in your plan works toward his ends: all your cash winds up in his pocket, all your happiness on his face. And perhaps that may be Gino-bili's secret, whispered advice to those—like me—confused by the apparent impasses that Luy's poem presents. Do not strive for prosperity and happiness by mirthlessly calculating a rational and efficient (but morally foul or aesthetically routine) plan. Do not become a calculating, sinister planner—a politician, a kidnapper. Instead, watch and know the plans of the calculating and the sinister.

Closely observing Ginobili's game with an adequate understanding of the history of on-court basketball play makes it clear that, far from some new breed, he is squarely in the incorrigible tradition of players past and present—the volatile force of Russell Westbrook, the whirling chaos of Earl Monroe, the sick deception of Larry Bird, the improvisational impossibilities of Michael Jordan, or, indeed, the quixotic fearlessness of Allen Iverson. Did these players play the right way? Do we remember them for their efficiency? To rephrase the lesson I attributed to Ginobili above, now within the context of the myth of the right way, do not fall prostrate before the altar of efficiency and its illusion that one good way is the right way and that this right way has a nationality or a skin color. In doing so, you may well turn your back on efficiency's diabolically creative other: invention and the risky, uncalculating experimentation that nourishes it and that, in basketball, at least, has always kept the game moving. Learn instead to disarm the efficient and to relieve them of their grimly stock-piled resources by having no plan other than knowing theirs and showing them that you have none yourself. They will never know what hit them.

THE MYTH OF THE MAN

July 8, 2010

He will not only have to play like a man,
but act like a man.—**Mike Lopresti**

O n Friday, July 9, 2010, residents of Cleveland, Ohio, awoke to a striking image when they unfolded their morning newspapers. From
top to bottom along the left-hand side of the page extended the
uniformed figure of the twenty-five-year-old Cleveland Cavaliers star
LeBron James, identifiable by the number (23) and name on the back of
his jersey, walking away from them. In the upper-right corner, a single
word—"Gone"—reported the news. A thin straight line led from James's
right hand to the italicized legend in the lower right corner: "7 years in
Cleveland. No rings."[1] Of course, the news was probably no news to most
of the readers of the *Cleveland Plain Dealer* on that Friday morning. After
all, the night before, one in four Cleveland televisions was tuned into an
hour-long special television program (entitled "The Decision") broadcast
on ESPN.[2] During the program, James—two-time reigning MVP of the
NBA, native of Akron, and a free agent—had ended a fevered national
debate about where he would play by announcing that he would be "taking
[his] talents to South Beach"—that is, exercising his contractual right to
join the Miami Heat and his fellow free-agent superstars Dwyane Wade
and Chris Bosh.[3]

James's decision and the program "The Decision" immediately pro-
voked outrage and condemnation, both in public and in the media. In
Cleveland, fans burned James's jerseys, and the Cavaliers' owner, Dan
Gilbert, posted an open letter on the team's webpage excoriating James

as a coward, a narcissist, and a traitor.[4] Local sportswriters chronicled and vented the anger of the region. Beyond Cleveland, James's national "Q score," used to measure public figures' popularity for marketing purposes, plummeted in the days and weeks following the decision.[5] Across the country, those columnists who did acknowledge James's right to join whatever team he wished focused their criticism on the television broadcast, on the manner in which James handled his free-agency period before his decision, and on the effect his decision (however legally legitimate) would have on his long-term reputation.[6] Even Larry Bird, Magic Johnson, and Michael Jordan expressed disappointment, noting that they would never have joined rival stars, since the point was to beat them. As Charles Barkley put it, James now would "never be Jordan. This clearly takes him out of the conversation. He can win as much as he wants to. There would have been something honorable about staying in Cleveland and trying to win it as The Man."[7]

While implying that he would never be "The Man" was neither the most common nor the most extreme criticism of James in the wake of his decision, it offers a useful avenue through which to explore critically how a number of myths reviewed in the preceding chapters converged to underwrite the widespread, intense backlash against James. Nearly every derogatory term leveled at James—from immature to traitor and whore—acquires its force in relation to a normative notion of masculinity from which James supposedly deviated. Moreover, in basketball culture this notion is in turn tied to other norms not only of gender but also of competition, play, morality, class, race, and national identity that extend in a series of complicated, intertwining paths from the game's invention through the various moments I have isolated up to the present day. This network of interrelated norms, expressed by various means and terms in the period following James's decision, is what I call "the myth of the Man." Adherents purveyed it as a capturing net through which to harness and discipline the radical autonomy—the "*free agency*," in both the narrow and broadest sense of the phrase—exercised by LeBron James, both on and off the court.

The Myth of the Man

The myth of the Man does not always use the term "man" but instead applies a variety of terms to James in a derogatory way. These terms can be usefully grouped into sets according to the tropes, or metaphors, of manhood they typically employ. Specifically, the myth of the Man comprises four sets of tropes of masculinity that its adherents accuse James of violating: (1) the Sports Man (tropes that equate a narrow definition of sportsmanship with an equally narrow definition of masculinity and exclude James from both); (2) the Grown Man (tropes that explain James's decision in terms of immaturity, childishness, or failure in other ways to be an adult man); (3) the Noble Man (tropes that identify masculinity with a code of honor associated with nobility and then exclude James from both); and (4) the Man's Man (tropes that associate James's decision with female stereotypes). These categories bleed together and, indeed, mutually reinforce one another. The term "whore," for example, marks James as not only a woman (and so not a Man's Man) but also as disloyal, duplicitous, and mercenary (and so not a Noble Man).

Sports Man tropes were mobilized most influentially—though not exclusively—by athletes.[8] In several interviews in the period following James's decision, Barkley commented that James, by leaving Cleveland to join rival stars in Miami, would now never be "the guy" or "the man" and that, even if he won championships in Miami, they would be less meaningful because he would not have won them as "the man." By "the man" (or "the guy"), Barkley had in mind an individual basketball player who accepts given circumstances (whether or not they are favorable to winning championships) and labors with determination, focus, and competitive intensity and will to rise above them. "The man," then, may or may not have championships to show for his efforts. But if he does not, then he will at least have remained "the man," and if he does, well, then he will have won them in the most meaningful way possible.

In making these comments, Barkley (who despite a very successful career never won a championship) joined Magic Johnson and Michael Jordan, both of whom, of course, did win championships and both of whom criticized James on similar grounds. All affirmed that in their careers, the thought of joining their rivals—Bird in Johnson's case and Isiah Thomas, Magic, or Bird in Jordan's case—never once crossed their minds. The only kind of thought they had about their rivals was how to beat them by raising their own performance and coaxing better performances out of whatever supporting casts they might have. All three made clear that in their opinion, James had violated a code of individual competitiveness that serves as something like the constitutive ground for the comparative measurement of greatness or, as the pundits put it, "legacy." When combined with the paradoxical tenet that team championships indicate individual greatness, a hierarchy of levels of possible greatness results: (1) Men with Championships (Jordan, Magic, Russell, Bird, Kobe

Bryant), (2) Men without Championships (Barkley, Reggie Miller, Karl Malone, John Stockton, Patrick Ewing), (3) non–Men with or without Championships (LeBron). No matter how many titles James might win, he had doomed himself forever to the ignominious third tier.

But Barkley not only skewered James for violating the competitive code and thus forfeiting his legacy as a Sports Man. He also frequently referred to James's relative youth in terms of immaturity, at one point describing his behavior as a "punk move."[9] In this, Barkley joined a chorus of critics, primarily in the media, who characterized James as not a man in the sense of not a *Grown* Man—not an adult but a child. Critics called James spoiled, immature, egotistical, entitled, coddled, irresponsible, selfish, and narcissistic.[10] Moreover, they infantilized him by implying that he had received "permission from his mother" to make the decision.[11] In the Cleveland area, writers patronized James by describing him as the ungrateful child of the region that had raised and loved him.[12] In this way, just as James had been "unmanned" within the codes of competitive sportsmanship, he is here rendered unmanly by the codes of adulthood.

Probably the most commonly employed tropes in the backlash against James's decision come from the category of the Noble Man. Although journalists—and Barkley himself, with his reference to the "honor" of remaining in Cleveland—again were quick to join in, Dan Gilbert was the first to mobilize noble codes of gentlemanly honor against James. In his open letter to Cavaliers fans, Gilbert referred to James as having "deserted" the team in a "cowardly betrayal" that he also described as a "shocking act of disloyalty" and a "shameful display of selfishness and betrayal."[13] Gilbert next reduced the price of life-size LeBron Fathead posters from $100 to $17.41, a price that represented "the birth year of the first traitor of note in American history, Benedict Arnold."[14] While some columnists argued that Gilbert's letter was out of line, many others joined in the use of such terms as "coward," "mercenary," "traitor," "treachery," and "betrayal" to describe the decision or James himself.[15] Here the definition of manhood is derived originally from aristocratic norms of honor, courage, and loyalty. While obviously anachronistic—and selectively applied, to say the least—sports (along with the military) may be the only contemporary cultural domain where such codes still carry normative force. After all, basketball, you may recall, was invented as a way to foster gentlemanly masculinity in the unruly young men who played the game.

Finally, the most direct challenge to James's masculinity involved journalists' actually comparing him to a woman. Thus, noting that James had joined his "pals Chris Bosh and Dwyane Wade," Maureen Dowd, an op-ed columnist for the *New York Times*, slyly mused, "It's usually women who get accused of needing to go places (restaurant bathrooms) together."[16] And another columnist, Sean Conboy, went further, writing, "In a world of attention whores, The King has ascended to the throne."[17] While certainly unsubtle, these isolated comments take on fuller force when situated alongside the other tropes mobilized by the myth of the Man in the backlash against James's decision. In the case of the other three tropes, James has fallen short of certain norms that can be associated only indirectly with masculinity: competitive intensity, maturity, honor. But when Dowd compares James to a woman or Conboy compares him to a prostitute, though still obviously metaphorical at a number of levels, the critique becomes more directly pointed, as though the writers believed that James was literally, biologically, female.

This can perhaps best be seen in the most spectacular expression of the myth of the Man (and the backlash to the decision), the three-hundred-page screed *The Whore of Akron: One Man's Search for the Soul of LeBron James*, by the Cleveland native and New Jersey resident Scott Raab, whom one reviewer characterized as "James' biggest, most belligerent detractor on Twitter well before *Whore of Akron* was announced." Raab employed the metaphor of prostitution not only most extensively but also most forcefully, using it as a gravitational center into which he drew all the other tropes that formed the myth of the man.[18] As a literary trope, the "whore" serves Raab's purpose well in that it bears—alongside the obvious connotation of femininity—a long-standing set of associations (duplicity, mercenary soullessness) that resonate with and evoke other tropes already at work in the myth of the Man.[19]

"For seven years," Raab explains, "LeBron did the same thing as any trollop worth her taxi fare: he made the right noises, told us how good it felt, how big we were, how he loved us, how special we were. Oh, we knew . . . that he was only a child, and a child born unto a hapless mother more or less a child herself. His vast sense of childish entitlement seemed to speak louder every season. But lord, the sex was fine."[20] There, as throughout the book, Raab yokes together femininity (in the figure of the trollop and the feminine pronoun), duplicity and betrayal (feigning sincerity to induce vulnerability), and immaturity (he was an entitled child). Elsewhere, Raab combines the trope of the whore and the child with the trope of ignoble treachery: "The Whore of Akron knows full well he has stomped on Cleveland's soul. . . . [He is] a native son who betrayed the fatherland."[21]

Raab seems obsessively thorough in foreclosing every avenue by which masculinity might be attributed to James. Elsewhere, he ladles in tropes that refer to the Sports Man, as when he writes, for example, "He is a hideously poor sportsman and more adept each season at acting every inch the prima donna bitch."[22] Raab closes the book with a patronizing lecture—"You're not a grown man. You're a kid and you're afraid"—in which he "explains" to James what he presumes the star's father never taught him: that "hard work is the only thing that makes it mean anything, the only thing that makes losing or winning worth the pain of trying."[23] With this, we come full circle, as Raab essentially echoes, albeit with greater complexity and venom, the criticisms first leveled at James by Barkley, Jordan, and others: that with his decision he had forfeited his man-ness. Most of the country—outside southern Florida, anyway—seemed to agree with a peculiar mixture of vitriolic, gleeful disappointment that, however great a talent James might possess, he could never be the man.

A Genealogy of Basketball *Ressentiment*

The myth of the Man works in part because it draws on elements of all of the other myths in the culture of basketball that I have analyzed thus far. These other myths serve as a kind of language, furnishing both a basic vocabulary and the elements of grammar and syntax that render new discourses within the culture of basketball legible or illegible, plausible or implausible. Norms of masculinity, racial attitudes, and moral values combine in various ways with platitudes about the sport itself. These combinations then attach themselves to individual figures, teams, events, or eras exploiting the strong affective investment fans already have in these icons and landmarks of basketball history. All of this is to say that we, as citizens of basketball, are *culturally predisposed* to accept—and, indeed, cling to and passionately purvey—any story that brings together the right combination of elements from previous myths. When this occurs, we can easily accept that a given player, team, or moment either embodies or, as in this case, betrays everything we believe to be true, good, and beautiful about basketball.

Each of the four types of tropes that make up the myth of the Man echoes a message we already believe on the basis of a previously compelling myth. The Sports Man appears first in the myth of creation (think muscular Christianity) and then again in the myths of the rivalry, the amateurs, and the greatest of all time (LeBron could be like Chamberlain but could never be Russell, Magic, Bird, or Jordan). The Grown Man works in part by implicitly (or explicitly) contrasting James with norms of masculine maturity that it associates with those same four figures but also by relying on stereotypes—first circulated (in the culture of basketball, at any rate) within the myth of the rivalry (Chamberlain), the myth of the garden (the ABA), the myth of the amateurs (the NBA of the late 1970s), and the myth of blackness (Iverson and the "hip-hop" generation)—of black male athletes as immature and irresponsible. The Noble Man also echoes norms of gentlemanly masculinity set forth in the myth of creation and recapitulated in the myth of the garden and the myth of the right way. But also, insofar as James was said to have betrayed a city that relied on him for social healing, the Noble Man also implicitly contrasts James with the myth of the garden (where the Knicks put aside egos to help heal New York), the myth of the rivalry (in which Russell remained loyal to Boston, even when it did not reciprocate), and the myth of the greatest of all time (in which Jordan remained loyal to Chicago, despite early missteps by management that jeopardized his legacy). Finally, the Man's Man again draws on the myth of creation. But because James as whore or woman appears concerned with the superficial (literally, jewelry, as in championship rings) in lieu of the substantive (hardness, work, sacrifice), the Man's Man also casts him into a suspect tradition of flashy superficiality or style previously associated with Wilt Chamberlain, the ABA, and Allen Iverson.

In addition to drawing energy from existing myths, these four tropes acquired force by mirroring what we had attributed, with love and admiration, to LeBron James in the first place. To banish James from the company of Sports Men revokes one of the first (and perhaps the best known) of the labels thrust on him: "the Chosen One." *Sports Illustrated* thus anointed James—as in chosen to be the next Jordan—on its cover when he was still a high school junior.[24] Claims that he was a spoiled child, immature, and entitled reverse the image of preternatural maturity. From early in James's high school career, observers praised not only his physical but also his intellectual and emotional maturity.[25] After the decision, James in effect was cast from being a miraculous Man-Child to a monstrous Child-Man. Of course, with the nickname "King James" obviously connoting the highest rank of nobility, critics, like children first discovering the workings of puns, gleefully dethroned James in the wake of the decision. He went from King James to Benedict Arnold, the King of the Attention Whores, LeFraud, and the counterfeit King.[26] Finally, the duplicitous femininity ascribed to James after the decision contrasts with the hard masculinity so often emphasized in journalists' admiring accounts of James's physique. Before the decision, James was not only obviously a "man"; he was also physically the ideal of manhood: tall, fast, and powerfully muscular. But even more important, his physical power was *useful*, acquired in the course of and for the end of perfecting his craft. After the decision, James's physique, no longer the sign of hard work and the guarantor of dominance, became the flashy, unearned token of a false promise that would never be fulfilled.

In a sense, all these facets of our image of James combine to form a single image of promise, a promise we imagine that LeBron James made to us but that in fact we attributed to him. *We chose* LeBron James to embody the promise—so desperately needed after so many disappointments, after hip-hop, after the international debacles—of Heir to Jordan, the greatest of all time, which is to say, an heir to basketball perfection and to the perfection that is basketball. James was first constructed as a second coming, messianic imagery making him both man and god.[27] LeBron James was born in 1984, the year that the twenty-one-year-old rookie Michael Jordan first set the league ablaze. As Jordan matured and began to pile up scoring titles, MVP trophies, and championships, LeBron bounced around from one Akron project to another, twelve times between the ages of five and eight. By the time Jordan retired for the second time in 1998, clearly the greatest of all time but with no heir apparent, the NBA seized by the abhorrent hip-hop revolution, James was just entering eighth grade but already creating a sensation on his Amateur Athletic Union youth team. Our search for the next Jordan amped up, and there we found LeBron. From that moment, he never escaped our crosshairs.[28]

This so-called conversation about the greatest of all time is first and foremost *our* conversation, a thing of our own making. It is as if we just want the excitement of imagining we want a next Jordan—despite our investment in his unsurpassable greatness—and of arguing about whether we have got one or not. We played out a faux one-on-one battle with our MJ and LBJ dolls in which it appeared to be close, but we never really wanted or expected Jordan to be surpassed, or even equaled. LeBron's decision to go to Miami provided the pretext by which we could disqualify him from a contest in which, until that moment, he was more or less where Jordan had been seven years into *his* career. LeBron's first "crime" was to refuse to play passively his role in our drama. Instead, he took it *seriously* and *acted out*. *We* called him "the Chosen One," and he had the audacity to write it in his skin. Then, even worse, he nicknamed himself. Forget for a moment what the nickname was. Just think for a second about what it might mean, in a country in which for generations white men gave black men their names, for a powerful, poor, young black man to name himself and in so doing to appoint himself King.

LeBron offended us by wanting to be the author of the drama we had scripted for him. And this leads me to what I suspect is, from the perspective of the deepest needs of adherents of the myth of the Man, LeBron's more serious transgression, for he took control of not only the cultural dramas we had cast him in but also, with other players, aspects of the sport that— in sway of the myth of foundation—we reserve for owners. As an unnamed TV executive told Maureen Dowd, explaining why everyone was going to root against Miami after the decision, "These three players have attempted to hijack the league and said, 'We're all good buddies who are going to gang up and go to one team and dictate who wins championships.'"[29] That, of course, is something that only owners are allowed to do, as only a small minority of mainstream observers at the time wryly pointed out.[30]

At one level, this offends our deep national investment in the hierarchies of private property ownership within capitalism. What could be more offensive than the workers colluding to determine, without consulting their owners, where they would work and which factory will be most productive? Well, I will tell you what could be more offensive: if those workers were young, already highly paid black men. But notice that I say "offensive" and not, say, "terrifying." While the specter of a workers' revolution or of a collective insurgency of poor African American men might well terrify the Donald Sterlings of the world, the truth is that the vast majority of those who tore so viciously into LeBron James after the decision are not the Donald Sterlings of the world. They are, rather, also workers who are bossed by owners of their own. And if they are *offended* by LeBron's decision it might be because they have not had the courage to make the decision themselves, and they will be goddamned if some spoiled young black kid is going to get there first.

Two events that seemed to anger critics even more than the decision bear this out. First, a few months after the decision, having been asked whether race played a part in the backlash, James replied, "I think so, at times. There's always—you know, a race factor."[31] Second, a few months after that, as the nation's basketball fans and media pundits gloated over the defeat of Miami in the NBA finals at the hands of the Dallas Mavericks (led by the foreign, white superstar Dirk Nowitzki), James was asked what it was like to have so many millions rooting against him.[32] He replied, "All the people that were rooting for me to fail . . . at the end of the day, tomorrow they have to wake up and have the same life that [they had] before they woke up today. They got the same personal problems they had today. And I'm going to continue to live the way I want to live and continue to do the things I want to do."[33] The indignation and outrage these two episodes provoked indicates, contrary to popular explanations, that James hit too close to home, essentially saying, "You're angry because a black man like me is doing what you, white men, are afraid to do—namely, what I want." After all, these statements apparently did not offend everyone equally. While James's Q-score plummeted among white fans, it dipped only slightly among black fans.[34]

Via the myth of the Man, the basketball world hysterically chanted—like the boys in *Lord of the Flies*, intoxicated by unanimity—over and over again, "LeBron is not a Man! LeBron is not a Man!" The words resonated with the vitriolic resentment its adherents felt toward James, not because he failed to be "a Man" or "the Man," but because he behaved as a *free* man. By doing so, he forced us to see, first, how the league—indeed, the entire basketball culture—we loved was structured like a plantation, running smoothly only insofar as its black players agreed to limit their own freedom; and second, and more painful still, the ways in which we were unfree in our own lives. We thought we had scripted James's life for our entertainment. Instead, he wrote his own story and showed us that our lives were scripted by others.

Henry Miller once observed, "Every day we slaughter our finest impulses. That is why we get a heartache when we read those lines written by the hand of a master and recognize them as our own, as the tender shoots which we stifled because we lacked the faith to believe in our own powers."[35] Nietzsche called it *ressentiment*.[36] It means resentment, of course, but the specific form of resentment we feel when someone else is doing what we wish we could—or, rather, wish we had the courage to—do. Simultaneously exposed to and separated from what we could but will not do, we feel not inspiration but pain. As the philosopher Gilles Deleuze explains, "The man of *ressentiment* experiences every being and object as an offence in exact proportion to its effect on him. Beauty and goodness are, for him, necessarily as outrageous as any pain or misfortune that he experiences. . . . [He] is venomous and depreciative because [he] blames the object in order to compensate for [his] own inability to escape."[37] *Ressentiment* is what we feel when we have enslaved ourselves, forgotten that we did it, and then despise those—like LeBron James—who have refused to do so as though they were evil and trying to get away with something, or worse, as though they were responsible for our enslavement.

Inventing Free Agency

Chris Ballard of *Sports Illustrated* concluded his book *The Art of a Beautiful Game: A Thinking Fan's Tour of the NBA* (2009) with a chapter devoted to "the anatomy of LeBron James." For Ballard, James "represents the apex of [basketball's] physical skill. And it is skill that is married to an innate feel for the game. Here is a man who passes like a point guard, runs like a sprinter, leaps like a high jumper and . . . hits like a linebacker. If you were to create the prototype for the NBA player of the future, it would look an awful lot like James."[38] Ballard succinctly voices what has amazed fans about James on the court since even before he entered the league: all of the qualities constituting the Platonic ideal of basketball, all those skills or qualities that the basketball gods distributed among the pantheon of all-time greats, seem to come together in James. He combines athletic ability (hops like Jordan, strength like Shaq, speed and quickness like Iverson), fundamental skills (ball handling and passing like Magic, rebounding and hustle like Bird, defense like Russell, and, increasingly, jump shooting like Reggie Miller), as well as the "IQ" and unselfishness to do everything (like Oscar Robertson) or just that one thing (like Russell) that his team needs on a given night. As Ballard noted, even James's penchant for passing up a shot to a more open teammate near the end of some close games (which has elicited some criticism) makes it seem as if he "has skipped a step in his evolution as a dominant NBA player." After all, it took even the greatest of all time "the better part of his career before he trusted his teammates in those final critical moments."[39]

Noting (pre-decision) LeBron James's carefully polished public persona, some NBA writers suggested that perhaps he would embody "the one NBA archetype that not even [Michael Jordan] fully realized: the emperor."[40] This certainly fits with my characterization of this era as "Basketball Empire." But to say that LeBron embodies all of the best of basketball that preceded him is also to situate him, as Ballard appropriately does, on a horizon—or, rather, it is to recognize that James stands as a kind of threshold between basketball as we have known it, with all of its possibilities and limitations, and a future version of itself that will still be called basketball but whose precise dimensions and forms we cannot yet imagine. In other words, if James embodies the emperor, he is the sort of emperor who does not simply reign over an inherited territory or empire but redefines the territory and the history that came before it. Reflecting on the fact that the emperor who ordered the building of the Great Wall of China "also decreed the burning of all the books that had been written before his time," Jorge Luis Borges wonders whether the emperor "wanted to recreate the beginning of time."[41]

James does not so much seem to be the second coming of Jordan, a repetitive ending of all time, as his antithesis, a kind of Promethean emperor who takes the throne only to set history and time back in motion. James's celebrated passing ability and unfailing unselfishness on the court (he recently surpassed Jordan's wing man, Scottie Pippen, to become the NBA all-time assist leader among forwards)—more than his strength or speed—may be the best emblem for my invention. James is the player who deploys his strengths to create opportunities for others on the court. Whereas Jordan's struggle to understand teamwork eventually redounds to his credit in the bildungsroman of the myth of the greatest of all time, James's inherently collaborationist disposition frequently appears as a strike against him. Yet even in the depths of his darkest moment, when pressed on the night of the decision as to how much "looking at your peers with multiple [championships]" influenced his decision, LeBron James gave the interrogating journalist a history lesson, reminding him that all of his "peers" won championships as members of teams. Magic had Kareem and James Worthy. Bird had Dennis Johnson and Kevin McHale and Robert Parish. Jordan had Pippen and then Rodman. And more recently, Duncan had David Robinson and then Tony Parker and Ginobili. In the NBA, James concluded, "you become a superstar individually but you become a champion as a team. And I understand that, and I know the history of the game."[42] James here articulates the view that he has consistently demonstrated on the court, from the time he was in high school through his most recent games: that individual greatness is no end in itself; it is a means to elevate a community.

In July 2014, almost four years to the day after the infamous decision, James exercised his free agency once again, this time to leave the Miami Heat and return home to northeastern Ohio, to the Cleveland Cavaliers, to the very same owner who had slandered him, to the very same fans who had burned his jersey. He even let those fans choose whether he would wear the number 6, as he had in Miami, or the number 23, as he had during his first seven seasons in Cleveland.[43] They chose 23, and in accepting their decision he allowed them, in effect, to unburn the jerseys. The usual story of this Return of the King is that LeBron, having weakly, immaturely, selfishly, whorishly abandoned Cleveland to secure his championship rings, had grown up, come to his senses, and come home to win (at least) one more for hard-luck Cleveland fans whose last major sports title came in 1964. Maybe. That certainly feeds our appetite for moralizing bildungsroman stories and allows Scott Raab and other critics to feel both absolutely justified in originally purveying the myth of the Man and entitled now to welcome James home (since he has, after all, learned his lesson).[44]

But maybe we can tell a better story. LeBron did:

Remember when I was sitting up there at the Boys & Girls Club in 2010? I was thinking, this is really tough. I could feel it. I was leaving something I had spent a long time creating. If I had to do it all over again, I'd obviously do things differently, but *I'd still have left*. Miami, for me, has been almost like college for other kids. These past four years helped raise me into who I am. I became a better player and a better man. *I learned from a franchise that had been where I wanted to go.*[45]

Maybe LeBron left Cleveland because he knew he had something to learn before he could use his strengths to deliver the title to Cleveland and that he could learn that something only by leaving home. Maybe LeBron, ever the point guard, ever the pleaser, loved Cleveland so much that he left, and suffered the hatred of the hoops universe, so that he could return, now more powerful (on and off the court) than ever before and lend that power to the region he loved. This difference from the conventional interpretation is subtle but important. In the conventional story, James made a childish error in 2010. In this story, James made a difficult but necessary *decision* that he would make again (even if he might do it "differently"), one that admittedly transformed and improved him ("a better player and a better man") but that did not entail a shift from child to adult. Even here, James subtly eludes our efforts to tell his story for him.[46]

In this, James may the Baruch Spinoza of basketball history. For one thing, Spinoza was also the subject of vitriolic censure. Raised in the Jewish community of Amsterdam in the seventeenth century, Spinoza so earnestly and uncompromisingly pursued a philosophy of freedom that he was both condemned by Christian authorities and excommunicated by his fellow Jews, to which Spinoza replied, "All the better, they do not force me to do anything that I would not have done of my own accord. . . . I enter gladly on the path that is opened to me."[47] But the comparison of James with Spinoza rests on something more than a dignified response to unjustified public calumny.

Spinoza condemned traditional morality, which he argued depended on ignorance and fostered slavish obedience, in favor of an ethics of radical freedom, self-awareness, and joy. Spinoza's ethics, like James's game, is predicated on the relationship; on the interconnected, interdependence of all beings, like players on a team. Understanding the web of cause and effect, how our encounters with others affect us, and vice versa, is at the root of Spinoza's ethical vision. From there, in Spinoza's ethics, "that individual will be called *good* (or free, or rational, or strong) who strives, insofar as he is capable, to organize his encounters, to join with whatever agrees with his nature, to combine his relation with relations that are compatible with his, and thereby to increase his power."[48] Remember LeBron asserting, on the night of the decision, "You become a superstar individually, but you become a champion as a team"? Spinoza agreed, for the goodness cultivated by the free, rational, or strong individual, to merit its name, was necessarily a goodness "common to all . . . and can be enjoyed by all equally."[49]

Moreover, the path to ethical goodness, for Spinoza as for LeBron, is in a certain sense a path that has to be walked (and thereby created) anew by every individual in every situation. It cannot be found by obeying the commands of a conventional morality that presents its norms as eternal and universally applicable. The complexity of the world, the diversity of circumstances, and the unique makeup of individuals mean that there is no single formula for ethical virtue. It must, instead, be forged through trial and error by following one's inclinations and measuring the results, using joy as the best indicator of an increase in power and so, therefore, of ethical virtue. This striving for ethical goodness, following the indications of increasing joy, could lead to what Spinoza called "beatitude," which coincides with "being at rest in oneself" (*acquiescentia in se ipso*) also defined as "joy, accompanied by the idea of the self as cause."[50] Spinoza's life and ethics illuminate the novelty and the power of both James's style of play on the court, which combines individual power and unselfishness in measures that vary according to the circumstances, and the trajectory of his career, which eludes all of the predetermined cultural and economic narratives.

The myths of the cultures of basketball uphold a static image of the game, as though it had not changed in essence since 1891. Whatever changes these myths do accommodate must still conform to the moralizing parameters supposedly embodied by this static image of the sport. These myths express an unconscious tension with respect to the increased presence and then dominance of black men in basketball. The result is what Deleuze calls an "apparatus of capture": a kind of net—at once symbolic and material, at once moral and tactical, stylistic and social—used to arrest the experimental creative force of players and the unpredictable, chaotic flow of the game.[51] Confronted with the creative technical, tactical, and stylistic innovations of basketball players, the myths of basketball culture either appropriate them by rewriting them in preexisting terms (Dr. J.'s iconoclastic jam becomes fine art) or reject them as cancerous foreign bodies (the dunks of a latter generation are judged, by comparison, as thuggish).

Thus, we tried to capture LeBron James by, among other things, plotting him on a graph established by Jordan. But maybe all along he was, as Nietzsche put it, "transvaluing all values," changing, in other words, the rules of the game, inaugurating a new order, with new standards.[52] In this sense, perhaps he is a traitor, not in the derogatory sense implied by the petty and petulant complaints of his resentful critics but "a traitor to the world of dominant significations, and to the established order."[53] Perhaps LeBron James has betrayed the racializing pseudo-moral order constructed through the myths of basketball culture and given it an inventive twist. Perhaps LeBron is the paradigm that does away with all paradigms.

If the apparatus of capture, to put it most simply, is thinking that seeks to conserve predetermined identities and the institutions whose powers depend on the stability of those identities, Deleuze contrasted it with what he sometimes called "nomad thought," which "breaks free from the models and stereotypes that would predetermine our thought processes."[54] I see in nomad thought the same tendencies I associated with inventive, elusive Athena, daughter of the cunning Metis in Chapter 1. And I believe James may merely be the best known among a growing host of contemporary NBA players who embody with their play and their demeanor this nomad thought as so many countless predecessors have done, going all the way back to James Naismith and the original eighteen incorrigibles. James may *temporarily* inhabit any number of the predetermined identities offered up by the myths of basketball culture. But for that very reason he exceeds any single one of them. For that reason, he eludes any fixed label or teleological narrative we try to impose on him. For that reason, he remains—like the sport itself (and regardless of what feeble efforts may be made to arrest its inventive, fluid, unending process of becoming)—radically free.

NOTES

INTRODUCTION

Epigraph: Rasheed Wallace, quoted in Justin Rogers, "Rasheed Likens NBA Zero-Tolerance Policy to Slavery," MLive, November 6, 2006, http://blog.mlive.com/fullcourt press/2006/11/rasheed_likens_nba_zerotoleran.html, accessed September 4, 2015.

1. Tony Gervino, "With 'Ball Don't Lie,' Wallace Keeps Technicals Flowing," *New York Times*, December 4, 2012, sec. B.

2. Terry Eagleton, *Literary Theory: An Introduction*, 2d ed. (Oxford: Basil Blackwell, 2003), 94.

3. National Basketball Association, "Official Rules of the National Basketball Association, 2014–2015," 11, http://mediacentral.nba.com/media/media central/ Official-NBA-Rule-Book.pdf, accessed September 4, 2015.

4. Ibid., 17.

5. Ibid., 44–46, 57–58.

6. On racial bias, see Alan Schwarz, "Study of NBA Sees Racial Bias in Calling Fouls," *New York Times*, May 2, 2007, http://www.nytimes.com/2007/05/02/sports/ basketball/02refs.html?pagewanted=all&_r=0.

7. John Searle, *Expression and Meaning: Studies in the Theory of Speech Acts* (Cambridge: Cambridge University Press, 1979), 16. For a philosophical history of the concept, see Kent Bach, "Speech Acts," in *Routledge Encyclopedia of Philosophy*, ed. Edward Craig (London: Routledge, 1998), 8230–8235. For a history of its use in literary studies, see Jonathan Culler, *Literary Theory: A Very Short Introduction* (Oxford: Oxford University Press, 1997), 94–107. For two passing mentions of officials' calls as speech acts, see Donald J. Mrozek, "'It Ain't Nothin' until I Call It': What Belongs in a Course in American Sport History," in *Sport in the Classroom: Teaching Sport-Related Courses in the Humanities*, ed. David L. Vanderwerken (Cranbury, NJ: Associated University Presses, 1990), 21; Spencer K. Wertz, "Time Out: Teaching Sport and Philosophical Analysis," in *Sport in the Classroom:*

Teaching Sport-Related Courses in the Humanities, ed. David L. Vanderwerken (Cranbury, NJ: Associated University Presses, 1990), 87. Finally, for a critique, see J. S. Russell, "The Concept of a Call in Baseball," *Journal of the Philosophy of Sport* 24 (1997): 22–23.

8. For summaries of realism, see Edward Craig, "Realism and Anti-Realism," in Craig, *Routledge Encyclopedia of Philosophy*, 7236–7239; Alexander Miller, "Realism," in *Stanford Encyclopedia of Philosophy*, ed. Edward N. Zalta, http://plato.stanford.edu/ archives/win2014/entries/realism, accessed September 4, 2015. On the correspondence theory of truth, see Richard Kirkham, "Truth, Correspondence Theory of," in Craig, *Routledge Encyclopedia of Philosophy*, 8696–8698, and David Marian, "The Correspondence Theory of Truth," in Zalta, *Stanford Encyclopedia of Philosophy*, http://plato.stan ford.edu/entries/truth-correspondence, accessed September 4, 2015.

9. William James, "Pragmatism," in *William James: Writings, 1902–1910*, ed. Bruce Kuklick (New York: Library of America, 1987), 520.

10. Ibid., 574.

11. Thomas McLaughlin, *Give and Go: Basketball as a Cultural Practice* (Albany: State University of New York Press, 2008), 23–45.

12. On autonomist politics, see Harry Cleaver, *Reading Capital Politically* (Austin: University of Texas Press, 1979); Michael Hardt, "Translator's Foreword: The Anatomy of Power," in Antonio Negri, *The Savage Anomaly: The Power of Spinoza's Metaphysics and Politics*, trans. Michael Hardt (Minneapolis: University of Minnesota Press, 2003), xi. On horizontalism, see Marina Sitrin, "Horizontalism and the Occupy Movements," *Dissent*, 2012, http://www.dissentmagazine.org/article/horizontalism-and-the-occu py-movements, accessed September 4, 2015.

13. Lars Anderson and Chad Millman, *Pickup Artists: Street Basketball in America* (London: Verso, 1998); Pete Axthelm, *The City Game: Basketball in New York from the World Champion Knicks to the World of the Playgrounds* (New York: Pocket Books, 1971); Todd Boyd, *Young, Black, Rich, and Famous: The Rise of the NBA, the Hip Hop Invasion, and the Transformation of American Culture* (Lincoln: University of Nebraska Press, 2008); Nelson George, *Black Men and Basketball* (Lincoln: University of Nebraska Press, 1999); Wright Martindale Jr., *Inside the Cage: A Season at West 4th Street's Legendary Tournament* (New York: Simon Spotlight Entertainment, 2005); Steven A. Riess, *City Games: The Evolution of American Urban Society and the Rise of Sports* (Urbana: University of Illinois Press, 1989); Murry Nelson, "Telander, Rick Heaven Is a Playground," *Journal of Sport History* 37, no. 3 (2011): 490–491.

14. On the concept of "supplement," see Jacques Derrida, *Of Grammatology*, trans. Gayatri Chakravorty Spivak (Baltimore: Johns Hopkins University Press, 1997), 144–157. For the source of my use of "other," see Robert Miles and Malcolm Brown, *Racism*, 2d ed. (New York: Routledge, 2004), 19–53.

15. David J. Leonard, *After Artest: The NBA and the Assault on Blackness* (Albany: State University of New York Press, 2012), 9–13.

16. Robert A. Segal, *Myth: A Very Short Introduction* (Oxford: Oxford University Press, 2004), 4–6.

17. Jay Caspian Kang, "Person of Interest: Rasheed Wallace," *Grantland*, March 6, 2012, http://grantland.com/features/a-los-angeles-lakers-rumor-spurs-writer-look-back-rasheed-wallace-nba-career, accessed September 4, 2015; FreeDarko Collective, "Rasheed Wallace: Family Man," in *FreeDarko Presents . . . The Macrophenomenal Pro Basketball Almanac: Styles, Stats, and Stars in Today's Game* (New York: Bloomsbury, 2008),

161–167; Netw3rk, "Why We Watch: Rasheed Wallace, Outlaw," *The Classical*, November 14, 2012, http://theclassical.org/articles/why-we-watch-rasheed-wallace-outlaw, accessed September 4, 2015.

18. Susan Birrell and Mary McDonald, "Reading Sport, Articulating Power Lines: An Introduction," in *Reading Sport: Critical Essays on Power and Representation*, ed. Susan Birrell and Mary McDonald (Boston: Northeastern University Press, 2000), 11.

19. Friedrich Nietzsche, *On the Genealogy of Morality*, ed. Keith Ansell-Pearson, trans. Carol Diethe (Cambridge: Cambridge University Press, 2006), 1–120.

20. William Morgan, *Why Sports Matter Morally* (New York: Routledge, 2006), 14.

CHAPTER 1

Epigraph: Selby Kiffer, quoted in Richard Sandomir, "Basketball's Beginnings Are Headed for Auction," *New York Times*, October 26, 2010, sec. B.

1. Richard Sandomir, "At Auction, Naismith Rules Set a Record," *New York Times*, December 11, 2010, http://query.nytimes.com/gst/fullpage.html?res=9C04E7DD1F3 BF932A25751C1A9669D8B63.

2. For examples, see Richard Davies, *Sports in American Life: A History* (Oxford: Blackwell, 2007), 106; Zander Hollander, ed., *The Modern Encyclopedia of Basketball* (New York: Four Winds, 1969), 3; Leonard Koppett, *24 Seconds to Shoot: The Birth and Improbable Rise of the NBA* (New York: TOTAL/Sports Illustrated Classics, 1999), 1; Walter LaFeber, *Michael Jordan and the New Global Capitalism* (New York: W. W. Norton, 2002), 33; Michael Mandelbaum, *The Meaning of Sports: Why American Watch Baseball, Football, and Basketball and What They See When They Do* (New York: Public Affairs, 2004), 201; Robert C. Peterson, *Cages to Jump Shots: Pro Basketball's Early Years* (Lincoln: University of Nebraska Press, 2002), 15.

3. Nelson George, *Elevating the Game: Black Men and Basketball* (Lincoln: University of Nebraska Press, 1999) 3; John Grissmer, *The Perfect Game: Jim Naismith Invents Basketball* (Indianapolis: Author House, 2010), 46; Marc T. Horger, "Play by the Rules: The Creation of Basketball and the Progressive Era, 1891–1917," Ph.D. diss., Ohio State University, Columbus, 2001), 14; "James Naismith," *Naismith Memorial Hall of Fame*, 2009, http://www.hoophall.com/hall-of-famers/tag/james-naismith; Maura Mandt and Josh Swade, "There's No Place like Home," *30 for 30* documentary, ESPN, October 16, 2012; John P. McCarthy, *Coaching Youth Basketball*, 2d ed. (Cincinnati: Betterway, 1996), 2; Peterson, *Cages to Jump Shots*, 15; Rob Rains and Helen Carpenter, *James Naismith: The Man Who Invented Basketball* (Philadelphia: Temple University Press, 2009), 45.

4. Allen Guttman, *A Whole New Ball Game: An Interpretation of American Sports* (Chapel Hill: University of North Carolina Press, 1988), 72; Peterson, *Cages to Jump Shots*, 15; Richard Sandomir, "Basketball's Beginnings Are Headed for Auction," *New York Times*, October 26, 2010, sec. B.

5. Kiffer, quoted in Richard Sandomir, "Basketball's Beginnings Are Headed for Auction," *New York Times*, October 26, 2010, sec. B; emphasis added.

6. Mandt and Swade, "There's No Place like Home"; Sandomir, "Basketball's Beginnings Are Headed for Auction."

7. William J. Baker, "Introduction," in James Naismith, *Basketball: Its Origins and Development* (Lincoln: University of Nebraska Press, 1996), x–xvii; Horger, "Play by the Rules."

8. Peterson, *Cages to Jump Shots*, 20.

9. Armand D'Angour, *The Greeks and the New: Novelty in Ancient Greek Imagination and Experience* (Cambridge: Cambridge University Press, 2011), 140–141.

10. David A. Leeming, *Creation Myths of the World: An Encyclopedia* (Santa Barbara: ABC-CLIO, 2007), 7.

11. Alfred Sohn-Rethel, *Intellectual and Manual Labor: A Critique of Epistemology* (London: Macmillan, 1978).

12. Dominick Cavallo, *Muscles and Morals: Organized Playgrounds and Urban Reform, 1880–1920* (Philadelphia: University of Pennsylvania Press, 1981); D. J. Mrozek, *Sport and American Mentality, 1880–1910* (Knoxville: University of Tennessee Press, 1983).

13. Horger, "Play by the Rules," 5.

14. Clifford Putney, *Muscular Christianity: Manhood and Sports in Protestant America, 1880–1920* (Cambridge, MA: Harvard University Press, 2001).

15. Rains and Carpenter, *James Naismith*, 26.

16. C. Howard Hopkins, *History of the Y.M.C.A. in North America* (New York: Association Press, 1951), 251–259; Putney, *Muscular Christianity*, 70.

17. James Naismith, *Rules for Basket Ball* (Springfield, MA: Springfield Printing and Binding, 1892), 3. See also Steven J. Overman, *The Protestant Ethic and the Spirit of Sport: How Calvinism and Capitalism Shaped America's Games* (Macon, GA: Mercer University Press, 2011), 160–161, 176–177.

18. Naismith, *Basketball*, 184.

19. Ibid., 184–189.

20. Thomas J. McLaughlin, *Give and Go: Basketball as a Cultural Practice* (Albany: State University of New York Press, 2008).

21. Bill Bradley, *The Values of the Game* (New York: Artisan, 1998).

22. John Wooden, *They Call Me Coach* (New York: McGraw Hill, 2004), 85–93.

23. Phil Jackson and Hugh Delehanty, *Sacred Hoops: Spiritual Lessons of a Hardwood Warrior* (New York: Hyperion, 1995); Phil Jackson and Charley Rosen, *More than a Game* (New York: Fireside, 2002).

24. Leeming, *Creation Myths of the World*, 5. Metaphors of a spiritual fall thus make their way into contemporary critiques of the sport's development: see, e.g., Harvey Araton, *When the Garden Was Eden: Clyde, the Captain, Dollar Bill and the Glory Days of the New York Knicks* (New York: HarperCollins, 2011); Harvey Araton, *Crashing the Borders: How Basketball Won the World and Lost Its Soul at Home* (New York: Free Press, 2005); Terry Pluto, *Falling From Grace: Can Pro Basketball Be Saved* (New York: Simon and Schuster, 1995).

25. For an example, see R. Scott Kretchmar, "Basketball Purists: Blind Sentimentalists or Insightful Critics?" in *Basketball and Philosophy*, ed. Jerry Walls and Gregory Bassham (Lexington: University Press of Kentucky, 2008), 31–43. For a general critique of moralizing stances on the game's styles, see McLaughlin, *Give and Go*.

26. Sigmund Freud, *The Interpretation of Dreams: The Complete and Definitive Text*, ed. and trans. James Strachey (New York: Basic, 2010), 585–604; Fredric R. Jameson, *The Political Unconscious: Narrative as a Socially Symbolic Act* (Ithaca, NY: Cornell University Press, 1981).

27. George, *Elevating the Game*, 87.

28. Quoted in Naismith, *Basketball*, 33.

29. Gerald Bruns, *Inventions: Writing, Textuality, and Understanding in Literary History* (New Haven, CT: Yale University Press, 1982), 1–13; John Muckelbauer, *The Future of Invention: Rhetoric, Postmodernism, and the Problem of Change* (Albany: State University of New York Press, 2008); Richard Toye, *Rhetoric: A Very Short Introduction* (Oxford: Oxford University Press, 2013); Eric Charles White, *Kaironomia: On the Will-to-Invent* (Ithaca, NY: Cornell University Press, 1987).

30. Naismith, *Basketball*, 38.

31. McLaughlin, *Give and Go*, 16.

32. Grissmer, *The Perfect Game*, 42–43, 55–56, 93.

33. James Naismith, "How Basketball Started and Why It Grew," in *Aims and Methods in School Athletics* (New York: Wingate Memorial Foundation, 1932), 234; Naismith, *Basketball*, 63–65. For commentary on the evolution of the dribble, see FreeDarko Collective, *FreeDarko Presents the Undisputed Guide to Pro Basketball History* (New York: Bloomsbury, 2010), 6; Horger, "Play by the Rules," 28–31; Peterson, *Cages to Jump Shots*, 26–27.

34. Leonard Koppett, *The Essence of the Game Is Deception: Thinking about Basketball* (Boston: Little, Brown, 1973), 12–17.

35. Kieran Egan, *The Educated Mind: How Cognitive Tools Shape Our Understanding* (Chicago: University of Chicago Press, 1997), 53–58.

36. Bethlehem Shoals, "Down By Law: James Naismith, the Peach-Basket Patri-arch," in FreeDarko Collective, *FreeDarko Presents the Undisputed Guide to Pro Basketball History*, 13–15.

37. Ilya Prigogine and Isabelle Stengers, *Order Out of Chaos: Man's New Dialogue with Science* (New York: Bantam, 1984); Isabelle Stengers, *Power and Invention: Situating Science*, trans. Paul Bains (Minneapolis: University of Minnesota Press, 1997).

38. D'Angour, *The Greeks and the New*, 139.

39. Homer, *The Odyssey*, trans. Robert Fagles (New York: Viking, 1996), 13:338–339.

40. Marcel Detienne and Jean-Paul Vernant, *Cunning Intelligence in Greek Culture and Society*, trans. Janet Lloyd (Atlantic Highlands, NJ: Humanities, 1978), 21; Susan Deacy, *Athena* (New York: Routledge, 2008), 7.

CHAPTER 2

Epigraph: Donald Sterling, quoted in Tim Marchman, "Donald Sterling Thinks He Owns His Players; He's Not Alone," Deadspin, April 28, 2014, http://deadspin.com/donald-sterling-thinks-he-owns-his-players-hes-not-alo-1567516088.

1. James Naismith, *Basketball: Its Origins and Development* (Lincoln: University of Nebraska Press, 1996), 110.

2. E. J. Hobsbawm, *Nations and Nationalism since 1780: Programme, Myth, Reality* (New York: Cambridge University Press, 2000).

3. Benedict Anderson, *Imagined Communities: Reflections on the Origin and Spread of Nationalism* (London: Verso, 1991).

4. Ernest Renan, *Qu'est-Ce Qu'une Nation* (Paris: Calmann Lévy, 1882), 7.

5. Homi K. Bhabha, "DissemiNation: Time, Narrative, and the Margins of the Modern Nation," in *Nation and Narration*, ed. Homi K. Bhabha (New York: Routledge, 2000), 291–322.

6. John A. Fortunato, *The Ultimate Assist: The Relationship and Broadcast Strategies of the NBA and Television Networks* (Cresskill, NJ: Hampton, 2001); Frank P. Jozsa Jr., *The National Basketball Association: Business, Organization and Strategy* (Hackensack, NJ: World Scientific, 2011); Connie Kirchberg, *Hoop Lore: A History of the National Basketball Association* (Jefferson, NC: McFarland, 2007); Leonard Koppett, *24 Seconds to Shoot: The Birth and Improbable Rise of the NBA* (New York: TOTAL/Sports Illustrated Classics, 1999); Terry Pluto, *Tall Tales: The Glory Years of the NBA, in the Words of the Men Who Played, Coached, and Built Pro Basketball* (New York: Simon and Schuster, 1992); Charley Rosen, *The First Tip-Off: The Incredible Story of the Birth of the NBA* (New York: McGraw-Hill, 2009); David Surdam, *The Rise of the National Basketball Association* (Urbana: University of Illinois Press, 2012).

7. "13 Arena Chiefs Form New Pro Basket League," *Chicago Daily Tribune*, June 7, 1946.

8. "Pro Basketball Leagues Merge," *Chicago Daily Tribune*, August 4, 1949, sec. B.

9. Mark Vancil, *The NBA at Fifty* (New York: Park Lane, 1996); emphasis added.

10. "NBA Season Recaps," *NBA*, July 4, 2013, http://www.nba.com/history/nba-season-recaps/index.html; Sam Goldpaper, "The First Game: Nov. 1, 1946: New York vs. Toronto," *NBA Encyclopedia Playoff Edition*, http://www.nba.com/history/first game_feature.html, accessed January 30, 2015.

11. Jan Hubbard, ed., *The Official NBA Encyclopedia*, 3rd ed. (New York: Doubleday, 2000).

12. Kirchberg, *Hoop Lore*, 300–301.

13. Rosen, *The First Tip-Off*.

14. Koppett, *24 Seconds to Shoot*, viii.

15. Bill Simmons, *The Book of Basketball: The NBA According to the Sports Guy* (New York: Ballantine and ESPN, 2010), 87.

16. Fortunato, *The Ultimate Assist*, 2001; Jozsa, *The National Basketball Association*; Surdam, *The Rise of the National Basketball Association*, 57.

17. Robin Deutsch and Douglas Starks, "The Roots: Early Professional Leagues," in Hubbard, *The Official NBA Encyclopedia*, 45; Haskell Cohen, "History of the National Basketball Association," in *Official National Basketball Association Guide* (St. Louis: Sporting News, 1958), 5–7.

18. Michael Schumacher, *Mr. Basketball: George Mikan, the Minneapolis Lakers, and the Birth of the NBA* (Minneapolis: University of Minnesota Press, 2008), 142.

19. "National Basketball Association," *Wikipedia*, June 14, 2014, http://en.wiki pedia.org/wiki/National_Basketball_Association.

20. Walter Benjamin, "Theses on the Philosophy of History," in Walter Benjamin, *Illuminations: Essays and Reflections*, ed. Hannah Arendt, trans. Harry Zohn (New York: Shocken, 1968), 256–257; Michel Foucault, "Nietzsche, Genealogy, History," in Michel Foucault, *Language, Counter-Memory, Practice: Selected Essays and Interviews*, trans. Daniel F. Bouchard and Sherry Simon (Ithaca, NY: Cornell University Press, 1988), 139.

21. Donald M. Fisher, "The Rochester Royals and the Transformation of Professional Basketball," *International Journal of the History of Sport* 10, no. 1 (April 1993): 20–48; Murry R. Nelson, *The National Basketball League: A History, 1935–1949* (Jefferson, NC: McFarland, 2009); Robert C. Peterson, *Cages to Jump Shots: Pro Basketball's Early Years* (Lincoln: University of Nebraska Press, 2002), 121–141.

22. Surdam, *The Rise of the National Basketball Association*, 192–193.

23. Nelson, *The National Basketball League*, 229. See also Fisher, "The Rochester Royals and the Transformation of Professional Basketball," 22; Kirchberg, *Hoop Lore*, 52.

24. Nelson, *The National Basketball League*, 6.

25. Fisher, "The Rochester Royals and the Transformation of Professional Basketball," 23; FreeDarko Collective, *FreeDarko Presents the Undisputed Guide to Pro Basketball History* (New York: Bloomsbury, 2010), 27; Kirchberg, *Hoop Lore*, 59; Koppett, *24 Seconds to Shoot*, 35; Nelson, *The National Basketball League*, 7, 225; Peterson, *Cages to Jump Shots*, 166.

26. Susan J. Rayl, "The New York Renaissance Professional Black Basketball Team, 1923–1950," Ph.D. diss., Pennsylvania State University, State College, 1996; Nelson George, *Elevating the Game: Black Men and Basketball* (Lincoln: University of Nebraska Press, 1999), 45–48.

27. Nelson, *The National Basketball League*, 1.

28. FreeDarko Collective, *FreeDarko Presents the Undisputed Guide to Pro Basketball History*, 16.

29. Albert G. Applin, "From Muscular Christianity to the Market Place: The History of Boys' and Men's Basketball in the United States, 1891–1957," Ph.D. diss., University of Massachusetts, Amherst, 1982, 32–50; Marc T. Horger, "Play by the Rules: The Creation of Basketball and the Progressive Era, 1891–1917," Ph.D. diss., Ohio State University, Columbus, 2001, 33–37; Peterson, *Cages to Jump Shots*, 28–31.

30. L. W. Allen, "Basket Ball at Hartford, Conn.," *Physical Education*, June 1894.

31. Peterson, *Cages to Jump Shots*, 32–36.

32. Horger, "Play by the Rules," 99.

33. FreeDarko Collective, *FreeDarko Presents the Undisputed Guide to Pro Basketball History*, 16.

34. Matt Moore, "More Sterling Tape: 'Do I Make the Game or Do (Blacks) Make the Game?'" *CBS Sports*, April 27, 2014, http://www.cbssports.com/nba/eye-on-basketball/24541798/extended-sterling-tape-do-i-make-the-game-or-do-blacks-make-the-game.

35. Tim Marchman, "Donald Sterling Thinks He Owns His Players; He's Not Alone," *Deadspin*, April 28, 2014, http://deadspin.com/donald-sterling-thinks-he-owns-his-players-hes-not-alo-1567516088; Dave Zirin, *Bad Sports: How Owners Are Ruining the Games We Love* (New York: New Press, 2012).

36. David West, Twitter post, April 26, 2014, https://twitter.com/D_West30/status/460199784611983361.

37. Marshall Berman, *All That Is Solid Melts into Air: The Experience of Modernity* (New York: Penguin, 1988); Stephen Kern, *The Culture of Time and Space, 1880–1918* (Cambridge, MA: Harvard University Press, 1983).

38. Robert Reach, "Basket Ball as an In-Door Game for Winter Amusement and Exercise," *Physical Education*, May 1893; "Clippings," *Physical Education*, March 1893; Greg Gubi, *The First Decade of Women's Basketball, 1892–1905: A Time Capsule of Media Reports from the Dawn of the Game* (N.p.: Lost Century of Sports Collection, 2011).

39. George C. Hepbron, "Order vs. Chaos in Basket Ball," in *Spalding's Official Basket Ball Guide* (New York: American Sports Publishing Company, 1902), 5–13.

40. Tim Elcombe, "Philosophers Can't Jump: Reflections on Living Time and Space in Basketball," in *Basketball and Philosophy*, ed. Jerry Walls and Gregory Bassham (Lex-

ington: University Press of Kentucky, 2008), 217; Yago Colás, "Getting Free: The Arts and Politics of Basketball Modernity," *Journal of Sport and Social Issues* 39.4 (August, 2015), 267-286; Thomas J. McLaughlin, *Give and Go: Basketball as a Cultural Practice* (Albany: State University of New York Press, 2008), 112.

41. Leonard Koppett, *The Essence of the Game Is Deception: Thinking about Basketball* (Boston: Little, Brown, 1973), 15.

42. Lars Anderson and Chad Millman, *Pickup Artists: Street Basketball in America* (London: Verso, 1998).

43. National Basketball Association, "Constitution and By-Laws of the National Basketball Association," 2012, 59, http://mediacentral.nba.com/media/mediacentral/ NBA-Constitution-and-By-Laws.pdf, accessed September 6, 2015.

44. David Wolf, *Foul! Connie Hawkins* (New York: Holt, Rinehart, and Winston, 1972); Bethlehem Shoals, "Missing in Action: Stokes, Hawkins, and Careers That Never Were," in FreeDarko Collective, *FreeDarko Presents The Undisputed Guide to Pro Basketball History*, 70–71.

45. David J. Leonard, *After Artest: The NBA and the Assault on Blackness* (Albany: State University of New York Press, 2012), 122–126.

46. National Basketball Association, "Constitution and By-Laws of the National Basketball Association," 53.

47. Quoted in George, Elevating the Game, 145.

CHAPTER 3

Epigraph: Bill Russell and Taylor Branch, *Second Wind: The Memoirs of an Opinionated Man* (New York: Random House, 1979), 158.

1. Chris Flink, Twitter post, November 16, 2013, https://twitter.com/cfCollision/ status/401770894671896576.

2. David K. O'Connor, "Wilt versus Russell: Excellence on the Hardwood," in *Basketball and Philosophy*, ed. Jerry Walls and Gregory Bassham (Lexington: University Press of Kentucky, 2008), 128.

3. Bill Simmons, *The Book of Basketball: The NBA According to the Sports Guy* (New York: Ballantine and ESPN, 2010), 59.

4. Ibid., 585.

5. Ibid., 584.

6. Thomas Aquinas, *Summa Theologica*, accessed February 2, 2015, http://www .basilica.org/pages/ebooks/St.%20Thomas%20Aquinas-Summa%20Theologica.pdf; René Descartes, *Discourse on Method and Meditations on First Philosophy*, trans. Donald A. Cress (Indianapolis: Hackett, 1980); Plato, "Phaedo," in *Plato: Collected Dialogues*, ed. Edith Hamilton and Huntington Cairns, trans. Hugh Tredennick (Princeton, NJ: Princeton University Press, 2009), 40–98; Plato, "Republic," in Hamilton and Cairns, *Plato*, 575–844.

7. Thomas McLaughlin, *Give and Go: Basketball as a Cultural Practice* (Albany: State University of New York Press, 2008), 183.

8. Jimmy Breslin, "Can Basketball Survive Wilt Chamberlain?" *Saturday Evening Post*, December 1, 1956; "Sport: Wilt the Stilt," *Time*, December 12, 1955; Jeremiah Tax, "Here Comes the Big Fellow at Last," *Sports Illustrated*, October 26, 1959, http:// www.si.com/vault/1959/10/26/598614/here-comes-the-big-fellow-at-last; Barry

Gotteherer, "When Wilt and Russell Meet," *Sport*, March 1960; John Taylor, *The Rivalry: Bill Russell, Wilt Chamberlain and the Golden Age of Basketball* (New York: Ballantine, 2006), 8–9.

9. Leonard Koppett, *24 Seconds to Shoot: The Birth and Improbable Rise of the NBA* (New York: TOTAL/Sports Illustrated Classics, 1999), 153–154; Taylor, *The Rivalry*, 5–6, 64–65, 208–210, 330.

10. Taylor, *The Rivalry*, 7, 83, 121–122, 170.

11. Ibid., 141, 246.

12. Ibid., 42, 87, 89, 99, 144, 192, 208–210.

13. Gregory J. Kaliss, "A Precarious Perch: Wilt Chamberlain, Basketball Stardom, and Racial Politics," in *Fame to Infamy: Race, Sport, and the Fall from Grace*, ed. David C. Ogden and Joel Nathan Rosen (Jackson: University Press of Mississippi, 2010), 152–153.

14. Taylor, *The Rivalry*, 129, 235, 238–243.

15. Ibid., 111.

16. Ibid., 144, 239–243, 319; Simmons, *The Book of Basketball*, 80–83.

17. Bethlehem Shoals, "The Nuclear Option: Wilt Chamberlain, the Man Who Went Too Far," in FreeDarko Collective, *FreeDarko Presents The Undisputed Guide to Pro Basketball History* (New York: Bloomsbury, 2010), 49–50.

18. O'Connor, "Wilt versus Russell," 118–121, 126–127.

19. Kieran Egan, *The Educated Mind: How Cognitive Tools Shape Our Understanding* (Chicago: University of Chicago Press, 1997), 40.

20. Albert G. Applin, "From Muscular Christianity to the Market Place: The History of Boys' and Men's Basketball in the United States, 1891–1957," Ph.D. diss., University of Massachusetts, Amherst, 1982, 262–272.

21. Ibid., 268; "North-South All-Star Game and the Chuck Taylor All-Star Team," *Big Blue History*, accessed February 2, 2015, http://www.bigbluehistory.net/bb/north-south_frame.html.

22. "NBA and ABA Career Leaders and Records for Win Shares per 48 Minutes," *Basketball-Reference*, accessed February 2, 2015, http://www.basketball-reference.com/leaders/ws_per_48_career.html; "NBA and ABA Career Leaders and Records for Player Efficiency Rating," *Basketball-Reference*, accessed February 2, 2015, http://www.basketball-reference.com/leaders/per_career.html.

23. Claude Johnson, *Black Fives: The Alpha Physical Culture Club's Pioneering African-American Basketball Team* (New York: Black Fives, 2012), 34–36; Susan J. Rayl, "The New York Renaissance Professional Black Basketball Team, 1923–1950," Ph.D. diss., Pennsylvania State University, State College, 1996, 11–17.

24. Rayl, "The New York Renaissance Professional Black Basketball Team," 25–64.

25. Nelson George, *Elevating the Game: Black Men and Basketball* (Lincoln: University of Nebraska Press, 1999), 36–37.

26. Ibid., 87. See also Milton S. Katz, *Breaking Through: John B. McLendon, Basketball Legend and Civil Rights Pioneer* (Little Rock: University of Arkansas Press, 2010), 29.

27. Arthur Ashe, *A Hard Road to Glory: A History of the African-American Athlete, 1919–1945* (New York: Warner, 1988), 49; George, *Elevating the Game*, 71–81; Gary Sailes, "An Examination of Basketball Performance among African American Males," *Journal of African-American Men* 1, no. 4 (1996): 37–46.

28. George, *Elevating the Game*, 42, 44–51; Ashe, *A Hard Road to Glory*, 50–52.

29. Robert C. Peterson, *Cages to Jump Shots: Pro Basketball's Early Years* (Lincoln: University of Nebraska Press, 2002), 109.

30. David Surdam, *The Rise of the National Basketball Association* (Urbana: University of Illinois Press, 2012), 84–85; Koppett, *24 Seconds to Shoot*, 40–41.

31. Ron Thomas, *They Cleared the Lane: The NBA's Black Pioneers* (Lincoln: University of Nebraska Press, 2002), 3.

32. Terry Pluto, *Tall Tales: The Glory Years of the NBA, in the Words of the Men Who Played, Coached, and Built Pro Basketball* (New York: Simon and Schuster, 1992), 75–79; Gary Pomerantz, *Wilt, 1962: The Night of 100 Points and the Dawn of a New Era* (New York: Three Rivers, 2005), 9, 53, 204; Surdam, *The Rise of the National Basketball Association*, 82–83; Taylor, *The Rivalry*, 109–110, 261–262.

33. Aram Goudsouzian, *King of the Court: Bill Russell and the Basketball Revolution* (Berkeley: University of California Press, 2010), 155.

34. Bill Russell, *Go Up for Glory* (New York: Berkley, 1966), 73.

35. Wayne Embry, *The Inside Game: Race, Power, and Politics in the NBA* (Akron: University of Akron Press, 2004), 161; A. L. Hardman, "Baylor's Refusal to Play Here Brings ABC Protest," *Charleston Gazette-Mail*, January 18, 1959, http://www.wvculture.org/history/africanamericans/baylor03.html; Pluto, *Tall Tales*, 71–75; Karen Russell, "Growing Up with Privilege and Prejudice," *New York Times Magazine*, June 14, 1987.

36. Goudsouzian, *King of the Court*; Gotteherer, "When Wilt and Russell Meet"; Pomerantz, *Wilt, 1962*, 50–55; Taylor, *The Rivalry*, 11–12.

37. "Art on the Court," *Sports Illustrated*, December 9, 1957, http://sportsillustrated.cnn.com/vault/articlemaga/MAG1132873/index.htm.

38. John McPhee, *A Sense of Where You Are: Bill Bradley at Princeton* (New York: Farrar, Straus and Giroux, 1999), 6; "Sport: Little Man, What Now?" *Time*, February 22, 1960.

39. Breslin, "Can Basketball Survive Wilt Chamberlain?" 104; "Notes on College Sports: Dominance of Big Men Ruining Basketball as Team Game, Utah Coach Declares," *New York Times*, December 28, 1956; Jimmy Jemail, "The Question," *Sports Illustrated*, December 21, 1959, http://sportsillustrated.cnn.com/vault/article/MAG1133916/index.htm.

40. Pomerantz, *Wilt, 1962*, 55.

41. Michael Novak, *The Joy of Sports: End Zones, Bases, Baskets, Balls, and the Consecration of the American Spirit* (New York: Basic, 1976), 109–110.

42. Glyn Hughes, "Managing Black Guys: Representation, Corporate Culture, and the NBA," *Sociology of Sport Journal* 21 (2004): 164.

43. Wilt Chamberlain and David Shaw, *Wilt: Just like Any Other Seven-Foot Black Millionaire Who Lives Next Door* (New York: Macmillan, 1973), 162; Taylor, *The Rivalry*, 222, but also 193–197, 202, 261–264, 279, 322.

44. Goudsouzian, *King of the Court*, 214–215.

45. Chamberlain and Shaw, *Wilt*, 110.

46. Wilt Chamberlain Archive, "Bill Russell Ran All 5 Positions on Offense," video file, YouTube, June 24, 2013, https://www.youtube.com/watch?v=SF22xiRxHv8; Jaranarm, "Wilt Chamberlain—Block Party," video file, *YouTube*, October 13, 2012, https://www.youtube.com/watch?v=splnUR-52jM.

47. Yago Colás, "Bill Simmons Is Wrong! (but Also . . .) On Russell and Chamberlain's Supporting Casts," *Between the Lines*, July 15, 2014, http://yagocolas.com/2014/07/15/bill-simmons-is-wrong-but-also-on-russell-and-chamberlains-supporting-casts.

48. Pluto, *Tall Tales*, 330–349; Goudsouzian, *King of the Court*, 113–115; Koppett, *24 Seconds to Shoot*, 151–152, 161–162, 180–183; Bob Ryan, "The Incomparable Wilt Chamberlain," *Total Basketball* (Toronto: Sport Media Publishing, 2003); Shoals, "The Nuclear Option"; Bethlehem Shoals, "Pride of the Celtics: Bill Russell and the Price of Winning," in FreeDarko Collective, *FreeDarko Presents the Undisputed Guide to Pro Basketball History*, 41–45; Zachariah Blott, "Giving Bill Russell's Offense Its Proper Due," *Behind the Basket*, November 16, 2011, http://www.behindthebasket.com/btb/2011/11/16/giving-bill-russells-offense-its-proper-due.html; Will Clapton, "The Best Defensive Centers of All Time," *Basketball Journalist*, August 21, 2011, http://basketballjournalist.blogspot.com/2011/08/best-defensive-centers-of-all-time.html.

49. Dave Hickey, "The Heresy of Zone Defense," in *Air Guitar: Essays on Art and Democracy* (Los Angeles: Art Issues Press, 1997), 155.

50. Ibid., 155–156.

51. Nicholas Dixon, "On Winning and Athletic Superiority," *Journal of the Philosophy of Sport*, no. 11 (1999): 10–26.

52. Stephen Mumford, *Watching Sport: Aesthetics, Ethics and Emotion* (New York: Routledge, 2012), 11–12; Bethlehem Shoals, "Somewhere between Winning and Losing," Good Men Project, February 1, 2011, http://goodmenproject.com/featured-content/somewhere-between-winning-and-losing.

53. Peter May, "Russell Mourns Loss of Friend and Foe," *Boston Globe*, October 14, 1999.

CHAPTER 4

Epigraph: Bethlehem Shoals, "The Get Along Gang: Why Everybody Loves the New York Knicks," in FreeDarko Collective, *FreeDarko Presents the Undisputed Guide to Pro Basketball History* (New York: Bloomsbury, 2010), 80.

1. Thomas Rogers, "Fans Take Sting Out of Knicks Defeat," *New York Times*, April 20, 1969.

2. "Knicks Look to a New Season and Start of Dynasty," *New York Times*, April 19, 1969; Nelson George, *Elevating the Game: Black Men and Basketball* (Lincoln: University of Nebraska Press, 1999), 174.

3. George, *Elevating the Game*, 174–175; J. Gabriel Boylan, "The Knickerbookers: From Hard Court to Hard Cover," in FreeDarko Collective, *FreeDarko Presents the Undisputed Guide to Pro Basketball History* 81–82.

4. Harvey Araton, *When the Garden Was Eden: Clyde, the Captain, Dollar Bill and the Glory Days of the New York Knicks* (New York: HarperCollins, 2011), 25.

5. R. Scott Kretchmar, "Basketball Purists: Blind Sentimentalists or Insightful Critics?" in *Basketball and Philosophy: Thinking Outside the Paint*, ed. Jerry Walls and Gregory Bassham (Lexington: University Press of Kentucky, 2008), 31–43.

6. Pete Axthelm, *The City Game* (New York: Pocket Books, 1971), 18–27; Frank Deford, "In for Two plus the Title," *Sports Illustrated*, May 18, 1970, http://www.si.com/vault/1970/05/18/611328/in-for-two-plus-the-title.

7. Stanley Cohen, *The Game They Played* (New York: Carroll and Graf, 1977); Axthelm, *The City Game*, 22–23.

8. Leonard Koppett, "Transition of a Team," *New York Times*, February 11, 1969; Phil Berger, *Miracle on 33rd Street: The New York Knickerbockers' Championship Season, 1969–1970* (New York: Contemporary, 1994), 3–6; Axthelm, *The City Game*, 26–28.

9. Leonard Koppett, "Knicks' Five-Year Rebuilding Program Has Blossomed into 'Sudden' Success," *New York Times*, November 2, 1969, sec. S; Lewis Cole, *Dream Team: The Candid Story of the Champion 1969–1970 Knicks—Their Collective Triumphs and Individual Fates* (New York: William Morrow, 1981), 73–91; Axthelm, *The City Game*, 28–32; Araton, *When the Garden Was Eden*, 25–90.

10. Cole, *Dream Team*, 133.

11. Ibid., 35. For other examples, see Araton, *When the Garden Was Eden*, 34; Frank Deford, "The Knicks Drive in High," *Sports Illustrated*, April 27, 1970, http://www.si.com/vault/1970/04/27/the-knicks-drive-in-high; Deford, "In for Two plus the Title"; Jerry Kirshenbaum, "Overdue Winner in New York," *Sports Illustrated*, December 8, 1969, http://www.si.com/vault/1969/12/08/611305/overdue-winner-in-new-york; Koppett, "Transition of a Team"; Leonard Koppett, "'Textbook' Knicks Play Royals Here," *New York Times*, December 9, 1969; Robert Lipsyte, "Nate the Great and Friends," *New York Times*, November 3, 1969; Lawrence Shainberg, "In a Game of Individuals, They Are a Community," *New York Times Magazine*, January 25, 1970.

12. Deford, "In for Two plus the Title."

13. Araton, *When the Garden Was Eden*, 53–66, 101; Axthelm, *The City Game*; Shainberg, "In a Game of Individuals, They Are a Community"; Bethlehem Shoals, "The Get Along Gang: Why Everybody Loves the New York Knicks," in FreeDarko Collective, *FreeDarko Presents the Undisputed Guide to Pro Basketball History*, 74–80.

14. Milton Gross, "Pearl in NY! 'I'd Go in a Minute,'" *Boston Globe*, October 28, 1970; "Monroe Dealt to Knicks," *Washington Post*, November 12, 1971; "Earl Monroe: A Spectacular Shooter and a Master Showman," *New York Times*, November 14, 1971; Shoals, "The Get Along Gang," 79–80; Douglas Warshaw, "BackTalk: When Stars Collide in New York," *New York Times*, March 7, 2004; Earl Monroe, *Earl the Pearl: My Story* (New York: Rodale, 2013), 293, 297–305.

15. Dave Anderson, "From the Subway to Success," *New York Times*, May 13, 1973, sec. S; Araton, *When the Garden Was Eden*, 262–263, 273–290; Leonard Koppett, "Knicks' Perfect Championship Blend: Teamwork and Poise under Pressure," *New York Times*, May 12, 1973; Leonard Koppett, "One More For The Knicks," *New York Times*, May 13, 1973, sec. S.

16. George, *Elevating the Game*, 174.

17. Araton, *When the Garden Was Eden*, 295.

18. Fredric Jameson, *Archaeologies of the Future: The Desire Called Utopia and Other Science Fictions* (London: Verso, 2007).

19. Leonard Koppett, *24 Seconds to Shoot: The Birth and Improbable Rise of the NBA* (New York: TOTAL/Sports Illustrated Classics, 1999), 218.

20. Ibid.

21. Neil Isaacs, *All the Moves: A History of College Basketball*, Revised and Updated (New York: Harper Colophon, 1984), 76–101.

22. George, *Elevating the Game*, 75.

23. Shoals, "The Get Along Gang," 74.

24. Araton, *When the Garden Was Eden*, 55.

25. Amy Bass, *Not the Triumph but the Struggle: The 1968 Olympics and the Making of the Black Athlete* (Minneapolis: University of Minnesota Press, 2002); David K. Wiggins, *Glory Bound: Black Athletes in White America* (Syracuse, NY: Syracuse University Press, 1997), 104–122; Dave Zirin, *What's My Name, Fool? Sports and Resistance in the United States* (Chicago: Haymarket, 2005), 53–100.

26. Araton, *When the Garden Was Eden*, 60.

27. Ibid., 60–61.

28. Ibid., 63; Axthelm, *The City Game*, 85.

29. Araton, *When the Garden Was Eden*, 61.

30. Ibid., 127–132.

31. Ibid., 12–13. See also, Cole, *Dream Team*, 315–317.

32. Ibid., 57–59.

33. Ibid., 59.

34. Aram Goudsouzian, *King of the Court: Bill Russell and the Basketball Revolution* (Berkeley: University of California Press, 2010), 136–138, 152–160, 214–215, 220–222.

35. Julius Erving, *Dr. J: The Autobiography* (New York: Harper, 2013), 79; Lyle Spencer, "NBA at 50: The Greatest in History," in *The Official NBA Encyclopedia*, ed. Jan Hubbard (New York: Doubleday, 2000), 232–233; Bethlehem Shoals, "Three on a Match: Elgin Baylor, Jerry West, and Oscar Robertson," in FreeDarko Collective, *FreeDarko Presents The Undisputed Guide to Pro Basketball History*, 53–54.

36. Kretchmar, "Basketball Purists," 40.

37. Aram Goudsouzian, "'Can Basketball Survive Chamberlain?' The Kansas Years of Wilt the Stilt," *Kansas History* 28 (Autumn 2005): 160.

38. David W. Houck, "Attacking the Rim: The Cultural Politics of Dunking," in *Basketball Jones: America above the Rim*, ed. Todd Boyd and Kenneth L. Shropshire (New York: New York University Press, 2000), 151–169.

39. Terry Pluto, *Loose Balls: The Short, Wild Life of the American Basketball Association* (New York: Simon and Schuster, 1990); *Long Shots: The Life and Times of the American Basketball Association*, documentary, HBO Films, 1997; Terry Pluto, "American Basketball Association, 1967–1976," in *Total Basketball* (Toronto: Sport Media Publishing, 2003); John Gardella, "Red, White and Blue: The Colorful ABA," in Hubbard, *The Official NBA Encyclopedia*; George, *Elevating the Game*, 179–185; Bethlehem Shoals, "Notes from the Underground: What the Hell Was the ABA," in FreeDarko Collective, *FreeDarko Presents the Undisputed Guide to Pro Basketball History*, 111–117; Bill Simmons, *The Book of Basketball: The NBA According to the Sports Guy* (New York: Ballantine and ESPN, 2010), 111–117.

40. Bethlehem Shoals, "Choose Your Weapon: Larry Bird, Magic Johnson, and the Real Merger," in FreeDarko Collective, *FreeDarko Presents the Undisputed Guide to Pro Basketball History*, 113.

41. Pluto, *Loose Balls*, 26.

42. Ibid.

43. Erving, *Dr. J*, 292–293.

44. Todd Boyd, *Young, Black, Rich, and Famous: The Rise of the NBA, the Hip Hop Invasion, and the Transformation of American Culture* (Lincoln: University of Nebraska Press, 2008), 98; George, *Elevating the Game*, 185; Shoals, "Notes from the Underground," 88.

45. George, *Elevating the Game*, 180–181.
46. Erving, *Dr. J*, 292.
47. Axthelm, *The City Game*, 115.
48. Gardella, "Red, White and Blue," 62–63.
49. Shoals, "Notes from the Underground," 83, 86–87.
50. Bill Bradley, *The Values of the Game* (New York: Artisan, 1998), 148.
51. Pluto, "American Basketball Association," 442.
52. George, *Elevating the Game*, 176.
53. Monroe, *Earl the Pearl*, 361.

CHAPTER 5

Epigraph: Larry Bird and Earvin Magic Johnson with Jackie MacMullan, *When the Game Was Ours* (Boston: Mariner, 2010), 308.
1. Seth Davis, *When March Went Mad: The Game That Transformed Basketball* (New York: Holt, 2010), 4.
2. Bill Gorman, "NBA Finals TV Ratings, 1974–2008," TV by the Numbers, May 22, 2009, http://tvbythenumbers.zap2it.com/2009/05/22/nba-finals-tv-ratings-1974–2008/19324.
3. Alan Hahn, *New York Knicks: The Complete Illustrated History* (New York: MBI, 2012), 117; Nelson George, "All Eyez on Spre," *Village Voice*, February 9, 1999, 40.
4. Arthur Ashe, *A Hard Road to Glory: A History of the African-American Athlete, since 1946* (New York: Amistad, 1993), 68; Bird and Johnson, *When the Game Was Ours*, 79, 94–96; Steve Cady, "Basketball's Image Crisis," *New York Times*, August 11, 1979; Davis, *When March Went Mad*, 138–139; John Feinstein, *The Punch: One Night, Two Lives, and the Fight That Changed Basketball Forever* (Boston: Little, Brown, 2002), xi; John A. Fortunato, *The Ultimate Assist: The Relationship and Broadcast Strategies of the NBA and Television Networks* (Cresskill, NJ: Hampton, 2001), 25; David Halberstam, *Playing for Keeps: Michael Jordan and the World He Made* (New York: Random House, 1999), 115–116; David Halberstam, *The Breaks of the Game* (New York: Hyperion, 2009), 13–14; Lee Daniel Levine, *Bird: The Making of an American Sports Legend* (New York: McGraw-Hill, 1988), 198–200; Scott Ostler, "NBA, like Walton, Tries a Comeback," *Los Angeles Times*, October 10, 1979, sec. B; Bill Simmons, *The Book of Basketball: The NBA According to the Sports Guy* (New York: Ballantine and ESPN, 2010), 130–137. For critiques of this consensus and alternative accounts, see Todd Boyd, *Young, Black, Rich, and Famous: The Rise of the NBA, the Hip Hop Invasion, and the Transformation of American Culture* (Lincoln: University of Nebraska Press, 2008)), 30–43; Matthew Schneider-Mayerson, "'Too Black': Race in the 'Dark Ages' of the National Basketball Association," *International Journal of Sport and Society* 1, no. 1 (2010): 223–233; Tom Ziller, "Punch-Dunk Lovetron: The NBA's Lost Years Reconsidered," in FreeDarko Collective, *FreeDarko Presents the Undisputed Guide to Pro Basketball History* (New York: Bloomsbury, 2010), 99–103.
5. Mike Granberry, "Clippers Are a Player Away," *Los Angeles Times*, October 14, 1979.
6. Kareem Abdul-Jabbar, *Giant Steps: The Autobiography of Kareem Abdul-Jabbar* (New York: Bantam, 1983), 314.
7. Earvin "Magic" Johnson, *My Life* (New York: Fawcett, 1992), 108–109.
8. Bob Ryan, "Bird Does Job," *Boston Globe*, October 13, 1979.

9. David DuPree, "Boston 'Pro Fans' Welcome Back Celtics Who Hustle," *Washington Post*, October 21, 1979.

10. Larry Bird, *Drive: The Story of My Life* (New York: Bantam, 1989), 80; DuPree, "Boston 'Pro Fans' Welcome Back Celtics Who Hustle"; Bob Ryan, "'New' Celtics Rout Cavaliers," *Boston Globe*, October 14, 1979.

11. Bird and Johnson, *When the Game Was Ours*, 79.

12. Bob Logan, "Spotlight Is on Individual Stars," *Chicago Tribune*, October 5, 1979.

13. Bob Ryan, "LA Agog over Bird versus Magic," *Boston Globe*, December 29, 1979.

14. Bob Ryan, "The Two and Only," *Sports Illustrated*, December 14, 1991.

15. Ibid.

16. Doris Sommer, *Foundational Fictions: The National Romances of Latin America* (Berkeley: University of California Press, 1991).

17. Jere Longman, "NBA's Biggest Rivals Really Pals," *Chicago Tribune*, June 8, 1987, 9; Mark Whicker, "Bird, Johnson Take Seven-Year Rivalry to MTV," *Houston Chronicle*, February 16, 1986, 6; Bird, *Drive*, 188; Bird and Johnson, *When the Game Was Ours*, 278; Johnson, *My Life*, 222–225; Hank Hersch and Mark Bechtel, *Classic Rivalries: The Most Memorable Matchups in Sports History* (New York: Sports Illustrated Books, 2003); Ezra Edelman, *Magic and Bird: A Courtship of Rivals*, documentary, HBO Films, 2010; "Magic/Bird," 2012, http://www.broadway.com/shows/magicbird.

18. Johnson, *My Life*, 223.

19. Bird and Johnson, *When the Game Was Ours*, 239.

20. Ibid., 278; Johnson, My Life, 354; Jack McCallum, *Dream Team: How Michael, Magic, Larry, Charles, and the Greatest Team of All Time Conquered the World and Changed the Game of Basketball Forever* (New York: Ballantine, 2012).

21. "Earvin Johnson Seeks a Trade," *New York Times*, November 19, 1981, sec. B.

22. Randy Harvey, "Just Call Him Earvin Johnson," *Los Angeles Times*, November 24, 1981, sec. D; Jim Murray, "Whatever Magic Wants, He Gets," *Los Angeles Times*, November 24, 1981, sec. D; George Vecsey, "Sports of the Times: A Power Play, Off the Court," *New York Times*, November 21, 1981, http://www.nytimes.com/1981/11/21/sports/sports-of-the-times-a-power-play-off-the-court.html.

23. D. Stanley Eitzen, "The Sociology of Amateur Sport: An Overview," *International Review for the Sociology of Sport* 24 (1989): 97.

24. Ibid.

25. Allen Guttman, *From Ritual to Record: The Nature of Modern Sports* (New York: Columbia University Press, 2004), 31.

26. Dave Anderson, "Sports of the Times: Another Coach Is an Undercut Victim," *New York Times*, November 22, 1981, http://www.nytimes.com/1981/11/22/sports/sports-of-the-times-another-coach-is-an-undercut-victim.html; Harvey, "Just Call Him Earvin Johnson."

27. Scott Ostler, "Magic Touch," *Los Angeles Times*, December 3, 1981, sec. G.

28. Harvey, "Just Call Him Earvin Johnson"; "Readers Write: The Magic Has All But Disappeared," *Los Angeles Times*, November 25, 1981, sec. D.

29. Bob Ryan, "Pistons Give Bird New Tag—Overrated," *Fort Lauderdale Sun Sentinel*, May 31, 1987, http://articles.sun-sentinel.com/1987-05-31/sports/8702190443_1_dennis-rodman-kevin-mchale-bleep-danny-ainge.

30. Jeffrey Lane, *Under the Boards: The Cultural Revolution in Basketball* (Lincoln: University of Nebraska Press, 2007), 142–143; Boyd, *Young, Black, Rich, and Famous*,

45–69; Nelson George, *Elevating the Game: Black Men and Basketball* (Lincoln: University of Nebraska Press, 1999), 222–225; Dennis Rodman, *Bad As I Wanna Be* (New York: Delacorte, 1996), 131–133; David L. Andrews and Michael L. Silk, "Basketball's Ghettocentric Logic," *American Behavioral Scientist* 53, no. 11 (2010): 1629.

31. Ira Berkow, "Sports of the Times: The Coloring of Bird," *New York Times*, June 2, 1987, http://www.nytimes.com/1987/06/02/sports/sports-of-the-times-the-coloring-of-bird.html.

32. Bird and Johnson, *When the Game Was Ours*, 89.

33. Ibid., 216–217; Levine, *Bird*, 317; Bird, *Drive*, 184–186; Johnson, *My Life*, 229–230; Scott Ostler, "Those Unfortunate Remarks about Larry Bird Just Don't Fly," *Los Angeles Times*, June 1, 1987, http://articles.latimes.com/1987-06-01/sports/sp-5447_1_dennis-rodman.

34. Bethlehem Shoals, "Choose Your Weapon: Larry Bird, Magic Johnson and the Real Merger," in FreeDarko Collective, *FreeDarko Presents the Undisputed Guide to Pro Basketball History* (New York: Bloomsbury, 2010), 113.

35. Greg Bach and National Alliance for Youth Sports, *Coaching Basketball for Dummies* (Hoboken, NJ: John Wiley, 2007), 137–138.

36. Boyd, *Young, Black, Rich, and Famous*, 100.

37. Leonard Koppett, *The Essence of the Game Is Deception: Thinking about Basketball* (Boston: Little, Brown, 1973), 21.

38. Simmons, *The Book of Basketball*, 17.

39. Herbert Simons, "Race and Penalized Sports Behaviors," *International Review for the Sociology of Sport* 38, no. 1 (2003): esp. 10–14; George, *Elevating the Game*, 119–132; Boyd, *Young, Black, Rich, and Famous*, 141.

40. Lane, *Under the Boards*, 138–139.

41. Boyd, *Young, Black, Rich, and Famous*, 99.

42. Bethlehem Shoals, "Sweet Fields of Unfastened Terrain," *McSweeney's*, October 12, 2006, http://www.mcsweeneys.net/articles/sweet-fields-of-unfastened-terrain.

CHAPTER 6

Epigraph: "Michael Jordan Biography," NBA.com, http://www.nba.com/history/players/jordan_bio.html, accessed September 11, 2015.

1. Bethlehem Shoals, "The Invention of Air: The Brash, Brilliant Doodles of a Young Jordan," in FreeDarko Collective, *FreeDarko Presents the Undisputed Guide to Pro Basketball History* (New York: Bloomsbury, 2010), 119.

2. OfficialHoophall, "Michael Jordan's Basketball Hall of Fame Enshrinement Speech," YouTube, February 21, 2012, https://www.youtube.com/watch?v=XLzBMGXfK4c.

3. Roland Lazenby, *Michael Jordan: The Life* (Boston: Little, Brown, 2014), 423.

4. Phil Jackson and Hugh Delehanty, *Sacred Hoops: Spiritual Lessons of Hardwood Warrior* (New York: Hyperion, 1995), 89.

5. Lazenby, *Michael Jordan*, 423.

6. Ibid., 435–436; Bob Greene, *Hang Time: Days and Nights with Michael Jordan* (New York: Doubleday, 1992), 256; David Porter, *Michael Jordan: A Biography* (Westport, CT: Greenwood, 2007), 67–68; Sam Smith, *The Jordan Rules* (New York: Pocket Books, 1994), 348.

7. Shoals, "The Invention of Air," 119.

8. Chris Baldick, *Oxford Concise Dictionary of Literary Terms* (New York: Oxford University Press, 2001), 27.

9. Yago Colás, "Michael Jordan and the *Bildungsroman* Index (BRI)," *Between the Lines*, October 1, 2014, http://yagocolas.com/2014/10/01/michael-jordan-and-the-bildungsroman-index-bri.

10. "Collector's Issue: The Greatest Ever," *Newsweek*, November 1993; Michael Hoechsmann, "Just Do It: What Michael Jordan Has to Teach Us," in *Michael Jordan, Inc.: Corporate Sport, Media Culture and Late Modern America*, ed. David L. Andrews (Albany: State University of New York Press, 2001), 269; Fred Kriger, "A Night to Remember," ESPN, June 11, 1997, https://espn.go.com/sportscentury/features/00242495.html; Jackie MacMullan, "Chicago Bulls," *The Official NBA Encyclopedia*, ed. Jan Hubbard (New York: Doubleday, 2000), 81; William C. Rhoden, *Forty Million Dollar Slaves: The Rise, Fall, and Redemption of the Black Athlete* (New York: Random House, 2006), 198; Bill Simmons, *The Book of Basketball: The NBA According to the Sports Guy* (New York: Ballantine and ESPN, 2010), 165; Art Thiel, "Michael Jordan: Modern-Day Icon," *The Official NBA Encyclopedia*, ed. Jan Hubbard (New York: Doubleday, 2000), 21; Pat Williams, *How to Be like Mike: Life Lessons about Basketball's Best* (Deerfield Beach, FL: HCI, 2001).

11. Greene, *Hang Time*.

12. Michael Jordan, *For the Love of the Game*, ed. Mark Vancil (New York: Crown, 1998), 63.

13. Thomas McLaughlin, *Give and Go: Basketball as a Cultural Practice* (Albany: State University of New York Press, 2008), 42.

14. David Harvey, *A Brief History of Neoliberalism* (New York: Oxford University Press, 2007); Robin D. G. Kelley, *Yo' Mama's Disfunktional! Fighting the Culture Wars in Urban America* (Boston: Beacon, 1997).

15. Andrews, *Michael Jordan, Inc.*; Loïc Wacquant, *Urban Outcasts: A Comparative Sociology of Advanced Marginality* (London: Polity, 2007).

16. David L. Andrews, Ronald L. Mower, and Michael L. Silk, "Ghettocentrism and the Essentialized Black Male Athlete," in *Commodified and Criminalized: New Racism and African-Americans in Contemporary Sports* (New York: Rowman and Littlefield, 2010), 73.

17. Michael Omi and Howard Winant, *Racial Formation in the United States from the 1960s to the 1990s* (New York: Routledge, 1994), 125–136.

18. David L. Andrews, "The Fact(s) of Michael Jordan's Blackness: Excavating a Floating Racial Signifier," *Sociology of Sport Journal* 13 (1996): 113–119; C. L. Cole, "Nike's America/America's Michael Jordan," in Andrews, *Michael Jordan, Inc.*, 65–103.

19. Walter LaFeber, *Michael Jordan and the New Global Capitalism* (New York: W. W. Norton, 2002).

20. Andrews, "The Fact(s) of Michael Jordan's Blackness," 119–130.

21. Francis Fukuyama, *The End of History and the Last Man* (New York: Free Press, 1992), xi.

22. Ibid., 51.

23. James Atlas, "What Is Fukuyama Saying? And to Whom Is He Saying It?" *New York Times Magazine*, October 22, 1989.

24. Fukuyama, *The End of History and the Last Man*, 307.

25. "Google Books Ngram Viewer," https://books.google.com/ngrams/graph?content=greatest+basketball+player+ever&year_start=1800&year_end=2000&corpus=15&smoothing=3&share=&direct_url=t1%3B%2Cgreatest%20basketball%20player%20ever%3B%2Cc0.

26. Frank P. Jozsa Jr., *The National Basketball Association: Business, Organization and Strategy* (Hackensack, NJ: World Scientific, 2011), 230.

27. National Basketball Association, "Michael Jordan Highlights from Early in His Career," YouTube, September 3, 2009, https://www.youtube.com/watch?v=MC3vanBCDmE.

28. Shoals, "The Invention of Air," 122.

29. Ibid.

30. Eric Charles White, *Kaironomia: On the Will-to-Invent* (Ithaca, NY: Cornell University Press, 1987), 13.

31. For a critique, see Jacques Derrida, *Specters of Marx: The State of the Debt, the Work of Mourning, and the New International*, trans. Peggy Kamuf (New York: Routledge, 1994), 56–75.

32. Michael Hardt and Antonio Negri, *Empire* (Cambridge, MA: Harvard University Press, 2000).

33. Ibid., 393–411.

34. Antonio Negri, *Time for Revolution*, trans. Matteo Mandarini (London: Bloomsbury, 2013), 165.

CHAPTER 7

Epigraph: Michael Wilbon, "There's No Dressing Up Bad Attitudes," *Washington Post*, October 15, 2005, http://www.washingtonpost.com/wp-dyn/content/article/2005/10/14/AR2005101402133.html, accessed September 11, 2015.

1. Jeffrey Lane, *Under the Boards: The Cultural Revolution in Basketball* (Lincoln: University of Nebraska Press, 2007), 36.

2. David Andrews, Mower, and Michael Silk, "Ghettocentrism and the Essentialized Black Male Athlete," in *Commodified and Criminalized: New Racism and African-Americans in Contemporary Sports* (New York: Rowman and Littlefield, 2010), 69–93; David Andrews and Michael Silk, "Basketball's Ghettocentric Logic," *American Behavioral Scientist* 53, no. 11 (2010): 1626–1644; Todd Boyd, *Young, Black, Rich, and Famous: The Rise of the NBA, the Hip Hop Invasion, and the Transformation of American Culture* (Lincoln: University of Nebraska Press, 2008), 154–156; David J. Leonard, *After Artest: The NBA and the Assault on Blackness* (Albany: State University of New York Press, 2012); Larry Platt, *Only the Strong Survive: The Odyssey of Allen Iverson* (New York: Harper, 2003), 118–119.

3. William James, "Pragmatism," in *Writings, 1902–1910*, ed. Bruce Kuklick (New York: Library of America, 1987), 524.

4. Terry Armour, "Bulls 108, 76ers 104: Iverson Wins the Battle, but Bulls Take the War," *Chicago Tribune*, March 13, 1997; Raad Cawthon, "Sixers Lose, but Put Up a Fight[;] Bulls Barely Escape; Iverson Gets 37 Points," *Philadelphia Inquirer*, March 13, 1997, sec. E.

5. Kathryn T. Stofer, James R. Schaffer, and Brian A. Rosenthal, *Sports Journalism: An Introduction to Reporting and Writing* (Lanham, MD: Rowman and Littlefield, 2010),

146; Steve Craig, *Sports Writing: A Beginner's Guide* (Shoreham, VT: Discover Writing Press, 2002), 62; Joe Gisondi, *Field Guide to Covering Sports* (Washington, D.C.: CQ Press, 2011), 12.

6. "Bulls Overcome Iverson," *New York Times*, March 13, 1997, sec. B.

7. Ibid.

8. Terry Pluto, *Falling from Grace: Can Pro Basketball Be Saved* (New York: Simon and Schuster, 1995), 116. For context, see Gitanjali Maharaj, "Talking Trash: Late Capitalism, Black (Re)Productivity, and Professional Basketball," in *SportCult*, ed. Randy Martin and Toby Miller (Minneapolis: University of Minnesota Press, 1999), 227–240.

9. Grant Farred, *In Motion, At Rest: The Event of the Athletic Body* (Minneapolis: University of Minnesota Press, 2014), 25–67; Leonard, *After Artest*, 191–192.

10. "Bulls Overcome Iverson."

11. "Excursions into Otherness: Understanding Dennis Rodman and the Limits of Subversive Agency," in *Sport Stars: The Cultural Politics of Sporting Celebrity*, ed. David L. Andrews and Steven J. Jackson (New York: Routledge, 2001), esp. 37–46; Yago Colás, "The Freedom in Dennis Rodman," Between the Lines, August 24, 2013, http://yago colas.com/2013/08/24/the-freedom-in-dennis-rodman.

12. Lisa Guerrero, "One Nation under a Hoop: Race, Meritocracy, and Messiahs in the NBA," in *Commodified and Criminalized: New Racism and African-Americans in Contemporary Sports*, ed. David J. Leonard and C. Richard King (Lanham, MD: Rowman and Littlefield, 2011), 142–143.

13. "Bulls Overcome Iverson."

14. R. Scott Kretchmar, "Basketball Purists: Blind Sentimentalists or Insightful Critics?" in *Basketball and Philosophy: Thinking Outside the Paint*, ed. Jerry Walls and Gregory Bassham (Lexington: University Press of Kentucky, 2008): 34–35, 39; Pluto, *Falling from Grace*, 84.

15. Bill Yousman, "Blackophilia and Blackophobia: White Youth, the Consumption of Rap Music, and White Supremacy," *Communication Theory* 13, no. 4 (2003): 3375.

16. Richard Campbell and Jimmie L. Reeves, *Cracked Coverage: Television News, the Anti-Cocaine Crusade and the Reagan Legacy* (Durham, NC: Duke University Press, 1994); Herman Gray, *Watching Race: Television and the Struggle for "Blackness"* (Minneapolis: University of Minnesota Press, 1995); Robin D. G. Kelley, *Yo' Mama's Disfunktional! Fighting the Culture Wars in Urban America* (Boston: Beacon, 1997).

17. David L. Andrews, *Michael Jordan, Inc.: Corporate Sport, Media Culture and Late Modern America* (Albany: State University of New York Press, 2001); Boyd, *Young, Black, Rich, and Famous*; Lane, *Under the Boards*.

18. Andrews and Silk, "Basketball's Ghettocentric Logic," 1626; Lane, *Under the Boards*, 52–53.

19. Samuel Davis, "Controlling Hip-Hop Culture 'Blackness': The Racial Politics of the National Basketball Association," master's thesis, Indiana University, Bloomington, 2013); Leonard, *After Artest*, 15; Maharaj, "Talking Trash," 234.

20. Joshua Kjerulf Dubrow and jimi adams, "Hoop Inequalities: Race, Class and Family Structure Background and the Odds of Playing in the National Basketball Association," *International Review for the Sociology of Sport* 47, no. 1 (2012): 51.

21. Boyd, *Young, Black, Rich, and Famous* 71–85; Mike DeBonis, "The World's Most Dangerous Basketball Team: How the Georgetown Hoyas Changed College Basketball," *Slate*, March 2007, http://www.slate.com/articles/sports/sports_nut/2007/03/

the_worlds_most_dangerous_basketball_team.html; Curry Kirkpatrick, "Hang on
to Your Hats . . . and Heads," *Sports Illustrated*, March 19, 1984, http://www.si.com/
vault/1984/03/19/569018/hang-on-to-your-hatsand-heads; Bishop Morin, "Basket-
brawl," *Sports Illustrated*, February 29, 1988; Leonard Shapiro, *Big Man on Campus:
John Thompson and the Georgetown Hoyas* (New York: Henry Holt, 1991).

22. Boyd, *Young, Black, Rich, and Famous*, 130–131; Greg Garber and Kory Kozak,
"Twenty Years Later, UNLV Still Indignant," *ESPN*, April 10, 2010, http://sports.espn
.go.com/ncb/tournament/2010/columns/story?id=5045144; Don Yaeger, *Shark Attack:
Jerry Tarkanian and His Battle with the NCAA and UNLV* (New York: HarperCollins,
1993).

23. Mitch Albom, *Fab Five: Basketball, Trash Talk, the American Dream* (New York:
Warner, 1993); Boyd, *Young, Black, Rich, and Famous*, 137–144; Jason Hehir, *Fab Five*
(ESPN Films, 2011); Lane, *Under the Boards*.

24. Curry Kirkpatrick, "And a Little Child Led Them," *Sports Illustrated*, April 6,
1981, http://www.si.com/vault/1981/04/06/825512/and-a-little-child-led-them-as-
though-drawing-inspiration-from-the-book-of-isaiah-baby-faced-isaiah-thomas-
spurred-indiana-to-a-fourth-ncaa-championship.

25. Ze'ev Chafets, *Devil's Night and Other True Tales of Detroit* (New York: Vin-
tage, 1990); Jerry Herron, *AfterCulture: Detroit and the Humiliation of History* (Detroit:
Wayne State University Press, 1993).

26. Michael Arace, "Pistons Go out like Thugs," *Vancouver Sun*, May 28, 1991, C7.
Boyd, *Young, Black, Rich, and Famous*, 105–123; Dennis Rodman, *Bad As I Wanna Be*
(New York: Delacorte, 1996), 32–48; Isiah Thomas, *Bad Boys! An Inside Look at the
Detroit Pistons' 1988–1989 Championship Season* (Grand Rapids, MI: Masters, 1989),
22–27.

27. Quoted in FreeDarko Collective, *FreeDarko Presents the Undisputed Guide to Pro
Basketball History* (New York: Bloomsbury, 2010), 159.

28. Leonard, *After Artest*, 20, 140–148; Lane, *Under the Boards*, 46–49.

29. Leonard, *After Artest*, 31–51; Farred, *In Motion, At Rest*, 25–67.

30. John Feinstein, *The Punch: One Night, Two Lives, and the Fight That Changed
Basketball Forever* (Boston: Little, Brown, 2002).

31. Harvey Araton, *Crashing the Borders: How Basketball Won the World and Lost Its
Soul at Home* (New York: Free Press, 2005), 8.

32. Hans Ulrich Gumbrecht, *In Praise of Athletic Beauty* (Cambridge, MA: Harvard
University Press, 2006), 189.

33. Leonard Koppett, *The Essence of the Game Is Deception: Thinking about Basketball*
(Boston: Little, Brown, 1973), 20.

34. Gumbrecht, *In Praise of Athletic Beauty*, 190.

35. Ibid.

36. Ibid., 198.

37. Ibid., 199.

38. Koppett, *The Essence of the Game Is Deception*, 15.

39. T. S. Eliot, *Four Quartets* (San Diego: Harcourt, 1971), 39.

40. Koppett, *The Essence of the Game Is Deception*, 45, 47.

41. Alexander Wolff, *Big Game, Small World: A Basketball Adventure* (New York:
Warner, 2002), 126.

42. Platt, *Only the Strong Survive*, 102–106.

43. Bethlehem Shoals, "Sweet Fields of Unfastened Terrain," McSweeney's, October 12, 2006, http://www.mcsweeneys.net/articles/sweet-fields-of-unfastened-terrain; Bethlehem Shoals, "In the Land of Spiny Columns," FreeDarko, August 19, 2007, http://freedarko.blogspot.com/2007/08/in-land-of-spiny-columns.html.

44. Greg Bach and National Alliance for Youth Sports, *Coaching Basketball for Dummies* (Hoboken, NJ: John Wiley, 2007), 46–47.

45. Shoals, "Sweet Fields of Unfastened Terrain."

46. Davis, "Controlling Hip-Hop Culture 'Blackness,'" 10.

47. Jorge Luis Borges, "Kafka and His Precursors," in *Selected Non-Fictions*, ed. and trans. Eliot Weinberger (New York: Penguin, 1999), 363–366.

CHAPTER 8

Epigraph: Henry Abbott, "Playing the Right Way with Larry Brown," True Hoop, July 31, 2013, http://espn.go.com/blog/truehoop/post/_/id/755/playing-the-right-way-with-larry-brown.

1. "Detroit Believes in Upset of Lakers," ESPN, June 6, 2004, http://sports.espn.go.com/nba/playoffs2004/news/story?id=1816507.

2. Chris Broussard, "Striking a Blow for the Right Way," *New York Times*, June 17, 2004, http://www.nytimes.com/2004/06/17/sports/pro-basketball-striking-a-blow-for-the-right-way.html; Michael Pinto, "Pistons Shock NBA World, Win Championship in 2004," NBA, May 21, 2013, http://www.nba.com/2013/history/05/17/2004-pistons-win-championship.

3. Broussard, "Striking a Blow for the Right Way."

4. Henry Abbott, "Playing the Right Way with Larry Brown."

5. Howard Beck, "Brown: The Man and the Mantra," *New York Times*, November 2, 2005, http://www.nytimes.com/2005/11/02/sports/basketball/02knicks.html?_r=0.

6. Howard Beck, "Brown's History Attracts Knicks," *New York Times*, July 21, 2005, http://query.nytimes.com/gst/fullpage.html?res=9C07E6DD173FF932A15754C0A9639C8B63.

7. Tom Lyons, "What Wins Basketball Games," Strauss Factor Laing and Lyons, 2005, http://www.sfandllaw.com/Articles/What-Wins-Basketball-Games-a-Review-of-Basketball-on-Paper-Rules-and-Tools-for-Performance-Analysis.shtml.

8. Dean Oliver, *Basketball on Paper: Rules and Tools for Performance Analysis* (Dulles, VA: Brassey's, 2004), 63.

9. "Q&A: Brown Discusses 'Right Way' to Play Basketball," NBA, April 19, 2012, http://www.nba.com/2012/news/features/04/18/larry-brown.

10. Abbott, "Playing the Right Way with Larry Brown."

11. Ibid.

12. Broussard, "Striking a Blow for the Right Way."

13. Larry Platt, *Only the Strong Survive: The Odyssey of Allen Iverson* (New York: Harper, 2003), 177–182.

14. Bethlehem Shoals, "One Shining Moment, the Realest Legacy of Allen Iverson," in FreeDarko Collective, *FreeDarko Presents the Undisputed Guide to Pro Basketball History* (New York: Bloomsbury, 2010), 182.

15. Chris Jones, "The New Black Guys," *Esquire*, February 2004.

16. Jonathan Feigen, "World Championships Fiasco Has U.S. Seeking Remedies," *Houston Chronicle*, September 9, 2002, http://www.chron.com/sports/article/World-Championships-fiasco-has-U-S-seeking-2083275.php; Steve Rushin, "The Ecstasy of Defeat," *Sports Illustrated*, September 16, 2002.

17. Harvey Araton, *Crashing the Borders: How Basketball Won the World and Lost Its Soul at Home* (New York: Free Press, 2005), 145.

18. R. Scott Kretchmar, "Basketball Purists: Blind Sentimentalists or Insightful Critics?" in *Basketball and Philosophy: Thinking Outside the Paint*, ed. Jerry Walls and Gregory Bassham (Lexington: University Press of Kentucky, 2008), 32.

19. David L. Andrews, "The (Trans) National Basketball Association: American Commodity-Sign Culture and Global-Local Conjuncturalism," in *Articulating the Global and the Local: Globalization and Cultural Studies*, ed. Ann Cvetkovich and Douglas Kellner (Boulder, CO: Westview, 1997), 92.

20. Jones, "The New Black Guys," 52.

21. Jeffrey Lane, *Under the Boards: The Cultural Revolution in Basketball* (Lincoln: University of Nebraska Press, 2007), 201.

22. Oliver, *Basketball on Paper*.

23. Michael Lewis, "The No-Stats All-Star," *New York Times Magazine*, February 13, 2009, http://www.nytimes.com/2009/02/15/magazine/15Battiert.html?pagewanted=all&_r=0.

24. Michael Lewis, *Moneyball: The Art of Winning an Unfair Game* (New York: W. W. Norton, 2003).

25. Fran Blinebury, "Spurs Scour Globe for Players, Meld Them into NBA Champs," NBA.com, October 29, 2014, http://www.nba.com/2014/news/features/fran_blinebury/10/29/the-international-influence-spurs.

26. Araton, *Crashing the Borders*, 145.

27. Harvey Araton, *When the Garden Was Eden: Clyde, the Captain, Dollar Bill and the Glory Days of the New York Knicks* (New York: HarperCollins, 2011), 147.

28. Kretchmar, "Basketball Purists," 43.

29. Karl Marx, *The 18th Brumaire of Louis Bonaparte*, trans. Daniel Deleon (Chicago: Kerr, 1913), 83.

30. Yago Colás, "The Meanings of Manu: Style, Race and Globalization in the Culture of Basketball," in *Sport and Nationalism in Latin America*, ed. Hector Fernandez, Robert Irwin, and Juan Poblete (New York: Palgrave, 2015).

31. Gilles Deleuze, "Mediators," in *Negotiations: 1972–1990*, trans. Martin Joughin (New York: Columbia University Press, 1995), 133.

32. Luis Paz, "Siempre Es Hoy," *Página 12*, May 10, 2012, http://www.pagina12.com.ar/diario/suplementos/no/12-5932-2012-05-15.html.

CHAPTER 9

Epigraph: Mike Lopresti, "What LeBron Needs Is a Good Example," Cincinnati.com, February 4, 2003, http://www2.cincinnati.com/preps/2003/02/04/wwwpreplebroncol4.html.

1. "The Plain Dealer's Front Page: LeBron James Edition," *Cleveland Plain Dealer*, July 9, 2010, http://www.cleveland.com/frontpage/index.ssf/2010/07/the_plain_dealers_front_page_l.html.

2. David Bauder, "Was LeBron Special ESPN's Deal with Devil?" *Sporting News*, July 10, 2010, http://www.webcitation.org/68lgFnX3W.

3. Associated Press, "Nets One of Many Teams Courting LeBron," *The Trentonian*, July 1, 2010, http://www.trentonian.com/article/TT/20100701/SPORTS/307019959; Henry Abbott, "LeBron James' Decision: The Transcript," True Hoop, July 8, 2010, http://espn.go.com/blog/truehoop/post/_/id/17853/lebron-james-decision-the-tran script; Andrew Keh, "LeBron Live: Blogging the Decision," Off the Dribble, July 8, 2010, http://offthedribble.blogs.nytimes.com/2010/07/08/lebron-live-blogging-the-decision; Lynn Zinser, "The LeBron James Surreality Show," *New York Times*, July 8, 2010, http://www.nytimes.com/2010/07/09/sports/09leading.html?ref=sports.

4. Primovibe, "Cleveland Fans Burning LeBron James Jersey on National TV," YouTube, July 8, 2010, https://www.youtube.com/watch?v=hQ7LaEJ83tg&feature= player_embedded; ESPN.com News Services, "James Picks Heat; Cavs Owner Erupts," ESPN, July 9, 2010, http://sports.espn.go.com/nba/news/story?id=5365165.

5. Darren Rovell, "LeBron's Q Score Takes Huge Hit," CNBC, September 14, 2010, http://www.cnbc.com/id/39170785/LeBron_s_Q_Score_Takes_Huge_Hit.

6. Gregg Doyel, "LeBron Comes out Looking like Coward, not King," *CBS Sports*, July 8, 2010, http://www.cbssports.com/nba/story/13618008/lebron-comes-out-looking-like-coward-not-king; Kevin Hench, "LeBron Chooses Treachery over Honor," *Fox Sports*, July 10, 2010, http://www.foxsports.com/nba/story/lebron-james-bene dict-arnold-miami-heat-chris-bosh-dwyane-wade-071010; Sean Conboy, "The Emperor's New Clothes: The Farce of King James," *Pittsburgh Magazine*, July 9, 2010, http://www.pittsburghmagazine.com/core/pagetools.php?pageid=12478&url=%2FBest-of-the-Burgh-Blogs%2FPulling-No-Punches%2FJuly-2010%2FThe-Emperor-039s-New-Clothes-The-Farce-of-King-James%2F&mode=print.

7. ESPN.com News Services, "Jordan Wouldn't Have Called Magic, Bird," ESPN, July 19, 2010, http://sports.espn.go.com/nba/news/story?id=5391478; Mitch Lawrence, "Michael Jordan, Charles Barkley Bash LeBron James for Teaming with Wade and Bosh with Miami Heat," *New York Daily News*, July 19, 2010, http://www.ny dailynews.com/sports/basketball/michael-jordan-charles-barkley-bash-lebron-james-teaming-wade-bosh-miami-heat-article-1.464980.

8. Jeff Winn, *Real Sports with Bryant Gumbel*, HBO, July 14, 2010, http://www .hbo.com/#/real-sports-with-bryant-gumbel/episodes/0/160-160-july-14-2010/ video/gumbel-commentary-lebron-james.html/eNrjcmbO0CzLTEnNd8xLz KksyUx2zs8rSa0oUc-PSYEJBSSmp-ol5qYy5zMXsjGyMXIyMrJJJ5aW5BfkJFbalh SVpgIAXbkXOA==; ESPN.com News Services, "Jordan Wouldn't Have Called Magic, Bird"; Lawrence, "Michael Jordan, Charles Barkley Bash LeBron James for Teaming with Wade and Bosh with Miami Heat"; Barry Rothbard, "Magic Johnson Says He Wouldn't Have Joined Bird after LeBron James's Move," *Bloomberg*, July 20, 2010, http://www.webcitation.org/5u6UVAdjv; Mike Wise, "LeBron James May Have His Fun on ESPN, but Lose His Legacy on the Court," *Washington Post*, July 9, 2010, http:// www.washingtonpost.com/wp-dyn/content/article/2010/07/08/AR2010070806864 .html; William J. Simmons, "Welcome to the All-LeBron Sound-Off," ESPN, July 9, 2010, http://sports.espn.go.com/espn/page2/story?page=simmons/100709; Jonathan Abrams and Catharine Skipp, "Criticism Grows as James Arrives in Miami," *New York Times*, July 9, 2010, http://www.nytimes.com/2010/07/10/sports/ basketball/10heat.html?_r=0&gwt=pay.

9. Tom Weir, "Barkley Says LeBron's 'Decision' Was a 'Punk Move,'" *USA Today*, August 13, 2010, http://content.usatoday.com/communities/gameon/post/2010/08/charles-barkley-lebron-james-punk-heat/1#.VPIwuUJpejI.

10. Bill Plaschke, "Heat over Heart," *Los Angeles Times*, July 9, 2010, http://articles.latimes.com/2010/jul/09/sports/la-sp-plaschke-lebron-james-20100709; Terry Pluto, "In the End, LeBron James Inflicts Needless Pain on the Region That Raised and Loved Him," *Cleveland Plain Dealer*, July 9, 2010, http://www.cleveland.com/pluto/blog/index.ssf/2010/07/in_the_end_lebron_james_inflic.html; Adrian Wojnarowski, "State of LeBron: Live at 9, from His Ego," Yahoo! Sports, July 7, 2010, http://sports.yahoo.com/nba/news;_ylt=ApPH.1kBV4zKxDXoT372BFk5nYcB?slug=aw-lebrondecision070710.

11. Harvey Araton, "Miami in Pinstripes: The New Evil Empire," *New York Times*, July 8, 2010, http://www.nytimes.com/2010/07/09/sports/basketball/09araton.html; Maureen Dowd, "Miami's Hoops Cartel," *New York Times*, July 10, 2010, http://www.nytimes.com/2010/07/11/opinion/11dowd.html.

12. Pluto, "In the End, LeBron James Inflicts Needless Pain on the Region That Raised and Loved Him"; Ron Nurwisah, "Cleveland Plain Dealer's Final Word on LeBron James," *National Post*, July 9, 2010, http://news.nationalpost.com/2010/07/09/cleveland-plain-dealers-final-word-on-lebron-james.

13. Phil Lutton, "LeBron a Coward and Traitor, Says Cavs Owner," *Sydney Morning Herald*, July 9, 2010, http://www.smh.com.au/sport/basketball/lebron-a-coward-and-traitor-says-cavs-owner-20100709-103cz.html.

14. Tom Weir, "Fathead Suggests LeBron Is the New Benedict Arnold," *USA Today*, July 9, 2010, http://content.usatoday.com/communities/gameon/post/2010/07/lebron-james-fathead-dan-gilbert-benedict-arnold/1#.VOzdikJpejI.

15. Fran Blinbury, "Cleveland May Never Get Over 'The Defection,'" NBA.com, July 9, 2010, http://www.nba.com/2010/news/features/fran_blinebury/07/08/what.next.cavs; Hench, "LeBron Chooses Treachery over Honor"; Plaschke, "Heat over Heart."

16. Dowd, "Miami's Hoops Cartel."

17. Conboy, "The Emperor's New Clothes."

18. James Sullivan, "Scott Raab, *The Whore of Akron: One Man's Search for the Soul of LeBron James*," A.V. Club, January 11, 2012, http://www.avclub.com/review/scott-raab-emthe-whore-of-akron-one-mans-search-fo-67461.

19. Claire Thora Solomon, *Fictions of the Bad Life: The Naturalist Prostitute and Her Avatars in Latin American Literature, 1880–1920* (Columbus: Ohio State University Press, 2014), 3–4.

20. Scott Raab, *The Whore of Akron: One Man's Search for the Soul of LeBron James* (New York: Harper Perennial, 2011), 9.

21. Ibid., 120, 146.

22. Ibid., 108.

23. Ibid., 298–299.

24. Grant Wahl, "Ahead of His Class," *Sports Illustrated*, February 18, 2002; Simon Hart, "Basketball: Hype at New Heights," *Sunday Telegraph*, October 26, 2003.

25. Carolyn White, "Ohio Super Sophomore Sets Tongues Wagging," *USA Today*, February 6, 2001, sec. C; Bill Livingston, "James on Pace to Eclipse Stars," *Cleveland Plain Dealer*, February 26, 2001, sec. D.

26. Weir, "Barkley Says LeBron's 'Decision' Was a 'Punk Move'"; Meena Harten-stein, "Le Fraud: LeBron James May Deserve a New Nickname after Spurning New York Knicks, NYC," *New York Daily News*, July 8, 2010, http://www.nydailynews.com/sports/basketball/knicks/le-fraud-lebron-james-deserve-new-nickname-spurning-new-york-knicks-nyc-article-1.465467; David Ramsey, "All Hail LeBron, the Counter-feit King," *The Gazette*, July 8, 2010, http://gazette.com/article/101344.

27. Lisa Guerrero, "One Nation under a Hoop: Race, Meritocracy, and Messiahs in the NBA," in *Commodified and Criminalized: New Racism and African-Americans in Con-temporary Sports*, ed. David J. Leonard and C. Richard King (Lanham, MD: Rowman and Littlefield, 2011).

28. LeBron James and Buzz Bizzinger, *Shooting Stars* (New York: Penguin, 2009); Terry Pluto and Brian Windhorst, *The Franchise: LeBron James and the Making of the Cleveland Cavaliers* (Cleveland: Gray and Company, 2007).

29. Dowd, "Miami's Hoops Cartel."

30. Henry Abbott, "Name the Crimes of LeBron James," True Hoop, July 9, 2010, http://espn.go.com/blog/truehoop/post/_/id/17867/name-the-crimes-of-lebron-james.

31. CNN Wire Staff, "LeBron James Says Race a Factor in Reaction to Miami Heat Announcement," CNN, September 30, 2010, http://edition.cnn.com/2010/SPORT/09/30/lebron.james.race/index.html.

32. Bill Simmons, "It's Time for LeBrondown, Part II," Grantland, June 9, 2011, http://grantland.com/features/time-lebrondown-part-ii.

33. Kurt Helin, "LeBron Has a Few Arrogant Words for Those Who Hate Him," Pro-BasketballTalk, June 13, 2011, http://probasketballtalk.nbcsports.com/2011/06/13/lebron-has-a-few-arrogant-words-for-those-who-hate-him.

34. Shannon J. Owens, "Black Athletes Dislike More than Other Groups, Sur-vey Says," *Orlando Sentinel*, September 17, 2010, http://articles.orlandosentinel.com/2010-09-17/sports/os-shannonowens-liked-disliked-athlet20100917_1_afri can-american-athletes-woods-and-kobe-bryant-personality-groups; Vincent Thomas, "LeBron James and Black Protectionism," ESPN, September 20, 2010, http://sports.espn.go.com/espn/commentary/news/story?id=5596310.

35. Henry Miller, *Sexus* (New York: Grove, 1965), 35.

36. Friedrich Nietzsche, *On the Genealogy of Morality*, ed. Keith Ansell-Pearson, trans. Carol Diethe (Cambridge: Cambridge University Press, 2006), 1–120.

37. Gilles Deleuze, *Nietzsche and Philosophy*, trans. Hugh Tomlinson, European Perspectives (New York: Columbia University Press, 1983), 111–137, esp. 116.

38. Chris Ballard, *The Art of a Beautiful Game: The Thinking Fan's Tour of the NBA* (New York: Simon and Schuster, 2009), 196.

39. Ibid., 207.

40. FreeDarko Collective, "LeBron James: Inland Empire," in *FreeDarko Presents . . . The Macrophenomenal Pro Basketball Almanac: Styles, Stats, and Stars in Today's Game* (New York: Bloomsbury, 2008), 179.

41. Jorge Luis Borges, "The Wall and the Books," in *Selected Non-Fictions*, ed. and trans. Eliot Weinberger (New York: Penguin, 1999), 345.

42. Henry Abbott, "LeBron James' Post-Decision Interviews," *True Hoop*, July 9, 2010, http://espn.go.com/blog/truehoop/post/_/id/17856/lebron-james-post-decision-interviews.

43. Joe Gabriele, "It's Numbers Game," NBA, September 30, 2014, http://www
.nba.com/cavaliers/news/features/uniform-numbers-140930.

44. Joe Coscarelli, "Guy Who Called LeBron James the 'Whore of Akron' Forgives
Him Now," New York Magazine, July 11, 2014, http://nymag.com/daily/intelligencer
/2014/07/guy-who-called-lebron-a-whore-forgives-him-now.html.

45. LeBron James and Lee Jenkins, "I'm Coming Home," Sports Illustrated, July 11,
2014, http://www.si.com/nba/2014/07/11/lebron-james-cleveland-cavaliers; emphasis added.

46. See Colin McGowan, "LeBron James, Michael Jordan, and the Next Act," Vice
Sports, May 26, 2015, https://sports.vice.com/en_us/article/lebron-james-michael-
jordan-and-the-next-act

47. Steven Nadler, Spinoza: A Life (New York: Cambridge University Press, 1999),
154.

48. Gilles Deleuze, Spinoza: Practical Philosophy, trans. Robert Hurley (San Francisco: City Lights, 1988), 22–23.

49. Benedict de Spinoza, "The Ethics," in A Spinoza Reader: The Ethics and Other
Works, ed. and trans. Edwin Curley (Princeton, NJ: Princeton University Press, 1994),
217.

50. Ibid., 259–260; Giorgio Agamben, "Absolute Immanence," in Potentialities: Collected Essays in Philosophy, ed. and trans. Daniel Heller-Roazen (Stanford, CA: Stanford
University Press, 1999), 237.

51. Gilles Deleuze and Félix Guattari, A Thousand Plateaus, trans. Brian Massumi
(Minneapolis: University of Minnesota Press, 1987), 424–473.

52. Friedrich Nietzsche, "The Antichrist," in The Portable Nietzsche, by Friedrich
Nietzsche, ed. and trans. Walter Kaufmann (New York: Penguin, 1982), 656.

53. Gilles Deleuze and Claire Parnet, Dialogues (New York: Columbia University
Press, 1987), 41.

54. Jeff Bell, "Nomad Thought: Deleuze, Whitehead and the Adventure of Thinking," in Secrets of Becoming: Negotiating Whitehead, Deleuze, and Butler, ed. Roland Faber
and Andrea M. Stephanson (New York: Fordham University Press, 2011), 78; Deleuze
and Guattari, A Thousand Plateaus, 351–424.

INDEX

Baylor, Elgin, 62, 73, 80–81
beauty, 120, 132, 144, 160. *See also* style
bildungsroman, 109–110, 116, 162
Billups, Chauncey, 138
Bird, Larry: and LeBron James, 152–153,
    156, 161–162; and Earvin "Magic"
    Johnson, 87–93; portrayed as great
    white hope, 96–97; as savior of NBA,
    14, 87–93, 114, 122, 127; style of play,
    97–101, 110, 134, 150
Birrell, Susan, 11
Black Fives, 62
black freedom struggle, 62
Black Jesus (Earl Monroe), 75–76, 86, 150
blackness, 8–9, 80, 108, 111, 138, 142,
    145, 157; myth of, 15, 121–136, 157
blacks: cultural practices, 15, 28, 100, 122,
    125, 128, 142; political struggles, 9–10,
    13–16, 28, 50, 62, 64–66, 69, 78–82,
    85, 112–113, 126–130, 135, 138, 159,
    158–160; social conditions, 8–9, 13–14,
    27, 62, 86, 112–113, 122, 126–130; ste-·
    reotypes, 9, 13, 27, 108, 113, 125, 135.
    See also race
blacks and basketball: achievements,
    13–16, 28, 43, 51, 56, 61–66, 67, 69,
    77, 80, 82–86, 96, 146, 164; participa-
    tion, 8–9, 13–16, 28, 43, 50, 56, 61–66,
    77, 79, 80, 84, 87, 90, 115, 122, 138,
    164; stereotypes, 8–9, 13–14, 64–66,
    67, 70, 82, 85, 87–88, 91, 95, 99, 108,
    110, 111, 113, 123–126, 130, 135, 142,
    145, 146, 157; styles of play, 14, 15,
    28, 51, 60–66, 68, 69, 77, 81, 82–86,
    98–101, 122, 128, 135, 142, 146. *See
    also* blackness; white basketball uncon-
    scious
body: associated with blackness, 57–59,
    110; as creative material, 31–32, 67, 82,
    108, 117, 132; in definition of personal
    foul, 3, 5; of LeBron James, 157–158;
    in mind-body dualism, 55, 57–59; in
    YMCA philosophy, 25
Boozer, Bob, 62
Borges, Jorge Luis, 135, 161
Bosh, Chris, 151, 154
Boston Celtics, 55, 71–72, 76, 88–89, 91,
    96, 98, 100, 107–108, 124, 128
Bownes, Robert, 84
Boyd, Todd, 100

Bradley, Bill, 25–26, 73–74, 78–81, 85–86,
    96
Breslin, Jimmy, 60–61, 65
Broussard, Chris, 138
Brown, Larry, 15, 95, 138–143, 145
Bryant, Kobe 137, 153–154
Bulls. *See* Chicago Bulls
Buss, Jerry, 93, 95

capitalism, 14–15, 27, 38, 41, 45, 48, 51,
    110, 159
Cavaliers, 15, 151, 154, 162
Celtics, 55, 71–72, 76, 88–89, 91, 96, 98,
    100, 107–108, 124, 128
center (position), 40, 68, 88, 134, 138. *See
    also* positional revolution
Chamberlain, Wilt: and dunking, 64–65,
    82; as first black superstar, 14, 51;
    negative portrayals of, 55–62, 66–67,
    70, 124, 127, 156–157; and politics, 64,
    66, 86; and Bill Russell, 14, 51, 55–62,
    66–70, 86, 110; statistical achievements
    of, 55, 67, 107; style of play, 67, 136
Chicago Bulls, 72, 76, 105–109, 111, 121,
    123–124, 126, 128–129
cities: African Americans in, 8–9, 14–15,
    62–63, 84, 98, 100, 112, 122–127, 129,
    142; BAA franchises in, 39; Black Fives
    in, 62; immigration and, 24; NBL fran-
    chises in, 42; pickup basketball in, 8–9,
    63, 84, 86, 98, 100, 133
City College of New York, 72
Civil Rights Movement, 13, 61, 62, 75, 127
class: and basketball, 10, 13–14, 26, 29,
    35, 72, 75, 113, 127, 147; class bias, 22;
    class conflict, 27, 46, 72, 75, 94, 129;
    and gender, 14, 24, 152; lumpenprole-
    tariat, 147; middle class, 9, 13, 24, 26,
    29, 75, 88, 94, 113, 127; and race, 9–10,
    13, 26, 46, 88, 152; working class, 10,
    24, 74, 75, 88, 94, 96
Cleveland (city), 15, 89, 151–155, 162–163
Cleveland Cavaliers, 15, 151, 154, 162
Clifton, Nat, 64
Clippers, 45
coach, authority of, 82, 94–95, 98, 106,
    134–135, 137–145
Cold War, 14, 106, 113–114, 118
Cole, Lewis, 74
Coleman, Derrick, 101

college basketball: and amateurism, 87–91, 94; and gambling scandal, 73; at historically black colleges and universities, 63; and modern basketball state, 48–50; in myth of blackness, 128; in New York City, 39, 45, 73, 76–77, 82; postwar popularity of, 39, 45, 76; resurgence in 1970s, 87–89; style of play, 77, 82, 86
Conboy, Sean, 155
confidence. *See* humility
Converse, 61–62, 91, 96
Converse Classic, 61–62
Cooper, Chuck, 64
cooperation. *See* unselfishness
Cosby, Bill, 113
creation: basketball's myth of, 13, 19–24; of Larry Bird and Earvin "Magic" Johnson, 89, 91, 98–99; and "black basketball aesthetic," 82–84, 98–99, 101, 135, 146; creativity of basketball players, 16, 38, 47–48, 50–51, 134–136; Gilles Deleuze on, 148; disrupted by invention, 30–35; of dribble, 32; of Julius Erving, 68, 82–84; of Manu Ginobili, 148–150; of Michael Jordan, 106, 108, 117; and *kairos,* 118–119; moral functions of, 26–27, 59, 94, 112, 141; portrayal of basketball essence in, 31, 74, 94, 141; racial implications of, 27–29, 51, 56. *See also* improvisation; innovation; invention
crossover. *See* dribble

Dallas Mavericks, 159
Darth Vader, 116
Dean, James, 117
DeBusschere, Dave, 71, 74
deception, 31–32, 34–35, 99, 132–133, 149–150, 165
defense: associated with New York Knicks, 14, 74; associated with Bill Russell, 58–59, 65; and black revolution in basketball, 63–65; as constraint prompting creative innovation, 31–32, 68–69, 82, 98–99, 117, 131–133, 147–150; innovations in, 48, 63–64; and LeBron James, 161; and positional revolution, 83, 134; and Triangle Offense, 108–109; viewed morally, 13, 58, 65, 138–142
Deford, Frank, 75
Deleuze, Gilles, 148, 160, 164–165
Denver Nuggets, 83
Descartes, René, 57
desegregation, 13, 61–62, 77, 90
Detroit (city), 129
Detroit Pistons, 76, 95, 107–109, 128–130, 137–139, 141, 143
dichotomy, 48, 55, 60–61, 68–69, 109
Douglas, Bob, 63
Dowd, Maureen, 154–155, 159
Dream Team, 92, 107, 129–130, 143
dribble: and creativity, 29–32, 35, 48, 131–135, 147–148; crossover, 126, 129, 131–135; invention of, 29–32; and player autonomy, 29–32, 48, 63, 134–135
Dr. J (Julius Erving), 67–68, 83–86, 97–98, 100, 110, 136, 165
Duke University, 129, 145
dunk: and ABA, 82–86; and Kareem Abdul-Jabbar, 50–51; associated with black players, 51, 64, 82–86, 165; banned by NCAA, 50–51; and Wilt Chamberlain, 51, 64–65, 82; compared to crossover dribble, 133; and Julius Erving, 83–86, 165; as expressing autonomy, 48, 64, 82–86; as expressing creativity, 48, 64–65, 82–86; as expressing individuality, 48, 82–86; and Michael Jordan, 116–117, 120, 133; as moral aberration, 27, 50–51, 81–82, 85, 165; tactical value of, 51, 64, 82; temporality of, 116–117, 120
Durant, Kevin, 101

Earl the Pearl (Earl Monroe), 75–76, 86, 150
efficiency: and Allen Iverson, 126, 135; and Michael Jordan, 105; and playing the right way, 139, 144, 150. *See also* statistics
effort: associated with Larry Bird, 89–90, 93; associated with New York Knicks, 75; associated with Bill Russell, 58–60; and modern basketball state, 94; as moral virtue, 58–60, 75, 82, 89–90, 93, 94. *See also* morals
eligibility, 49–50
Eliot, T. S., 132–133

Mikan, George, 40
Miller, Henry, 160
Miller, Reggie, 154, 161
mind, 23, 25, 57–59
Minneapolis Lakers. *See* Los Angeles
  Lakers
Minor, Harold, 115
MJ. *See* Jordan, Michael
modern basketball state: challenged by
  ABA, 84–86; defined, 37–38; foundation of, 46–52, 77, 94; introduced,
  13–14; moral values of, 60, 65, 67, 93;
  playing style in, 50–51, 56, 62, 64–65,
  77, 84–86, 93, 99; racial dynamics of,
  14, 51, 56, 60–67, 77, 84–86, 90–99
modernism, 48
modernity, 47–48
modernization, 24, 47
Monroe, Earl, 75–76, 86, 150
morals: associated with styles of basketball play, 26–27, 51, 56–57, 79–82,
  84–85, 90, 98, 109–110, 124–126,
  139–141, 143–144, 146; in comparison
  of Wilt Chamberlain and Bill Russell,
  56–60, 66, 70; and imagined essence of
  basketball, 22, 25–29, 38, 60, 79–82,
  98, 106, 109–110, 140–141, 143–144,
  146; and invention of basketball, 22,
  24–29, 47; and LeBron James, 152, 156,
  162–165; and Michael Jordan, 106,
  109–110, 129; and modern basketball
  state, 38, 50; and New York Knicks,
  79–82, 85, 109–110; racialized, 20,
  27–29, 51, 70, 79–82 , 84–85, 90, 98,
  124–125, 130, 146, 152, 156; relationship to myths summarized, 12–15; and
  "the right way," 139–141, 143–146; in
  white basketball unconscious, 27–29,
  110, 124–125
Mourning, Alonzo, 130
Mumford, Stephen, 69
muscular Christianity, 24–25, 156
myth: defined, 9, 11; general function
  of, 4, 11, 13–14. 27–28, 35, 38, 60–61,
  76, 97, 109–110, 126–127, 135, 141,
  156–157, 164–165

Naismith, James: biography, 24–25; on
  creativity as invention, 29–31, 136,
  165; on dribbling, 31; on fast break,
  63; invention of basketball, 24–34, 47,

51, 82; in myth of creation, 19–23, 82,
  112, 140
Naismith Memorial Basketball Hall of
  Fame, 21, 92
narcissism, 59, 66, 82. *See also* individuality; morals; selfishness
National Basketball Association (NBA):
  attempts to control players, 5–9, 49–52,
  111, 122, 124, 127, 130, 141; decline
  in popularity in 1970s, 87, 91, 95, 130;
  desegregation of, 63–64; formation of,
  42–46, 61; globalization of, 106, 111–
  112, 114, 143–146; merger with ABA,
  82–83, 97–98; myth of foundation,
  38–42; rules on fouls, 5–9, 23; "saved"
  by Larry Bird and Earvin "Magic"
  Johnson, 88–91, 93; and statistics,
  144–145; style of play shaped by black
  players, 9, 72, 81–86, 97–101, 122, 127,
  135, 165; summary of myths, 12–16
National Basketball League (NBL), 39–40,
  42–43, 45–46, 48, 85
National Collegiate Athletic Association
  (NCAA), 13, 49–51, 73, 84, 87–89, 101,
  105–106, 129, 139
National Invitational Tournament (NIT),
  73
National League of Professional
  Basketball, 44
natural talent, 58–59, 65, 108. *See also*
  blacks and basketball; race
Negri, Antonio, 118–119
neoliberalism, 114, 118
Nets, 83
Nevada, Las Vegas, 128
New York City, 71–73. *See also* New York
  Knicks
New York Knicks, 1, 26, 71–82, 85–87,
  110, 127, 130, 157
New York Nets, 83
New York Renaissance Five, 43, 63
Nietzsche, Friedrich, 11, 160, 165
Nike, 34, 101, 110, 113–114, 133
Nine Queens, 147, 149–150
North Carolina College for Negroes, 63
Novak, Michael, 65
Nowitzki, Dirk, 159
Nuggets, 83

Obi-Wan Kenobi, 116
O'Connor, David, 60

Yago Colás teaches in the Department of Comparative Literature and in the Residential College at the University of Michigan.